G000108796

How to Write and Publish Local and Family History Successfully guides even complete novices through all the stages needed to produce and promote books, booklets, magazines, CD-ROMs and Web sites on local and family history. For those who are not novices the information will also act as a checklist for producing professional-looking publications.

All the advice is based on Bob Trubshaw's fifteen years of experience publishing local and family history books, booklets, magazines, CD-ROMs and Web sites. He has written and self-published 16 books and booklets; compiled and published two local history CD-ROMs; edited and published over 60 books, booklets and electronic publications for other authors; and edited nearly 50 issues of quarterly and annual magazines.

Quotes from reviews of Bob Trubshaw's previous book *How to Write and Publish Local History*

'Helpful, unassuming, practical and very much to the point, *How to Write and Publish Local History* is a most enjoyable read for any would-be author and is strongly recommended.'
Family and Community History

'It is truth universally acknowledged that all local historians want to publish books and booklets – as the pages of *Local History Magazine* prove. Publishers take on a rare few, but most decide to do it themselves. As I know from bitter experience it is very, very easy to produce a badly designed unattractive booklet, which doesn't sell, however interesting the contents might be.

'This important new book shows those who decide on self publishing the right way to go about it. It is based on the experiences of Bob Trubshaw who has published a number of local history books in the ten years his Heart of Albion Press has been running.

'The book is conveniently broken down into various sections including how to write history, dealing with printers, design and typesetting, and publicity and selling the book. Almost every page contains some tip or hint that might save hours of wasted time, often based on Trubshaw's own experiences. This advice is given in a jargon free, non-patronising style while assuming the reader is a complete novice. How I wish I had had this book years ago when first starting out in local history. If you are planning to publish your own researches or are involved in a local history society's publishing programme this book is an essential purchase.'
Simon Fowler *Local History Magazine*

'Helpful, not pompous, practical and very much to the point, *How to Write and Publish Local History* is a most enjoyable read for any would-be author and is strongly recommended.'
Open University Newsletter DA301 (Studying family and community history)

'This is a book which should be owned by everyone who is writing their village or town history for the Millennium, and there appear to be hundreds in preparation! Every aspect of the subject is covered: how to write your history, design and typesetting, legal matters, estimating costs, artwork and illustrations, proof-reading (essential!) and indexing. Having got your book written and printed it is too easy to just sit back in a glow of achievement, but this was not the purpose of the exercise, further chapters tell how to store, advertise and sell your completed book, who is legally

entitled to a free copy, and give suggestions on packaging for the mail. For those still eager for knowledge, a chapter on 'Further reading' at the end gives a list of useful books on writing, indexing, publishing, design and promotion.'
Julie Goddard *Family Tree Magazine*

'The shelves of any local studies library groan with the research of amateur local historians. And so they should. The honourable estate of amateur has rightly always been the backbone, or perhaps the lifeblood, of local history; much distinguished work has been achieved by self-styled 'amateurs'. Amateurs certainly – amateurish, definitely not. But oh how often sound and valuable work is let down by amateurish production. There is no excuse for this. Not these days, anyway.

'Bob Trubshaw has written an intensely practical guide (based firmly on his own experience) for self-publishing for local history. He runs the whole gamut, from the blank paper before anything is written, to the technique of peddling publications around bookshops. All the snags and tricks I can think of (and many that hadn't occurred to me) are here, concisely but comprehensively tackled and resolved, referenced and indexed. And in the shifting sands of DTP Trubshaw is right up to minute – indeed (if the truth be known) way ahead of most local historians. No-one, of course, in 120 pages can teach fine prose or classic typography. The budding Hoskins or Beresford requires flair, imagination and plenty of practice. But writing to publish also involves a great deal of nitty-gritty, and here Trubshaw is a star. Look no further!
John Chandler *3rd Stone*

'If ever a group of budding U3A writers wanted a step-by-step guide from inspiration to successful sales of their work, *How to Write and Publish Local History* is a very useful companion. R.N. Trubshaw is the author and it is he who, from his own Heart of Albion Press, publishes books and pamphlets on local history. The formality of his name on the title page is relaxed on the cover where he becomes Bob Trubshaw. That is indicative of the contents, professional but also user-friendly.

'There is advice on assembling ideas and the style and structure of writing. The confusion of footnotes, references, title pages and indices are carefully and logically untangled. Having written the text, what about illustrations and instructing the printer? Where can economies be made to keep the cover price within the scope of the reader's pocket? The die is cast. The size and price, and the budgeted profit too, have all been worked out. How is the publication to be sold and how many will be left unsold? A helping hand is given along the road.
David Ensor *U3A Sources* [Bulletin for the University of the Third Age]

Previous publications by Bob Trubshaw

Books

Little-known Leicestershire and Rutland (1996)
How to Write and Publish Local History (1999)
Explore Folklore (2002)
Explore Mythology (2003)
Rutland Village by Village (2003)
Good Gargoyle Guide: Medieval church carvings in Leicestershire and Rutland (2nd edn 2004)
Leicestershire Legends retold by Black Annis (2004)
Sacred Places: Prehistory and popular imagination (forthcoming 2005)

Booklets

Ancient Crosses of Leicestershire and Rutland 1990
Holy Wells and Springs of Leicestershire and Rutland 1990
Standing Stones and Mark Stones of Leicestershire and Rutland 1991
Good Gargoyle Guide: Medieval church carvings in Leicestershire and Rutland (1st edn) 1991
The Quest for the Omphalos (with John Walbridge) 1991
Grimr's Year 1991
Putting Things Straight 1992
Dragon Slaying Myths Ancient and Modern 1993
Gargoyles and grotesque carvings of Leicestershire and Rutland 1995

Electronic publications

Little-known Leicestershire and Rutland - the hypertext 1996
Little-known Leicestershire and Rutland CD-ROM (2002)
Grotesques and Gargoyles of Leicestershire and Rutland CD-ROM (2002)

Edited books

Wolds Reflections 1997
2000 Years of the Wolds (co-editor 2003)

Edited magazines

Mercian Mysteries (1990 to 1996)
At the Edge (1996 to 1998)
Wolds Historical Organisation Newsletter (co-editor 1992 to 2002)
The Wolds Historian (co-editor 2004 onwards)

HOW TO WRITE AND PUBLISH LOCAL AND FAMILY HISTORY SUCCESSFULLY

Books, booklets, magazines, CD-ROMs and Web sites

Bob Trubshaw

Heart of Albion

How to Write and Publish
Local and Family History Successfully
Books, booklets, magazines, CD-ROMs and Web sites

R.N. Trubshaw

Cover design and illustration by Tanya Goodwin
(www.vitaldesign.co.uk)

ISBN 1 872883 59 1

This book is a substantially rewritten and greatly expanded version of *How to Write and Publish Local History*, published by Heart of Albion Press in 1999.

Published by
Heart of Albion Press
2 Cross Hill Close, Wymeswold
Loughborough, LE12 6UJ

telephone 01509 880725
albion@indigogroup.co.uk

Visit our Web site: www.hoap.co.uk

Printed in the UK by Booksprint, Wellington, Somerset

Contents

List of illustrations

Acknowledgements

I am indebted to a number of people for help with preparing this book. David Lazell, Max Wade-Matthews and Peter Shaw all made helpful comments about the previous book, *How to Write and Publish Local History,* on which this book is based.

I am especially grateful to Joan Shaw for commenting in detail on drafts of the first two chapters, offered advice regarding family history research and for permission to reproduce old photographs. Grateful thanks also to Laighton Waymouth for reading Chapter 5, Sue Brown and Janet Spavold for checking the summary of their book in Chapter 2, Paul Nix and Peter Woodward for permission to reproduce the Memories of Nottinghamshire copyright assignment form, John Hamilton for permission to reproduce illustrations from *Glad for God,* Anne Tarver for permission to reproduce the map of Leicestershire place-names, and the late Alec Moretti for permission to use the graphs and data reproduced on page 92.

Would the author and/or copyright owner of 'How to do it not' on page 41 please make contact so that this can be correctly acknowledged in future editions.

Disclaimer

All information is given in good faith but the author accepts no responsibility for the consequences of following any advice given in this book. All addresses, including Web addresses, are correct at the time of writing but may change at any time in the future. Use a Web search engine to check physical addresses or to locate new Web addresses.

BEFORE WE BEGIN

The information in *How to Write and Publish Local and Family History Successfully* will guide even the complete novice through all the stages needed to produce and promote books, booklets, magazines, CD-ROMs and Web sites on local and family history. For those who are not novices the information will also act as a checklist for producing professional-looking publications.

The widespread use of computers for so-called 'desk-top publishing' has created one of the biggest changes in publishing since the invention of moveable type in the sixteenth century. A relatively low-cost computer, used skilfully, can produce results comparable with professional typesetting. This enables individuals and societies to produce short-run publications that would not interest major publishers. Indeed, most local interest titles are now produced by small publishers.

My experience with desk-top publishing goes back before the Windows operating system. During the last 15 years I have written and self-published 16 books and booklets, compiled and published two local history CD-ROMs, 150 substantial articles (and countless short reviews and the like), edited and published over 50 books, booklets and electronic publications for other authors, and edited nearly 50 issues of quarterly and annual magazines.

In 1999 I wrote and published *How to Write and Publish Local History.* This was an attempt to distil my experience down to provide concise guidance for anyone starting out with publishing local history books. It was in many ways the book I would like to have been able to learn from when I was starting out ten years previously.

In the five years since that book appeared there have been a number of changes to commercial printing technology and, more importantly, historians are increasingly using CD-ROMs and Web sites to publish their research. Also during the last five years I have been increasingly involved in the publication of family history, so now feel I can offer advice on this too. There are many similarities between publishing local and family history – indeed some books have their feet firmly in both. To avoid unduly cumbersome sentences throughout this book references to 'local history' should be read to include both local history in the stricter sense *and* family history. Only where there is a need to specifically distinguish between the two do I expressly refer to family history.

The idea of privately producing short-run books on local and family history is not new. What has changed over the last ten years is the ease with which highly presentable publications can be produced. Sadly, far too often the results do not look presentable and instead look unnecessarily amateurish. Any fool can produce a sloppy-looking booklet, CD-ROM or Web site – and a great many have. This book aims to help those who want to set their standards as high as realistically possible.

This book is much more than a revised edition of the 1999 book. All sections have been substantially rewritten and two entirely new sections have been added which offer detailed advice on preparing illustrations for publication and publishing on the Web and CD-ROMs. All the advice in this book is based on current UK practice.

This book is broken down into nine major sections:

1. writing and editing
2. legal matters
3. preparing illustrations for reproduction
4. an introduction to printing
5. an introduction to publishing
6. designing and typesetting books
7. designing Web sites and CD-ROMs
8. promotion and publicity
9. selling

Inevitably there are plenty of links between the different sections (indicated with 'see page so-and-so'), although I have tried to minimise extensive overlaps.

The main exclusion from this book is specific help on how to go about researching local and family history, simply because many books have already been written about different aspects. One of the best introductions is Kate Tiller's *English Local History: An introduction* (Sutton, 2nd edn 2002) which offers a broad range of useful information and has very helpful recommendations for further reading. Further sources for local historians can be found in *Local History: A handbook for beginners* by Philip Riden (Merton Priory Press, 2nd edn 1998); again this has a very useful list of further reading although does not list works that have appeared since 1998.

The long-standing 'bible' for novice genealogists is *The Oxford Guide to Family History* David Hey (Oxford UP 1993) but this has been overshadowed somewhat by Mark Herber's *Ancestral Trails: The complete guide to British genealogy and family history* (Sutton 2000); at 700 pages it lives up to its subtitle.

John Titford's delightful book *Writing and Publishing Your Family History* (Countryside Books 1996) will inspire any genealogist, however inexperienced, to go beyond merely 'ancestor spotting' (as Titford delightfully refers to the collecting of data about forebears) to creating more fully-fledged family histories and narratives. However the final section, relating to publishing, has understandably been overtaken by changes in technology since he wrote it nearly ten years ago.

Computer advice

With the exception of some of the advice in chapter 4 on preparing illustrations, this book is not a guide on how to use your computer and software. I have made recommendations about software available at the time of writing in late 2004; however inevitably these will become out of date. With hardware everything changes fast so any advice would be quickly out of date.

My practical advice will be limited to one obvious but all-too-often ignored suggestion: **Always make back ups regularly.** Plan for the worst case scenario. Hard drives crash when least expected. Computers get stolen without warning. Viruses can damage or wipe files long before you suspect their presence. Only 'forget' to make back ups if you are willing to risk your work being totally lost.

Back ups should preferably be kept in a different building to the computer itself so, in the event of theft or even fire, all your work will not be lost. If you work in an office during the day, then you may want to keep your back up CDs from your home computer in an office desk drawer. Even if this office location is not especially safe, the 'offsite' back up is unlikely to be damaged or lost at the same time as the home computer fails or goes. Those without office-based jobs may be able to arrange for a friend or neighbour to provide 'off site' storage for back ups.

Do not rely on single copies of CDs for back ups – for 'mission critical' files always burn at least two copies, then keep them in protective cases away from dirt and heat, with one copy in a different building to the other one.

If the amount of data you regularly back up exceeds the capacity of one or two CDs then purchase a pair of external hard drives which connect via USB2 or Firewire. Do daily back ups to one drive while keeping the other drive in another location. Not more than a week apart, swap the onsite and offsite drives and update the drive now brought onsite with all the files that have changed while it was offsite. The Windows 'My Briefcase' utility updates files on different drives although Microsoft's 'Backup Utility' (which comes on the Windows installation CD but is *not* installed by default) is more suitable. Best of all purchase a specialist back up program (such as Dantz Rerospect [www.dantz.com], Acronis Trueimage [www.acronis.com] or Bounce Back [www.cmsproducts.com]) – the cost is small compared to the consequences of losing data.

Chapter One

GETTING STARTED

What to write about?

Most people using this book will already have specific ideas on what they want to write about. However defining the topic or subject is a crucial step.

Local history research that is not well-defined risks becoming too big and complicated. Worse still, the process of research may become endless. Bear in mind that trying to track down all the details of a comparatively small village and the key inhabitants may initially seem a reasonable project but usually proves to be beyond the scope of most researchers. If research reveals large amounts of information then, sadly but all-too-often, the researcher loses interest in preparing it for publication so the effort is largely wasted. Some subjects may require access to original documents which are in difficult handwriting or Latin. Unless palaeography and translation skills are already developed then this could prove to be a stumbling block. Other projects may require access to documents stored in archives many miles from home.

A full appreciation of all the relevant sources is impossible at the start of any project. What is essential is a real interest in the subject. Local history is ultimately about people so the subject must be approached as, or transformed into, human history. Family history too needs to be about the human history – which is most certainly not the same as long lists of names with their associated dates of births and deaths, spouses and offspring.

The convergence of local and family history

The eighteenth century antiquarians who pioneered local history were mostly concerned with the descent of the manor and the pedigrees and houses of the landed classes. Nothing was said about the lives of the tenants, the 'ordinary' people who made up much of the population. This bias towards manorial history is reflected in many village histories, whereas urban histories give disproportionate attention to the leading figures of trade and industry. This bias is not simply because there is comparatively little written about 'ordinary' people, but more because considerable effort is needed to track down the records of such people to create some sort of social history.

However such effort is exactly what family historians revel in. Once the research extends beyond merely tracing descent through the male line then a more rounded account of the family becomes an exercise in social history. Once a number of such social histories of families have been researched (and, ideally, published) for a given place then the 'missing' history of ordinary people can be added to the traditional 'manorial history' of a village or the accounts of merchant families in towns. Appropriate family history and local history research thereby converge to produce a more complete social history.

Book, booklet, CD-ROM or Web site? One-off or series?

What is the difference between a book and a booklet? In most senses there is no difference apart from the way it is bound together because the same concepts apply to preparing both. Clearly a booklet is something less substantial than a book, but there is considerable middle ground.

However, another subtle overlap comes in. There is nothing to stop you producing booklets as a series (perhaps covering different aspects of a town) or producing them at regular intervals. In the last case you have, to all intents and purposes, a regular magazine. This brings yet another overlap – that between magazines and newsletters. Again, the difference is really one of size as publication involves similar considerations. At the other end of the scale, there are no fundamental differences between a book and annual journals or transactions. In this book all types of periodicals are considered to be the same as any other type of publication, except for one or two specific details, such as ISBN numbers (see page 122).

A research project may generate so much information and so many illustrations about a comparatively specialist topic that a book would be prohibitively expensive. A project may also be open-ended, and generate more and more information as others become aware of the author's interests. In such cases a CD-ROM or Web site might be the only affordable way of publishing the research. In Chapter 7 we will explore different forms of electronic publication.

So – book or booklet, CD-ROM or Web site, one-off or series, magazine or newsletter – this book will help you publish them all. For convenience, I will normally refer to the final item as a book, except where differences are important.

Self-publishing or group publishing?

For similar reasons of convenience, I will write as if one individual is doing the publishing. This does not mean that a local history society cannot be a publisher – many already are and hopefully this book will help many more.

Local history publications are often the result of collaborative work by a village history group. From the publication perspective this is not really important, although clearly there are a number of collective decisions which will be have to be made. However, it also means that some of the more onerous tasks (such as typing, proof reading and selling) can be shared.

Computer-aided research

You may find that database or spreadsheet software will (at least in the long run) greatly ease your work. Be prepared to spend quite some time getting to know how they work and how to set them up. The learning curve may be steep but the ability to quickly set up a new database or spreadsheet to analyse specific data will become an asset.

Microsoft Excel is the best-known spreadsheet software and fairly easy to use. Spreadsheets are useful for keeping lists of data, especially if some of this information is numerical. The main benefit of spreadsheets is the ability to perform numerical calculations on columns or rows of data.

Everything that can be done on a card file system can be done easily on a database. More importantly, information can be quickly accessed by topic. Unusual or unforeseen topics can be fairly quickly found using powerful automatic word search routines. Information can be easily pasted between databases and word processors. While in the middle of writing you can easily swap over to a database to check facts such as dates, the spelling of personal names, or bibliographical details. All these facilities greatly speed up the research and writing stages. Although databases make it easy to compile and, more importantly, recall all sorts of miscellaneous information, keeping track of the *sources* of all information is still essential (see also page 44).

The earliest Heart of Albion publications were, to all intents and purposes, the contents of a simple database interspersed with illustrations plus a brief introduction. The database had been created village-by-village for the county so exporting the contents in alphabetical order gave the basis of a gazetteer. Some expansion of abbreviations, general tidying up of sentences and grammar, and the correct numbering of references were all that was needed to produce a series of basic booklets.

There are a number of database programs. Microsoft's database software, Access, is anything but easy to set up and use; neither is it part of the standard Office package and is therefore expensive. Filemaker Pro (www.filemaker.com) is somewhat easier to set up and more affordable. Be prepared to seek expert help with either Access or Filemaker if you have no previous experience of setting up databases.

In contrast to so-called 'relational databases' such as Access and Filemaker, there are also 'freeform databases'. As their name implies, 'freeform' databases do not require information to be entered in pre-defined 'data fields'. Instead they simply swallow vast amounts of information and then provide sophisticated search facilities to find specific words or phrases. Probably the most widely used freeform database is AskSam (www.asksam.com). This requires almost no setting up and readily imports all types of text, such as word processing files, emails and Web pages; these can be imported as single files or by the folder full. Images can be included too, although at the risk of making the database files very large.

The real beauty of AskSam is that searching is done by Boolean logic (the posh name for the method used for advanced searches on Web search engines such as Google) combined with proximity searches (e.g. two or more different words within a specified number of words, sentences or paragraphs) and with 'fuzzy' searches (to allow for typing errors!). Once you have found data matching the search criteria this can either be copy and pasted into another program, or exported out as a word processor file. Since starting to use AskSam I have benefited greatly from the ability to quickly 'dump' information into AskSam files then retrieve it by searching on suitable keywords. AskSam's sister product called SurfSaver integrates with Web browsers to provide a searchable freeform database of downloaded Web pages – a very powerful tool for anyone whose research involves much 'surfing'.

Computer-aided research involving census returns

Local historians are frequently interested in analysing census returns. Databases provide an excellent method for handling such complex and inter-related information. The scope of this book cannot include advising on such a complex topic. However useful help can be found in *Computing for historians: an introductory guide* by Evan Mawdsley and Thomas Munck (Manchester University Press, 1993).

Do bear in mind that the effort of entering census data into a database is considerable. At an early stage it might well be worth trying to make sure the way you structure your database fields is compatible with other researchers in the area, so that computer-readable data can be easily and usefully swapped. Indeed, make sure that someone has not already entered the data you are interested in – a great many CD-ROMs of information useful to family and local historians have been produced. The best way to locate these is to enter appropriate words into a Web search engine.

Population studies are a major field of academic study; periodicals such as *Local Population Studies* and *The Local Historian* (usually available at county record offices or libraries) will provide an insight into current approaches and the relevant literature.

Computer-aided family history research

Several different software programs had been developed for family historians. The one most widely used is Family Tree Maker (www.genealogy.com/soft_ftm.html) but one of the pioneers, Brother's Keeper (ourworld.compuserve.com/homepages/Brothers_Keeper/) remains popular. But be warned – neither of these are particularly helpful when it comes to exporting the information to other programs for publication.

The main benefit of computers for family historians is the way search engines and email make it easy to identify and contact fellow researchers. As with everything else you must be careful to evaluate the reliability of all information and important points need to be double checked (including – or perhaps especially – information on the International Genealogical Index). But, at the very least, the Web can draw attention to sources that you might otherwise have missed.

One of the best ways of sharing information via the Web is to do just that – share it. Even quite a simple Web site can bring your research to the attention of others via search engines. There is no need to wait until you have crossed every 't' and dotted every 'i' – Web sites are especially useful for interim publication of work in progress.

Group research

If you are a member of a local history society or an adult education class then considerably more can be achieved (and more fun enjoyed along the way) if research is divided into overlapping projects.

In one successful project a number of people collaborated to research the history of the six largest families involved in the late eighteenth century enclosure of their village. These families inter-married, sold land and houses to each other, and otherwise interacted through the years. So those concentrating on, say, the 'Smiths' needed to liaise with those researching the 'Jones' or the 'Browns'. The result was a comprehensive study of the leading nineteenth century land-owning families, which in turn provided a detailed insight into village life at the time.

Another project straddling family history, social history and local history researched all the families living in a village in the seventeenth and eighteenth centuries, when it was nationally-important for pottery production. This built up a complex insight into the way families intermarried, how newcomers were integrated in the community, and how property rights were transferred. Among the surprises was the extent to which widows continued producing pottery after the death of their husbands, suggesting that these were typically 'family businesses' in which wives and daughters played a major part. (This research has been published as *Ticknall Pots and Potters* by Sue Brown and Janet Spavold, Landmark Publishing 2005.)

The benefits of collaborative efforts such as there are quickly apparent – different skills can be brought to bear, duplication of effort should be minimal, and the whole quickly becomes greater than the sum of the parts. The only possible problem might be that the group is so successful with its research that the sheer quantity of information becomes difficult to summarise or analyse! One incidental but nevertheless important benefit is that this approach provides a framework in which those group members who have little or no experience of local and/or family history research benefit from the expertise and guidance of more regular researchers.

The importance of oral history

Since the 1970s oral history recordings have begun to take the prominent place they deserve as a source of information for local and family history researchers. The types of recollections recorded by oral history should be regarded as quite distinct from documentary and photographic records. They are expression of individuals' memories. As numerous academic studies have shown, human memory is not 'objective' but subtly shaped by what we have been told happened and, to a varying extent, by what we think *should* have happened.

The basic assumption of all oral accounts is that the person is not so much telling you what they did, but *what they want you to think they did.* Frankly this remark applies to documentary sources too, which also can be 'selective', intentionally forged, or rely on hearsay (i.e. rely on oral history!). Just as documentary sources may contain unintended errors (local newspapers being notoriously prone to such problems) so too people's memories are fallible.

When interviewed people do not simply recount what they did – they also reveal what they wanted to do, what they believed they were doing, and what they now think they did. Memory is not something simple and transparent; rather memories are an intricate processes of recall which repeatedly selects, shapes, and reshapes the original experiences. Most people will, consciously or otherwise, tell the interviewer what they think the interviewer wants to hear. In most cases people will recall only events which they regard as distinctive or unusual, or which present the teller in a good light.

In general, although oral history can provide some details about events that would otherwise be forgotten, overall oral history tells us less about specific events than about their *current meaning* to the person interviewed. Even if the person being interviewed has only a limited awareness of wider historical issues, they will implicitly place their recollections within their prior assumptions about history – and assumptions about what historians are interested in!

The memories usually encountered in oral history interviews typically fall into three categories. There is 'global' information – actually usually national, and often ultimately derived from the mass media such as newspapers, radio and television. For example, recollections of what the Blitz was like in London during the Second World War from someone who was not living in London at the time fall into this category.

More interesting is 'local' information – such as what the Blitz was like from someone who was there at the time. Individual people are usually named, although there may only be fragments of a story (often triggered by mention of a specific building or person) rather than a more developed narrative. Some 'local' information can be recollections of purely personal events – for example, how the person felt on their wedding day.

In between the 'global' and 'local' information is another interesting category of information. This has been termed 'popular memory' and usually comprises short (and often seemingly 'rehearsed') narratives. These include supernatural legends – ghost stories and the like – and tales which have a 'moral' aspect, such as indicating how to behave at, say, weddings or funerals (usually because the tale clearly shows how things should *not* be done!). Such tales are clearly shared between people living in the same village, or those who worked or socialised together.

Too many local historians are so obsessed with getting at the facts that they tend to dismiss local legends and folklore whereas such lore may be a distinctive aspect of what bonds a group or community together. By their very nature these key aspects of collective identity are usually known only to those who 'belong' to a specific group. Such unique and easily-lost aspects of local history should never be ignored when encountered.

One variant of 'popular memory' is recollections from interviewees about what they recall older members of their families (such as parents) saying about significant events before the person being interviewed was born. For example in the 1940s the Irish government conducted a major oral history interview programme to find out what people 'remembered' about the famines of the 1840s. Such passed down recollections of more personal events can be thought of as 'family folklore' (see page 15).

More information about oral history

See the Oral History Society Web site (http://ohs.org.uk/) for extensive advice on all aspects of collecting, transcribing and publishing oral history.

The East Midlands Oral History Archive (EMOHA) has built up a useful collection of advisory leaflets, all of which can be downloaded from their Web site (www.le.ac.uk/emoha).

An academic journal, *Oral History Review*, is available online at www.historycooperative.org/ohindex.html; in the first issue the article by Rebecca Jones '*Blended Voices*: crafting a narrative from oral history interviews' (www.historycooperative.org/journals/ohr/31.1/jones.html) is especially relevant for anyone preparing interviews for publication.

Sounding Boards: Oral testimony and the local historian by David Marcombe (Department of Adult Education, University of Nottingham 1995) provides extensive practical suggestions and background advice.

For those who want to delve a bit deeper into the subject see the list of further reading on page 54.

How to record oral history

The origin of oral history in the 1970s coincides with the availability of affordable tape recorders. Such reel-to-reel tape recorders have been superseded by cassette tapes and more recently by mini-discs (although mini-disc recordings are tricky to transfer to computers for editing). Now recording direct to the hard drive of a laptop computer is the best option, using a suitable external microphone.

Another good way of recording is to use a video camera, probably with external microphones to get the best sound quality from both interviewee and interviewer. The aim is not to produce a sophisticated film, so putting the video camera on a tripod, pointing it at the interviewee (preferably from the side so they tend to forget about its presence) and then to all intents and purposes ignoring it is quite sufficient. By having a video, facial expressions and body language can add to the impact of the verbal reminiscences. With digital video cameras the image and sound can be readily imported into a computer for editing – for this reason alone consider this option rather than, say, mini-disc or cassette recordings.

When done properly oral history is much more than casually jotting down reminiscences. By interviewing a number of people with a common background a cumulative account of their experiences can be built up. Often this involves quite ordinary aspects of their lives – such as schooling, clothing, shopping, domestic chores – that are often too 'unremarkable' to form part of conventional records. Yet what was commonplace merely 40 or 50 years ago now seems increasingly distant from modern assumptions and expectations.

The person being interviewed needs to feel relaxed. This may mean that preliminary meetings and 'chats' are necessary to build up the required level of trust. Frustratingly not everyone who has an 'interesting story to tell' will want to be interviewed. And a great many will either refuse to be taped or videoed, or unexpectedly become tongue-tied in the presence of a microphone. As good shorthand is not a skill acquired by most local historians, this can cause significant problems.

The person interviewing needs to have a number of skills. They must be able to operate the tape recorder or video camera confidently. They must be able to listen and encourage the interviewee, without unnecessary interruptions. Questions must be open-ended (i.e. cannot be answered simply with a 'yes' or 'no') and not impose a bias (i.e. should take the form of ''What were your holidays like?' rather than 'You must have enjoyed your holidays'). Interviews usually benefit from being guided by pre-planned topics, but the interviewer must be alert enough to ask for more information about specific remarks. So ask for clarification on statements such as 'She used to live in Brown's old house' which leave anyone who does not know where Mrs Brown used to live (and she may have died or moved 30 or more years ago...) none the wiser.

Wherever possible make sure that there is only the interviewee and the interviewer (perhaps with a 'technical assistant') in the room. There is nothing worse than trying to interview someone while someone else is continually interjecting and telling them what they should be saying! The exception to this is organised 'reminiscence sessions' at elderly people's homes or monthly meetings for the elderly. Such sessions tend to stimulate reminiscences that might otherwise have not been recalled, but they can be dominated by a minority of contributors. They are usually a nightmare to record as often more than one person is speaking at one time, and it is difficult to place a microphone in a place where everyone is clearly recorded.

One very successful way of collecting reminiscences is to ask people to look out their old photographs. Even typical family photographs may be taken in front of significant buildings or show locations that have since changed substantially. If the owners of the photographs are agreeable then scan in these photographs (a portable scanner and a laptop computer means that the photographs never leave their owner's house). Now for the interesting stage. If Mrs A has talked about her photographs and allowed you to take copies, go along to see Mrs B down the road. Let Mrs B talk about her photographs, but then show her any of Mrs A's photographs that may contain people, buildings or locations that Mrs B would also know. You may find that Mrs B has recollections that add to those of Mrs A (or, indeed, may contradict what Mrs A said!). If appropriate permission has been granted then the more interesting of such photographs can be put on a Web site, together with the ability for anyone to email their recollections about the photographs. Not quite oral history as it was envisaged in the 1970s, but a way of potentially making contact with a wide range of previously-unknown 'informants'.

Oral history recordings may provide a rich resource for dialect studies. If you suspect that 'informants' have a distinctive dialect then be sure to ask where they grew up, and how long they have lived in their present village or suburb. Dialect researchers are especially interested in people who have lived most or all their lives in one locality. However a recording loses much of its value to dialect researchers if it is not known how long the speaker has lived in a location, or where they grew up.

The legalities of oral history

An oral history recording is usually only of real value if it can be placed in an archive, or the transcript published in some form. And this means that the person being interviewed must allow you to do this. In the absence of such consent it is unethical to publish such interviews and quite probably contravenes copyright (and there are separate rights in (a) the words spoken; (b) the recording; (c) any transcription of the recording). Bear in mind that copyright can only be assigned in writing, never just be 'word of mouth' (see pages 56 to 61).

Without such consent you will have to wait until 70 years after the death of the interviewee before being able to:

- copy the recording (even to make back ups or donate to a Record Office or other archive);
- play the recording in public or include on a Web site or CD-ROM;
- include a transcript in paper publications, exhibitions or Web sites;
- adapt in any way.

So even the most informative interview is to all intents and purposes a waste of time unless a suitable consent form is signed. Trying to get consent retrospectively is usually fraught and, if the interviewee has moved away or died, it may be difficult to contact anyone in the family who is authorised to give such consent.

Opposite: *A form devised for the Memories of Nottinghamshire project which collects scans of old photographs and recordings of reminiscences about the photographs.*

MEMORIES OF NOTTINGHAMSHIRE

COPYRIGHT ASSIGNMENT AND CONSENT FORM

FOR ORAL HISTORY RECORDINGS AND PHOTOGRAPHS

The purpose of this assignment and consent is to enable the Memories of Nottinghamshire project to permanently retain and use the photographs and recorded recollections of individuals.

As present owner of the copyright in the contributor content (i.e. the words recorded by and/or the photographs copied today by the Memories of Nottinghamshire project), I hereby assign copyright to the Memories of Nottinghamshire project on the understanding that the content will not be used in a derogatory manner.

I understand that no payment is due to me for this assignment and consent.

I understand that I am giving the Memories of Nottinghamshire project the right to make available the content of the recorded interview in the following ways:

- use in publications, including print, audio or video cassettes or CD-ROMs
- publication worldwide on the Internet
- public performance, lectures or talks
- public reference purposes in libraries, museums & record offices
- use on radio or television
- use in schools, universities, colleges and other educational establishments, including use in a thesis, dissertation or similar research

Do you want your name to be disclosed? YES/NO

Signed:

Print name:

Date:

Address (including postcode):

Name of interviewer(s)/recordist(s):

Brief details of deposited material (continued on a separate sheet if necessary):

Furthermore appropriate consent forms mean that a collection of oral history recordings will probably not need to be registered under the terms of the Data Protection Act (1988).

However the assignment of copyright is distinct from the 'moral rights' of the interviewee (see page 67). Moral rights cannot be assigned and so remain with the interviewee. This gives them the right to be named as the 'authors' of their words (although technically this right needs to be 'asserted') and, in any event, publishers are required not to adapt anyone's words in a way that might be deemed derogatory (such as by making alterations that give a false impression of what was said or meant).

One further legal issue should always be borne in mind – when publishing interviews make sure nothing is defamatory, otherwise an expensive legal action directed at the publisher may ensue.

Transcribing oral history interviews

After the interviews have taken place then transcriptions need to be made. This is very time-consuming – every hour of recording will take several hours of careful transcription. Transcription is more of an art than a science. Think of your role more as a translator than an editor and bear in mind the following guidelines:

- Never correct the interviewee's words, grammar or speech patterns (such idiosyncrasies are an important aspect of oral history)
- Never add words or otherwise change the content or intent (although parenthetical comments may be added if necessary to clarify ambiguities).
- Use em-dashes separated by a space (' — ') for brief pauses and for unfinished sentences.
- Use square brackets for relevant non-verbal events, such as [pause], [giggles] or [doorbell rings].
- Avoid including every pause, 'um' and 'ahh' (and 'uh' after words) but do include them they are significant to the specific part of the interview e.g. if the interviewee is finding it difficult to discuss say the death of a close friend or relative, or it is clear that the interviewee is choosing their words carefully to keep a skeleton in the closet!
- Likewise usually avoid the interviewer's noises of encouragement ('Ah yes', 'Oh really!', 'Hmmm') but do include them when they cause the interviewee to change tack or explicitly respond to them.

- If necessary adopt consistent spelling for dialect words.
- Adopt a 'house style' for quote marks etc (see page 51) and standardise font style and other typographical details (see page 141)
- Ask for help with any unintelligible sections of the recording. If necessary use square brackets such as [unintelligible because of traffic noise] to indicate words or passages that are not transcribed.

Note that person(s) transcribing the interview own the copyright to the transcript. This is in addition to the interviewee's rights to the words themselves (which should have been assigned using a consent form) and to the rights in the recording (owned, unless otherwise assigned, by the person who made the recording *or* the person or organisation who paid for the tapes etc on which the recording was made). Preferably transcriber(s) should assign copyright or, at the very least, make provision for copyright to be clearly assigned in the event of their death.

Family 'lore'

As already noted, oral history interviews can include passed down recollections of more personal events that can be thought of as 'family folklore'. However there is more to family 'lore' than such narratives. Indeed, often such tales are rarely told in their entirety but alluded to with a 'catch phrase' that means little to anyone else. Like nicknames and 'in' jokes, these sort of remarks simultaneously define who is part of the family (i.e. 'in the know') and bond the members of the family together. They are among the most interesting – and easily lost – aspects of any family's history.

For example, my mother and her mother-in-law could be reduced to fits of giggles by someone interrupting an appropriate conversation with 'You know where the Electricity Showrooms is... '. Anyone in that part of my family would also know exactly what was meant by 'Don't do an Aunt Beth...'.. Other examples of family lore include remarks such as 'Oh, remember the time at Andrew's wedding... ' which are never expanded on because everyone in the family recalls all too well what happened then.

Good examples of family lore and 'customary practices' can usually be found whenever the family gets together for fairly ritual events such as birthdays, Christmas, weddings, christenings and funerals. Most families do something a 'bit different' at such events. As an example of family customary practice, my mother's family (from rural Leicestershire) always had pork pie and toast for breakfast on Christmas Day. This was considered very odd by my father, who had grown up in the city of Leicester. The 'ritual' was adapted in later years by incorporating my mother's liking for Bucks Fizz. I suspect that few other families would even consider enjoying Bucks Fizz, pork pie and toast while opening their presents!

Weddings are especially interesting because here two families need to exchange the distinctive 'lore' that bonds each of the families together so that there is a sense of shared identity between the two sets of in-laws. So at a family wedding reception look out for the aunts from one family getting together with the aunts of the other family (and, all too often it is the aunts that spontaneously feel the need to share such family lore) and, after a few small sherries, explaining how a person acquired their rather scurrilous nickname, or exactly what did happen at Andrew's wedding (although you will be need to be part of the family for much longer before you are likely to know what Aunt Beth got up to...).

Nicknames

Nicknames used within the family or village are a valuable insight into the human nature of communities. In some families, especially in the second half of the nineteenth century and into the twentieth, baptismal names were rarely used and people known to their family and friends by entirely different names.

For example my maternal grandmother, born in 1904, has 'Sarah' as her first name on her birth certificate. However her father had just helped give birth to a calf while she was being born and both calf and daughter were always referred to as 'Dot'. In adult life she introduced herself as 'Dorothy'. Only in her 80s, when she had outlived most of her family and friends and went to live about twenty miles away did she decide to introduce herself as 'Sarah'.

While nicknames do not always get written down, they are an important aspect of family and local life and should be recorded whenever encountered. If the reference to the person is only a passing one, nicknames can be included as either 'Sarah "Dorothy or Dot" Dallaston' or 'Sarah ("Dorothy" or "Dot") Dallaston'.

From ancestor worship to 'real lives'

Such family lore and customs reveal that there is much more to a family than 'Biblical' lists of who begat who. While family trees are the backbone of family history research, unless fleshed out they are little more than ancestor worship, and only the start of the research needed for worthwhile writing and publication. Most certainly a family tree is not the end result of research – the lives of the people need to be developed into a story-like narrative which is easily digested by the readers and, so far is possible, makes entertaining reading.

Despite all the effort needed to track down the necessary information, families are not simply about names, births, marriages and deaths. These are landmarks in lives that are lived in communities, by people who have occupations or businesses, and who – if successful – will own and transfer property. Any one family interacts with any number of other families. Some people will have led lives that had a notable influence – for good or otherwise – on other peoples' lives.

Just as local history research needs to be developed so that it tells the story of the people rather than simply the place, so too the bare facts of family history research need to developed into brief accounts of families and their communities who are living – typically or otherwise – in the social milieu of their time. The emphasis should not be on individuals but on the *interactions* between individuals.

Look for contrasts within families. In *Glad for God* by John Hamilton (Heart of Albion 2003) the author compares the branch of the Bousfield family that stayed put in Nottinghamshire with the branch that moved down to Bedfordshire. The Nottinghamshire Bousfields remained with the Church of England and several of them ran local pubs. The Bedfordshire branch converted to Methodism and, in sharp contrast, became leading pioneers of the nineteenth century temperance movement. By putting these developments into the social and political context, locally and nationally, the contrasts in this one family became a microcosm of changing attitudes in England at that time.

Follow up anyone who is notable – or achieves notoriety! The Bedfordshire Bousfields included an important inventor of agricultural equipment. By tracing patents and the reviews of his new equipment in the trade press of the time, the author was able to write the first account of this man's previously overlooked achievements. Although starting out as fairly straightforward, albeit very thorough, family history research, the author achieved an account of much wider relevance and interest.

Gazetteers and guide books

Some types of local history books read – in whole or in part – as gazetteers, for example guide books which list villages in alphabetical order. The following remarks also apply to information about places which can be visited in the course of a walk, cycle ride or car tour. The main way such gazetteers and guides are used means they are read 'piecemeal' rather than from cover to cover. Aim for a standardised sequence of information rather than any attempt at 'literary variation'. Information which is needed most quickly – such as directions – should be at the start or end of the section, and perhaps typeset with a distinctive font or layout.

For example, a guide book to prehistoric monuments could have the following sequence (although not all categories of information may be available for every monument described):

- Name
- Parish
- OS 1: 50,000 sheet number and 6 or 8 figure grid reference
- Directions from nearest road
- Advice on access (e.g. permission must be obtained from nearby farm; footpath exceptionally muddy in wet weather)

- Type of archaeological monument (e.g. stone circle; hill fort; burial chamber; burial mound) and approximate date
- What can be seen (perhaps augmented by a sketch map, photograph or drawing)
- Any important lost or buried archaeological information
- Nearby archaeological sites relevant to the appreciation of this monument
- Summary of earliest archaeological investigations
- Any folklore or popular interpretations (or misunderstandings!) of the monument
- Current archaeological interpretation
- Whether or not any finds are in local museums (if important artefacts from the site are in museums then photographs or drawings are especially helpful)
- Bibliography of published archaeological information about this monument (unless clearly listed in an appendix)
- Any additional information helpful to the visitor (e.g. nearest refreshments or toilets)

This is probably a greater variety of information than encountered in most other types of guidebooks but hopefully provides a few clues for other subjects.

Old photographs

Be careful about planning books based mostly on old photographs. Considerable skill and some experience is essential to avoid poor-looking reproduction (see Chapter 4). Above all, the limited space devoted to text – usually just captions and a short introduction – means that the writing has to be exceptionally 'crisp' to avoid being merely pedestrian.

The skill is to write a caption that goes beyond stating the 'who, what, where and when' necessary to appreciate the photograph. The aim is to subtly and concisely 'tell a story' about the event or people depicted, and to make this part of a wider understanding of the locality – although some photographs will lend themselves to such narrative captions more easily than others. (See page 98 for more on writing captions.)

Transcribing documents

A different type of primary research may involve the preparation of transcriptions or translations of old documents. R.F. Hunnisett has provided detailed help in *Editing Records for Publication, Archives and the User* No.4 (1977).

There are some key issues which apply even when short extracts are being transcribed:

- Reproduce the text as accurately as possible.
- Do not add or omit without clear editorial marks.
- The heading should state where the document is stored and the repository's document reference.
- Abbreviations which are unambiguous should be expanded in square brackets.
- Abbreviations which are doubtful should be left unexpanded and with an apostrophe ' to shown the abbreviation.
- Alternatively, expand the abbreviation in a square bracket but end the expansion with a question mark '?'
- *Either* retain *all* original spelling, punctuation, paragraphing and capital letters, however inconsistent, *or* modernise all spelling, punctuation and capitals.
- Figures and numerals should be as the original i.e. Roman, Arabic or mixed.
- Rubrics and other headings should be underlined.
- If there have been alterations and the original version is legible, provide this in a footnote.
- Gaps, tears and illegible sections should be indicated thus: [...]
- Recurring phrases may be contracted (e.g. TRE for *Tempore Regis Edwardi* [i.e. early 1066] in Domesday surveys)
- To denote mistakes in the original thus: [sic]

Where and what to write about

The tendency of local history to be based on a specific parish dates back to the origins of local history research, when it was typically the local clergyman who took an interest in the parish records and recorded the recollections of his parishioners.

In some ways the parish may be too big a unit for a local history study as even a small village will yield endless sources of material for local history. The researcher may need to focus on specific aspects of the history rather than attempt to find out 'everything'.

Too many 'village history' publications are excessively parochial, as if the events described are entirely self-contained. However, no community exists in isolation so local events should be linked to relevant regional and national events. For instance, churchwardens do not remove screens and altars in the sixteenth century entirely of their own accord – the Reformation led to various mandatory laws. Workhouses do not appear in the early eighteenth century through local whim – they are a result of national legislation. Likewise if the church was rebuilt in the mid-nineteenth century it was almost certainly conforming to the Gothic Revival fashion which had started in the 1840s. Events at the local level fall into two broad classes – they either conform to regional or national trends, or they are in some way deviant. The writer should indicate where local events are normal in a wider context – or draw attention to the untypical local situation.

Local history is normally seen as the history of a place – probably a village, perhaps a town, or specific aspects of a larger settlement. However, one unusual research project involved the history of a road *between* towns, drawing upon old photographs, the history of inns, important houses and factories along the way. This particular project also revealed a surprising amount of folklore – especially previously unrecorded ghost stories.

Other approaches may involve the study of a specific subject (such as holy wells, church monuments, wind or water mills, framework knitting, etc.) on a regional basis. There may be practical reasons for limiting a project to a specific county. However sometimes there is much similarity between adjoining counties, especially when the county boundary is a river valley. In such instances a topographically-defined scope may be more suitable than one defined by the more arbitrary administrative boundaries – so the 'water mills of the Avon' may make more sense than a study restricted to one of counties through which the Avon flows, especially when the river forms a county boundary.

In a few instances a county boundary defines a significant contrast, as where the Roman Watling Street forms the county boundary between Leicestershire (originally part of the Danelaw and considered part of the East Midlands) and Warwickshire (not part of the Danelaw and regarded as part of the West Midlands). The accent changes markedly within a few parishes and comparative studies have revealed that inter-marriage between adjoining Leicestershire parishes was higher than between adjoining parishes that straddle Watling Street. Look out for similarly significant contrasts elsewhere.

Sometimes the survival of documents enables aspects of one place's history to be described in unusual detail. This may lend itself to regional comparisons between places with a common link. Academic historians are rather fond of such comparative studies but this does not mean that such studies need to be dry and dusty.

Despite the tendency for local history to be about geographically-defined areas, always bear in mind history is about *people,* not just places. Make sure the convenience of limiting a study to a specific village, town or county does not diminish the opportunities for bringing the topic to life.

Non-documentary sources

The conventional distinction between historians and archaeologists is that the latter are 'prehistorians', dealing with preliterate societies. But this distinction is now bunkum – much archaeological investigation has been directed at Roman and medieval remains, where documentary evidence may be available to help interpret the artefacts. And with the increasing interest in post-medieval and industrial archaeology, copious records may survive. For example, most episodes of *Time Team* confirm that at least some documentary evidence is available to help the interpretation of remains that are up to 1,000 years old.

Apart from archaeology there are other important aspects of local history that are best thought of as non-documentary. Among these are buildings (which might be thought of as 'standing archaeology'), natural landmarks, and every aspect of the 'countryside'. In my more flippant moments I refer to these as 'historical sources you can go out and kick'. Collectively they can be referred to as 'landscape archaeology', a term invented in the 1950s by its pioneer W.G. Hoskins.

In an attempt to understand the historical records about 'lost' medieval field villages, Hoskins did something decidedly heretical for an historian in the 1950s – he put down his old documents, put on a pair of comfortable boots, and went out to look at the present day fields and lanes in Leicestershire which overlaid the abandoned medieval villages he was reading about. And the results were far more exciting than he had expected. To his expert eye the modern landscape preserved evidence of not just the immediately previous field systems but, at least in some places, evidence for a whole sequence of changes. Ancient boundaries, field systems, and the 'humps and bumps' of long-since abandoned medieval houses could all be discerned if you knew where to look.

The publication of Maurice Beresford's book *The Lost Villages of England* in 1954 and Hoskins' book *The Making of the English Landscape* in 1955 alerted both specialists and the public to this exciting new concept of 'landscape archaeology'. Map-like aerial photographs of much of England taken by the RAF in the late 1940s, plus others taken specially, provided a novel and seductive way of experiencing these new approaches to past landscapes.

Hoskins famously observed that in the English landscape everything is much older than we think it is, as (apart from the field boundaries created during eighteenth century enclosures) much else dates back to the medieval era, in most cases to the formation of nucleated settlements and their associated 'great field' systems in the ninth or tenth centuries. About twenty years later further research revealed that in some places aspects of the landscape were much older than even Hoskins thought, as Iron Age and even Bronze Age boundaries and field systems seem to have persisted for over 2,000 years.

By the mid-1980s landscape archaeology had moved on and become concerned with physical evidence for changes in population, climate, land use, the technology of farming, settlement patterns, and the organisation of space. This approach was given the text book treatment by Michael Aston (later to don stripey jumpers and become the kingpin of *Time Team*) in his book *Interpreting the Landscape* (Batsford 1985). However such sophisticated analysis was achieved at the expense of effectively depopulating the landscape – there was no attempt to see the land through the eyes of the people who once lived there, still less about how social practices and customs influenced the use of the land or brought about changes. Local historians attempting to build on the insights of specialist landscape archaeologists need to address this academic weakness.

There are several useful books on landscape archaeology. Christopher Taylor brought Hoskins' *The Making of the English Landscape* up to date with a heavily annotated edition (Hodder and Stoughton 1988). The recent *Historic Landscape Analysis: Deciphering the countryside* by Stephen Rippon (Council for British Archaeology 2004) offers practical advice. For villages in the East Midlands and East Anglia Tom Williamson's *Shaping Medieval Landscapes: Settlement, society, environment* (Windgather Press 2003) offers a novel and persuasive argument for the formation of nucleated villages in the Anglo-Saxon era.

Must time dictate?

Conventional local history tells its tale through chronological ordering. The starting points vary but usually there is a superficial account of any archaeological finds, probably a translation of the entry in Domesday (although all-too-rarely is there any discussion of how this fits in with regional trends), a brief mention of the origin of the place-name (but rarely any suggestion of what broader significance this may have), transcriptions (often of dubious accuracy) of medieval and early modern documents, followed by a fits-and-starts coverage of the eighteenth century onwards depending on the availability of well-researched documentary sources, and perhaps concluding with recollections from people born about seventy years ago, together with a selection of old photographs. Non-documentary sources of information, such as topography and landscape archaeology, may sometimes be fitted into their respective time slots, together with detailed descriptions of historic buildings.

But is this really presenting the history of the place as above all a settlement of human families? The availability of detailed information for one period might mean that a thorough analysis and synthesis of just that part of the overall sequence would be far more worthwhile. This is especially true of, say, the nineteenth century, where even the most humdrum community will be documented in numerous ways.

In *Writing Local History* David Dymond (Phillimore, 2nd edn 1988) quotes a local historian in a commonly-encountered situation: 'It seemed such a pity to have all these bits and pieces lying about, so I decided to put them in chronological order.' Such an uncreative approach is surely the least satisfying solution to the circumstances! Each local history project will require its own approach. Convention is not necessarily the best guide.

The 'inevitable' march of progress

Far too often the chronological account builds up into a remorseless march of progress – the transport gets better, the schools get better, the population gets larger, local administration is reformed, piped water arrives, and so on and so on. Such 'triumphalist' accounts should ring loud alarm bells. 'Progress' is something which is only seen in retrospect, and usually only by ignoring a great many 'inconvenient' inconsistencies. Rather than fall for this propaganda – and it is propaganda – the local historian should assess the evidence as impartially as possible. For example, just how easily was Victorian prosperity achieved? Were there setbacks? How homogenous was nineteenth century society – was prosperity really shared by all, or just enjoyed most by those who left the records?

Everyone has heard the expression 'History is written by the victors'. It is equally true for local history. Records and historical accounts are usually written from the 'top down'. This means the attitudes of major landowners take precedence over the 'common people' – who usually left less in the way of written records, and whose names more often than not enter historical accounts only when they transgress the norms of the period and appear before the judiciary. Likewise the supremacist stance of the Church of England subtly or otherwise colours perceptions of the 'dissenting' denominations – note for a start the ideologically biased terminology of 'dissent'.

Such 'top down' bias is especially noticeable with the eighteenth and nineteenth century Enclosure Awards. The typical historical accounts of this era are written from the perspective of the larger landowners who usually benefited from these awards. But what happened to the people who lost commoners' rights and had to adapt to a new economic regime based on wage labour? Census data shows that most villages grew after parliamentary enclosure awards, suggesting that the requirements for wage labour were greater. But Poor Law records may offer conflicting evidence about the prosperity of these labourers. Some villages were more open than others to growth, usually when the land was mostly held by tenant farmers rather than by a resident landowner. Yet other villages also developed at this time in other ways – for example, becoming centres for framework knitting or lace-making. How does the settlement or region you are studying fit into these general trends? Was 'progress' that easily recognised at the time, or by all people?

Key players in the heritage industry, such as The National Trust, have long beguiled us with the illusion of stately homes and country houses that magically sustained themselves without human intervention. The reality – the luxury of a few was often sustained by near-slavery for a great many servants – has been conveniently excluded from the ideologically-loaded heritage myth that presents the past as a romantic idyll. While this is an extreme example, local historians should remain wary about accepting other deeply-rooted myths about British history that have been developed over the last hundred-or-so years.

When to start writing?

The simple answer is: sooner rather than later. Too many local historians enjoy researching ever-deeper into their subject but then fail to write up their efforts for the benefit of others. Claiming that one has not finished the research is no excuse – no subject can be fully researched, and no research remains complete or definitive for long. Frankly, if you are not willing to rise to the challenges of writing up your research for the benefit of other people, all the time spent researching might as well have been spent watching TV or talking down at the pub.

After a time sufficient information will have been obtained on a specific aspect which enables the basic interpretation to be made confidently. Further details may well emerge but these will not cause a fundamental revision. This is the time to begin writing up that aspect. Leave it longer and the quantity of 'secondary detail' will make it more difficult to get to grips with the main analysis.

Any item of local history writing longer than an essay can be broken into fairly self-contained sections. The writing of one section can proceed while another section still awaits further research.

With family history research writing drafts as you go is fairly essential. Tracing of names, dates and other 'primary' information usually concentrates on a specific branch of the family. The nitty gritty detail and the unresolved ambiguities may be forgotten after you have moved onto another chunk of research. Rather than leaving a rather messy set of notes and putting off the challenges of linking it all together, put together a reasonable draft *before* you move on to the excitement of generating yet more notes. Writing such a draft inevitably shows where more research might be needed. At this stage you may not know where to look for the necessary information or you may be unable to visit geographically-remote archives. Just leave suitable notes in the text while putting together a narrative that links together what you have discovered.

There is a maxim that says that all stories have a beginning, a middle and an end. However this is especially unhelpful for family history, where the beginning is lost in the mists of time, and the end has yet to come. The narrative aspect of family history needs to be less about the family 'as a whole' than the lives of the people – and these tales most certainly have apparent beginnings, middles and ends, even if they span several generations.

If all else fails begin by dealing with topics of regional or national importance, and introduce your ancestors into the 'bigger story'. So if you are having difficulty finding out details of your seventeenth century predecessors, summarise any previously-published historical accounts of the Civil War and Commonwealth era for the areas where they lived, and put your relatives' lives into this context.

Put concisely, if the foreground is rather devoid of detail, make the background more interesting. So, even if you have not traced all the individuals in the early seventeenth century, the geographical occurrence of a surname is probably easier to establish and this can be part of the story.

If you have a parallel interest in other aspects of history – say costume or traditional farming practices – then include appropriate details as background to your predecessors' lives.

Sometimes the sheer difficulties – and, less rarely, the satisfactions – of a particular episode of family history research will itself be a tale worth telling. This is an approach that needs to be handled carefully – concentrate only on the main aspects and avoid mentioning every minor detail. Still less keep harping on about how difficult it was – 'show don't tell' the reader the problems and allow them to infer your feelings at the time. Keep the reader wondering what happens next. If one particular anecdote starts rambling on then intervene a 'sub plot' before coming back to the original previous aspect. If appropriate make one story the 'framing story' inside which other narratives are interwoven. The 'How I did it' approach is difficult to pull off but can work well if there is a strong sense of suspense and plenty of verbal illustrations.

'I've not finished the research' is never an excuse

Putting off starting to write up because you think the research is not yet finished is never an excuse. No research is ever finished and with both local and family history the more information you collect then the more questions arise. Family history research is especially prone to being open-ended. However there is always a point at which enough is known about a topic to make a reasonable interpretation. This is the time to put the notes into a suitable order and begin to draw together your overview. Often the act of writing everything out will reveal critical gaps or at the very least sources that need to be checked or rechecked. This may also reveal problems with keeping track of the exact details of your sources – something that will be easier to correct earlier than later.

Always start to write up one project, even it means leaving a few gaps, before you move on to another project. If you find working through one folder of notes to prepare an article rather intimidating then how are you going to feel when you have a whole pile of folders of notes? Inexperience and lack of confidence with writing is certainly not helped by also having to deal with too much material. And, unless you have found a way of reversing the effects of human ageing, then the longer you put off writing up the less likely you are to start. Local and family historians can all make long lists of people those work was never written up and therefore to all intents and purposes lost when they became infirm or died.

By starting to write up sooner rather than later you are also gaining practice at the skills of putting information into order. This is not a skill that any of us are born with and, like any other skill, it only 'comes naturally' (if it ever does!) after considerable practice. However, the more you practice the easier it becomes.

There are plenty of opportunities to publish short articles. Local history magazines will be keen to include quite specialist and specific topics if they are written in an appropriate style. Aim to contribute one such article each year. With family history write up recent research as a 'newsletter' to be circulated to family members with their Christmas cards. Keep to a consistent design and layout so these accumulate into an attractive set of documents.

If all else fails

If you really cannot psyche yourself up for writing up an article – and we have all been there, for whatever reasons – then there is something else that you should do. Simply put all your notes into a 'time line'. This is especially helpful for family history where the commonest source of information is a list of names, dates of birth, marriage and death, etc.

By putting everyone's dates onto chronological sequence the bare bones of a story are already showing through:

1743 John Brown (II) baptised St Mary's church, Littlethorp

1745 Elizabeth Golightly born Littletown

1758 or 1759 John Brown (probable father of John Brown (II)) buried Littlethorp

1767 John Brown (II) marries Eliz. Golightly Littletown Baptist chapel

1789 John Brown (III) born Littletown

1792 Jane Brown born Littletown

1793 John Brown (III) buried Littletown Baptist chapel

1819 Thomas Hodgkinson named as licensee of The Three Crowns, High Street, Bigtown.

1821 Jane Brown marries Thomas Hodgkinson, SS Peter and Paul church, Bigtown

1821 John Hodgkinson baptised, SS Peter and Paul church, Bigtown

In practice you will probably have more exact dates for marriages, baptisms and deaths. You should also keep details of the sources for information with each entry. You may also want to add key regional and national events. Perhaps a spate of deaths coincides with an especially harsh winter, or poor harvests. Clearly if you know that any of the men have been killed or injured in a battle then you need to add pertinent details of the war to your time line.

It sounds rather tedious but this is an excellent way of structuring your information and offers benefits out of proportion to the effort needed to prepare the timeline.

This timeline may be sufficient to inspire you to write up *parts* of the family history as a specific story about certain people and events. Bear in mind that compiling details is not the same as writing – the latter needs a narrative, a 'story line', which provides a structure for all the 'facts'. And do not be tempted to include somewhat irrelevant information just because you happened to have tracked it down (even if considerable blood, sweat and tears were expended tracking it down – save that for another story!)

Beware that timelines are deceptive because what people do *not* do is also significant. Are there any reasons why Edna never married and remained a spinster? Why did George stay on the farm when both his brothers went off to the trenches in 1915? Likewise why did Mary stay in Dublin when her mother and sisters went to Liverpool? If one person never appears before the magistrates for being drunk and disorderly whereas known associates or relatives of his do, then this is interesting. Is there any suggestion that he had joined the Methodists?

If you have, or plan to create, a Web site for your family history (see Chapter 8) then such a timeline would be an excellent 'work in progress' to share with other researchers. The advantages of Web pages is that any references to a specific individual in the timeline could 'hyperlink' to a page specifically about that person, and vice versa; the same applies to places. You could also provide links to other peoples' Web sites; for example if one of your ancestors was killed in the Battle of Waterloo then rather than provide details of Wellington's campaign on your site you could link to appropriate military history sites.

Invent nicknames

With family histories first names may not be sufficiently unique, as with dynasties whose oldest sons are all called Thomas or John. The answer here is to nickname them. At an early stage of research this may have to be done as Thomas (1815–49), Thomas (1845–93), and so forth. At a later stage (but only when you have identified all the possible 'Thomases' etc) you might want to refer to them as Thomas (I), Thomas (II), etc. However this is rather dehumanising. Much better to call them 'Thomas the alehouse keeper', 'Thomas the orphan' (making it clear that he is the same as 'Thomas the cobbler' later in the narrative...) and so on.

People and places

If your ancestors grew up in a fairly small community then the more you find out about the people, the more you will be finding out about the places where they lived. If possible share notes with relevant local historians, or deliberately find out as much about the places' history as you sensibly can. This may well lead to an article which is as much about local history as it is about family history, especially if your ancestors were key members of the community, or inter-married in such a way that many of the inhabitants were relatives of your ancestors.

Articles for local history periodicals

Most of this book assumes that you will be both writing and publishing your research. However many researchers begin by writing articles to be published in relevant local history publications. You will probably be familiar with these publications as resources for your own researches. They broadly fall into four categories:

- 'heavyweight' transactions which normally record the history and archaeology of a county;
- lighter weight annual (or, exceptionally, more frequent) periodicals relating to a county or major city; these usually have the title along the lines of *Anyshire Historian*;
- quarterly or monthly newsletters, with short 'newsy' information;
- annual village-based or interest-based periodicals, again often called something like the *Newton Historian.*

The editors of transactions usually publish articles that are 'heavy' in both their content and style of writing. The other types of publication are usually edited by people who realise that a more lively style of writing is required, and are often happy to consider articles on quite narrow topics if they are well-researched and competently written. Such articles usually need to be under 3,000 words (and rarely over 5,000). This means they are an excellent way of sharing 'interim results' of larger projects, with the benefit that publication may draw other people's attention to your (perhaps rather specialist) interests, enabling them to share any relevant research with you.

Be sure to include key references to sources but, except for academic-style journals, aim to keep bibliographical details 'light'. Often a list of sources at the end is quite sufficient for articles, without many or any details in the text. Only with direct quotations do you need to provide clear details of the source.

When writing for a popular readership any technical terms (such as 'toft and croft', 'hearth tax', 'bastardy bond', etc) will usually need to be explained when first used; this is known as 'glossing' (from which the word 'glossary' derives).

So a sentence which originally read 'Thomas Hodgkinson's name appears on a bastardy bond of 1832, although this does not mean he is the father of Mary's child' could usefully be expanded to 'Thomas Hodgkinson's name appears on a bastardy bond of 1832. However as at least two bondsmen signed these documents (which ensured that a sum of money of between £40 to £50 was available to support the child until it reached about nine years of age) he is not necessarily the father of Mary's child.'

Never assume that all readers will be sufficiently familiar with all the terms you have learnt to bandy about comfortably. If someone already knows what the term means then they can happily skip on, the rest of the readers will be grateful for a reminder.

As a matter of interest, could you fairly exactly define 'toft and croft' or 'hearth tax' or have written the gloss about bastardy bonds? If, as I suspect, most readers will have only a vague idea of what these terms refer to and when they applied then the need for them to be glossed is self-apparent. There are many other terms that need glossing but I have picked on these three simply because I recently consulted several standard reference books on British history, local history handbooks and the like and none of these offered definitions of these terms. If I, with some background interest in such topics and well-stocked bookshelves, have difficulty pinning these terms down then I am sure most readers of popular articles will have greater difficulty. If, as I did with 'bastardy bond', you end up using a Web search engine to find a definition then you have to make an assessment of the source – not everything on the Web is necessarily well-researched! With luck you will find several definitions that say more or less the same thing.

All editors are happy to discuss ideas for articles and offer advice. Indeed most would much prefer to discuss an idea at the early stages rather than have to deal with something sent in out of the blue. Editors may have to take into consideration details which you will not be aware of, and normally have more experience of writing than most novice writers, so do not be surprised – still less offended – if there are requests for changes. All editors will fine tune references and typographical details to conform to the 'house style' of the publication.

Writing articles will build up your confidence sufficiently to tackle more substantial accounts of your research. Understandably, the very thought of writing a book of 30,000 to 60,000 words seems intimidating to anyone who has never written a book before (and, from personal experience, it only seems a little less challenging after writing several such books!). As the old Chinese maxim says, 'Every journey of a thousand miles begins with the first step', so breaking a major writing project down into article-sized 'steps' is an excellent way to avoid being intimidated by the overall aim.

The same is true not just for the written part but for building up experience with dealing with illustrations – photographs, maps, charts, etc. – and, where necessary, obtaining permissions for reproduction (see pages 56 to 61).

Writing articles has another advantage as it means that research is put down on paper before you with too much material to easily deal with (a well-known problem already mentioned in the previous section).

And, while this might seem a rather negative way of thinking, by working on articles you will learn from mistakes – such as not keeping sufficient details of sources – before the damage becomes too great.

There is another reason for writing articles and that is to promote books; this is discussed further on page 237.

The three elements of history

There is no such thing as 'truth' which can be discovered by ever-more exacting research. All historians evaluate their sources, reject those considered dubious or irrelevant, emphasise those which enhance their interpretation, and (subtly or otherwise) cajole the reader into sharing their views. Put another way, not all facts are equal. No two writers, no matter how esteemed, will interpret the same topic in exactly the same way.

Although no historian can ever reveal the 'truth' about the past, there is most certainly a correct approach to writing about the past. Three main elements should always be present:

> **Narrative** – the progression of circumstances with the emphasis on 'what happens next' and on 'what changed'.
>
> **Description** – 'what happened at a particular time'.
>
> **Analysis** – 'why this happened or that changed' and how events are connected with other local, regional or national activities. At times 'comparison' may be more relevant than 'analysis'.

Unfortunately local history publications all-too-often give copious descriptions, a little narrative, and maybe some analysis tacked on as an after-thought. This is neither competent writing nor rewarding reading. All three elements must be woven together. Description and explanation should be almost simultaneous. Details and broader viewpoints should be frequently interspersed. Description and opinions should be balanced.

Remember also that while dates are important to many aspects of history they are most certainly not the only aspect of history that is important. Dates tell us *when* something happened but do not, of themselves, say *why* they happened, still less why *you* think events happened as they did.

Writing history is essentially a way of creating narratives that put 'what happened at a particular time' into a wider context. At the same time, try to not simply 'tell' your readers, but 'show' them.

In recent years academic historians have realised that 'story telling' is an appealing way to present even the most intellectual ideas. Perhaps this 'historical storytelling' should not be a surprise as the main sources for academic historians have always been literary sources (such as letters and journalism) and judicial records (such as witness's statements), all of which are strongly narrative.

Only with much practice will the three elements of good local history writing come together naturally. Fortunately word processors readily allow ideas to be elaborated, cut about and frequently redrafted. There is no excuse for not taking full advantage of this benefit of computers!

Preparing for a first draft

When commencing work on a specific section or topic the first stage is to compile all relevant facts and data into some semblance of order. This may involve information being exported from databases, various sections of text being cut-and-pasted from word processor files, all interspersed with brief notes, perhaps citing sources or queries.

At this stage *actively* keep track of the *sources* of every item of information (see also page 44). Setting up a new database or document for this specific purpose may help keep bibliographical data safe and secure. While copying-and-pasting changes the details of sources can be lost or confused all too easily. And if you think you're going to remember exactly what came from where in a few months' time then you need to take a serious reality check, or at least be willing to put in vast amounts of effort later to re-establish and check the sources.

The importance of a synopsis

With all this fresh in your mind establish a synopsis listing the most important topics. More experienced writers may prefer this synopsis to be quite concise, but others will want to break topics down further, perhaps as far as paragraph themes. In attempting to set out this linear progression gaps or contradictions may emerge. This is quite normal. At worst considerably more research may be needed, at best it will bring into focus the inherent ambiguity of the situation.

While this book is about self-publishing, bear in mind one of the reasons why commissioning editors at 'real' publishers insist on seeing a detailed synopsis – it shows the author has thought in sufficient detail about the scope of the book to have avoided or resolved any problems with the progression of ideas. As most people reading this book will probably have less experience of writing than authors submitting to 'real' publishers they will benefit even more from the time needed to think through ideas in sufficient detail to prepare a synopsis. This is a lesson that I have learnt the hard way – believe me, major restructuring of a book halfway through the first draft is seriously dispiriting!

So, don't say I didn't warn you – adopt the stance of 'synopses are too much trouble' or 'I'm not the sort of writer who needs a synopsis' only if you are willing to risk all the time and trouble it will take to dig yourself out of whatever unexpected pitfalls arise while writing the book.

The first draft

When you have enough information on a specific aspect to make a confident interpretation there is nothing to do now except 'get stuck in'. No more procrastination or putting it off until tomorrow!

Nowadays writing skills cover a broad spectrum. Sadly, even those who have been through higher education rarely have the ability to write clearly and grammatically. The lucid style of historians such as W.G. Hoskins seems to belong to a lost era. However, this is no reason not to start writing, even if you consider your writing skills to be in need of considerable polish – there will be plenty of opportunities to put a shine on things later.

Local history is about ordinary people and everyday life, and therefore many readers will also be 'ordinary people' rather than history specialists. Those who write local history should be particularly concerned that their writing is both clear and stimulating.

The key thing to remember is that you are trying to inform and entertain the reader. Keep the ideas moving forward. Write as if some typical readers are sitting reading your work, or they are across the desk from you and you are reading it aloud to them. Your style will become warmer and more conversational. Above all, get quickly to the point – and keep to the point!

At this stage resist all temptations to get bogged down with niceties of style or fine detail. Leave notes to yourself to check out minor facts or make specific additions (use the 'highlighter' tool in your word processor to make these notes stand out). Unless you need to check continuity of an argument, do not keep stopping to read what you have just typed.

After a while a particular theme will have been concluded so take a break. However, come back as soon as possible (certainly the next day) otherwise continuity will be lost. 'Little but often' is far preferable to intensive but isolated episodes of writing.

Keep asking some basic questions:

- Who and what is this information for?
- Where and when do the readers need to know it?
- Are you informing, persuading, or both?

Keep your readers in mind. Are they likely to be young or old (or both)? What might they already know about the subject?

All local history writing needs to inform and engage the reader's imagination. Most local history writing – anything that will be read for pleasure rather than simply as part of wider research – needs to be entertaining. Unfortunately these simple and obvious objectives are rarely achieved by local history writers.

Writing for on-screen reading

How you write depends to a large extent on the expected readers and to some extent on the way it will be published. There are number of key differences between writing for paper publications and for electronic publications such as CD-ROMs and Web sites. Paper publications must be structured in a 'linear' way, where different ideas follow successively in different chapters, and ideas are explored successively.

In contrast Web sites and CD-ROMs allow (indeed require) ideas to cross-refer using hyperlinks, which means that readers will not have the same 'linear' experience of the information as with a book and can explore the information in many different ways.

Also Web sites and CD-ROMs need to use more illustrations, and can incorporate moving images, animations and sound in a way not possible with printed publications.

Quite often electronic publications will contain more information than even a large book, and can be 'open ended', as revisions and updates can easily be made, and Web sites may even encourage feedback from visitors.

When writing for Web sites and CD-ROMs remember that on-screen reading is different to using books. Most people 'skim' through text and only stop to read fairly short sections that grab their attention. Be sure to use much shorter paragraphs than are typical for books. Also provide plenty of subheadings and other clues as to what the text is about. Making sure the opening sentence of a paragraph gives a good idea of what the rest of the paragraph is about is also beneficial.

See page 163 for more detailed advice about writing for Web sites and CD-ROMs.

Style

Unless you are an experienced writer then the first draft or two should be concerned with getting the 'flow' of ideas into a sequence which works. Unfortunately, inexperienced writers rarely realise that this is a long way from a final draft. Somewhere between the first and final drafts the details of 'style' need to be tackled. Do not be surprised if this requires substantial rewriting! None of us are born with the ability to write clearly. It is a skill that needs to be developed.

After you have completed the draft of a section come back to it some days – preferably weeks – later. Now is the time to start polishing up the writing style.

Writing style is as individual as dress sense. The trick is to avoid *inappropriate* style or looking daft. One of the long-standing writing style gurus is William Strunk. Entering his name into a Web search engine will lead to numerous online versions of his book *Elements of Style*. Overleaf is the contents list for Strunk's guide.

Two other Web sites are especially relevant. One is called the 'Perdue OWL' (http://owl.english.purdue.edu/writers/introduction.html) which has masses of on-

INTRODUCTORY

ELEMENTARY RULES OF USAGE

- Form the possessive singular of nouns with 's
- In a series of three or more terms with a single conjunction, use a comma after each term except the last
- Enclose parenthetic expressions between commas
- Place a comma before 'and' or 'but' introducing an independent clause
- Do not join independent clauses by a comma
- Do not break sentences in two
- A participial phrase at the beginning of a sentence must refer to the grammatical subject
- Divide words at line-ends, in accordance with their formation and pronunciation

ELEMENTARY PRINCIPLES OF COMPOSITION

- Make the paragraph the unit of composition: one paragraph to each topic
- As a rule, begin each paragraph with a topic sentence; end it in conformity with the beginning
- Use the active voice
- Put statements in positive form
- Omit needless words
- Avoid a succession of loose sentences
- Express co-ordinate ideas in similar form
- Keep related words together
- In summaries, keep to one tense
- Place the emphatic words of a sentence at the end

A FEW MATTERS OF FORM

WORDS AND EXPRESSIONS COMMONLY MISUSED

WORDS COMMONLY MISSPELLED

Above: *The contents list for William Strunk's book* Elements of Style. *The full text is available as free downloads from various Web sites.*

line and off-line writing related resources, including a long list of further helpful links. The other is called 'Writing argumentative essays' (www.eslplanet.com/teachertools/argueweb/frntpage.htm). (These Web addresses are correct at the time of publication; if the sites move then try entering the name of the sites into a search engine.)

If you prefer the printed page to Web sites then track down the following books:

English for Journalists, Wynford Hicks (Routledge 1998)

Writing for Journalists, Winford Hicks, Sally Adams and Harriett Gilbert (Routledge 1999)

Building Arguments, Drew Hinderer (Wadsworth 1992)

Critical Thinking, William Hughes (Broadview 1992)

Critical Reasoning, Anne Thomson (Routledge 2nd edn 2002)

The next few sections make some specific suggestions for a 'makeover' of the first draft.

Involving the reader

Reduced to the most simple wording, a key piece of advice is simple: **Don't tell but show**. This means using 'action' verbs and nouns rather than 'impersonal' sentences. So *always* avoid such impersonal constructions along the lines of:

- It is said that...
- It was believed that...
- There is reason to suppose...
- There were thought to be...
- It seems that...
- It is possible that...

Where appropriate, use action verbs and nouns to put sight, smell and sound into the writing.

And, to provide an example of the maxim 'Don't tell but show', the next section is written in just such a manner. And, at the risk of being far too self-referential, this paragraph is an example of what the next section is trying to tell you...

Keeping the reader curious

The way journalists subtly keep readers' interest is to raise expectations for information about a specific topic. So, when a tabloid newspaper offers some attention-grabbing headline such as 'Newly wed wife has nookie with vicar', you can be sure that the first part of the article will contain more-or-less relevant facts, but the really interesting bit (for those who regard such revelations as interesting) will be at least half-way through, if not right at the end.

While local historians will rarely be dealing with extra-marital sex, the same sense of suspense and deferred satisfaction of curiosity can be used. Indeed it can be usefully combined with an opening paragraph that outlines the following section or chapter. So a section on the origins of a village could begin:

> The village of Longdale is first mentioned in the Domesday book of 1086. But it must have existed before this. Indeed the name itself probably predates the village as we think of it now.

This could be followed by a series of paragraphs discussing, firstly the Domesday evidence, then a summary of evidence (probably regional rather than specific to 'Longdale') for the nucleation of villages, leading on to a discussion of dating evidence for place-names in the region, and what types of land unit (and associated settlement patterns) would have been associated with such early place-names. Only then would the curiosity raised by the third sentence of the introduction have been satisfied – yet, all through what may be quite an involved discussion, the reader may have retained (if only subliminally) a sense of where it was all heading.

There are more direct ways of raising curiosity. These opening sentences could be reworded as one or more rhetorical questions:

> When was Longdale first mentioned in records? Did it exist before this? Could the name itself predate the village as we now think of it?

This still serves to outline the topics to be covered in the subsequent discussion and most certainly raises curiosity. However repeated use of such rhetorical questions ceases to work as an 'attention getter' and simply becomes an annoying mannerism. Far better to make a habit of raising curiosity with 'incomplete' statements that are 'completed' later, and save explicit questions for the 'big occasions' when you need to make sure the reader really is paying attention.

At the end of a chapter the summing up could provide a bridge to the next chapter by 'anticipating' some of the key points that will be explored next. So, for example:

> From all this evidence William Hastings was clearly thriving in the 1460s. He now needed to show off this increased status by fortifying his houses in Leicestershire, using what in the fifteenth century was the very latest in 'one-upmanship' materials. Unusually, detailed records for the construction of one of these have survived; the next chapter is devoted to this insight into one of the last medieval castles built in Britain.

Note all the uses of 'curiosity raisers', for example, the new high status building material is not named (it is brick) and the location of the building for which records have survived is not disclosed (it is Kirby Muxloe). Note also how information is subtly put into some sort of wider context – the houses were status symbols, the records are 'unusual', the castle was 'one of the last'. In just 70 words the reader has a sufficiently clear idea of why the next chapter is going to delve deeply into the minutiae of medieval building accounts and is curious to read on.

Structuring paragraphs

Each paragraph must deal with a single clearly-identifiable theme. If not, break into two or more shorter paragraphs, even if the result is a very short paragraph (as this one is!).

Make sure that there is a logical link to the paragraphs before and after. If not, think whether a linking sentence or paragraph is needed, or whether a subheading would work better. (Reread this section of this book and consciously think about how the paragraphs have been broken up, and where subheadings have been used.)

Bear in mind that the reader's attention is limited, and that people who spend a lot of time 'surfing' Web sites tend to skip read. The first and last sentences of a paragraph should contain the main or strongest ideas, just as the opening of each sentence should be well-founded. On the same basis the first and last paragraphs of each section and chapter should provide a clear basis for what is to come or analysis of what has been presented.

Eschew sesquipedalianism*

Each sentence *must* be as clear and concise as possible. Some authors use four words when one would do. Others use an exotic term when an everyday one would be clearer. They may think this displays erudition. Far from it. Instead, they are taunting their readers and revealing their incompetence in basic communication.

Some academics love to use – or, worse still, invent – long words. Amateur writers are often fooled into thinking that these give their writing more authority. Most certainly not! Unusual words and jargon are obstacles to effective communication and betray muddled thinking. Always eliminate them.

However do not confuse jargon with technical terms such as 'cost of living index' or 'mean household size'. These expressions (provided they are explained fully when first used) are acceptable where no other word or phrase will convey the specific concept.

Also watch out for innocent words being corrupted – 'function' and 'situation' are especially susceptible to being violated. 'Absolutely', 'accountability', 'committed to', 'embed', 'enhance', 'global', 'hopefully ' and 'robust' are among many other victims of repeated abuse.

Some words and phrases have meanings which are only loosely-defined, or where the meaning depends on the context. Examples include 'the people', 'progress', 'the middle ages' and 'capitalism', but there are plenty of other examples to watch out for. Either replace such phases with more exact terms, or include a 'tighter' definition when you first use them.

* If you really want to know, 'sesquipedalianism' is Latin for 'using words a foot-and-a-half long'.

Keep things concise

Why 'commence' when you could simply 'start'? 'Accordingly' is far more cumbersome than 'so'. Words with Anglo-Saxon origins are easier than ones from French, while words derived from Latin are least easy for the reader. So 'turn' rather than 'revolve' and 'set up' instead of 'establish'.

Always eliminate any unnecessary clauses such as 'It can be argued that... ' or 'It should go without saying that... ' or 'It is true to say that... ' (to which my mental response is 'Which parts of what you have written are *not* true then?'). I've even come across writers who think they should tell us that 'It may or may not be true that... '. If you have a tendency to draft such out-and-out 'padding' and nonsense then make sure it gets eliminated at the first opportunity.

Sometimes you may feel the need to tell the reader 'It is important to understand that... ' or 'It is probably significant that... '. Such remarks can be completely eliminated on the basis of 'Why are you telling this if it is not important?'. If emphasis is needed it should be added not with a passive phrase but with just one 'active' word, such as 'Importantly... ', 'Significantly...', or 'Probably...'.

Avoid clichés like the plague

> At the end of the day they have all been done a million times before, and are getting a little tired. To be sure, I'll be as happy as a lark if they were few and far between. The bottom line is you can't see the forest for the trees when you're between a rock and a hard place – it's a can of worms, just one more bone of contention. Go back to the drawing board to get the best of both possible worlds and face the challenge to make continuous improvements a blessing in disguise. Mind boggling as this maybe, when it comes to a head such core values are a defining moment of the cutting edge. Even if you draw a blank with each and every example, the fact of the matter is that it is easier said than done in the foreseeable future to expect these to be few and far between. Whether or not this is food for thought or simply flogging a dead horse, forward looking people will fully diversify and give 110 percent to get the message across. Have I made myself perfectly clear?
>
> Hard on the heels on this head count of the holy grails at the heart of the matter there is a heated argument that, even if it grinds to a halt, hopefully – if you get my drift – it goes without saying that in terms of the final analysis the real issues that are the key to the problem need to be put in place. Last but not least, in the nick of time – and make no mistake about it – meaningful dialogue is the only way of meeting the challenge.
>
> To be sure, this means taking it to the next level. Walk the talk and welcome to the world of mumbo-jumbo. When all is said and done,

seriously consider whether this serves a role or whether to start the ball rolling by taking on board viable alternatives.

I make that 69 clichés in three paragraphs, not forgetting the heading. (Whoops, there goes another one – make that two; which then makes a hat trick. Who's counting anyway? I can't keep up...).

None of these clichés help clear communication. They are corporate-speak 'fog' that betrays the muddled thinking of their perpetrators. If you are tempted by such fossilised phases then twist them round – remember, you heard it here worst: he who burns the candle at neither end will wait in pain for the light at the end of the puzzle.

Readability

What makes some writing easier to read than others? Paying attention to four related issues makes all writing easier to read:

- Avoid unnecessary long words (i.e. those with 3 or more syllables).
- Avoid sentences with several long words.
- Keep most sentences to 24 words or less (the *average* sentence length should not exceed 20 words).
- Vary sentence length.

Some word processing software (such as Word) includes options for 'readability index' tests. One of the best-known is called the 'Flesch Reading Ease', which is based on the average number of syllables per word and average number of words per sentence. The scores range from 0 to 100 and the higher the score the easier the document is to read. Aim for a score of at least 60 (*Reader's Digest* editors are said to aim for a score of 75 on this test) and make changes if you score under 40.

Other reading index tests present scores as equivalent to the reading ability in American school grades. The Gunning Fog Index is widely used in the publishing industry – make changes if you score over 6th grade.

Break up sentences when possible

Two types of sentence should usually be broken up:

- Where 'which' or 'who' are not followed by a restrictive clause then break into two sentences and substitute with 'this', 'these' or the appropriate personal pronoun.
- Where a conjunction ('and', 'but', 'or') is followed by a 'parenthetical expression' enclosed by commas. If splitting into two sentences will not work, then consider replacing the conjunction with a semi-colon.

Sentences beginning 'While', 'Whereas', 'Although', 'Where' are often long and complex. Two simpler sentences can usually be created, although the second may need to start with 'Therefore', 'Thus', or 'However'.

Constructions using 'both . . . and', 'neither . . . nor' are always clumsy and should be reworded.

Cut out all superfluous statements such as 'I do not know whether or not they are related'. Worst of all are phrases that read to the effect that 'This statement is either true or not.'

First person and objectivity

Avoid using 'I' too often. Never use 'we' to refer to the author (except where the work is really the result of a team effort).

Never use impersonal constructions ('It is said that . . .', 'It is believed . . .', etc. – see page 35) to give a false objectivity to the author's beliefs or opinions.

Passive sentences

Involving the reader also means minimising the use of so-called 'passive sentences'. These are sentences that make an object or idea into the improbable instigator of some action. We use them all the time in conversation – 'The table's been booked for 8 p.m.' rather than 'I have booked a table for 8 p.m.' but they create an unnecessary distance between the writer and reader if used frequently.

Such passive sentences are regarded as necessary for 'academic' writing, but you should minimise their use when writing for a more general readership. So rather than 'This topic has been explored already ... ' try 'I have explored already ... ' or, involving the reader even more explicitly, 'We have already explored... '.

Tips on tense

Use the simple past ('went', 'announced') when the sentence includes some reference, possibly indirect, to the time or date when the event took place.

Use the present perfect ('have gone', 'have announced') when there is no reference to date – but avoid repeated use of the present perfect. Use the past tense when reporting what people said at a particular time.

Use the present tense when making a generalisation or drawing a wider conclusion from the evidence that is relevant to the present. In summary sections be sure to stick to one tense.

Tips on conjunctions

Two mistakes commonly made when speaking need to be eliminated in writing.

So:

- never use 'dates to' but always 'dates from'
- never use 'comprises of' but either 'comprises' or 'consists of'

Revisions to the draft

Once the first draft is well-advanced then go back and remove jargon and repeated words, tighten sentence structure, fill in minor gaps and maybe refine the basic structure and flow of ideas. Word processors – especially the built-in thesaurus – simplify all these tasks.

How to do it not

- Don't use no double negatives.
- Make each pronoun agree with their antecedent.
- Join clauses good, like a conjunction should.
- About them sentence fragments.
- When dangling, watch your participles.
- Verbs has to agree with their subjects.
- Just between you and i, case is important too.
- Don't write run-on sentences they are too hard to read.
- Don't use commas, which aren't necessary.
- Try to not ever split infinitives.
- Its important to use your apostrophe's correctly.
- Proofread your writing to see if you any words left out.
- Correct spelling is absoluteley essential.
- Don't abbr.
- You've heard it a million times: avoid hyperbole.

(Source unknown)

On a practical level, revisions may result in changes (such as deletions of substantial sections of text) which later you may want to 'undo'. My recommendation (based on problems resulting from *not* doing it this way!) is to keep the first draft (and also any subsequent completed drafts) 'tucked away' on the computer, and to revise a duplicate set of files. This way, going back to an earlier draft is always possible without delving into back up discs.

Referring to people

At a fairly late stage in the revision process read through checking specifically for references to people.

Firstly check that when a person is first mentioned you state their first name or, if this is not known, their initial(s). If all else fails then they should be 'Mr Smith' or 'Mrs Brown'.

Subsequent references to this person should usually be by surname only. However this clearly does not work with family histories – and even here first names may not be sufficiently unique, as with families whose oldest sons are all called Thomas or John. The answer here is to 'nickname' them (see page 27) – but do so consistently!

Except when a person's first name or initials are unknown avoid the use of conventional titles such as 'Mr' and 'Mrs', unless it is important to distinguish a 'Mrs' from a 'Miss'. What must be avoided is referring to some people as Mr John Brown or Mrs Beth Smith and others simply as Thomas Brown or Ann Smith, without there being any obvious reason why some get labelled 'Mr' or 'Mrs' and some do not.

However titles such as 'Sir', 'Lord', 'Dr' and 'Professor' should be included, at least the first time the person is mentioned. If the local GP was always referred to as 'Dr Black' or a squire was always addressed as 'Sir John' then this is the way they should be referred to throughout the book.

The final draft

So, now you think you are nearly there! Go through the draft again several times. Check just one of the following points each time (and try not to get distracted by the other things to be checked until it is their turn):

- Is the tense, voice and mood of the verbs consistent?
- Is each sentence expressed as clearly and concisely as possible?
- Ask 'What is the point of this paragraph?'
- Is each paragraph free from unnecessary duplications of words and phrases?
- Is the logical progression of ideas quite clear? Put yourself in the mind of someone who is approaching this 'cold' – would they still find the ideas linked easily together?

- Do facts get in the way of the flow?
- Would subheadings help?
- Is all the information under a subheading related to that heading?
- Are there too many short sentences made up of short words? Even worse, are there too many sentences which contain more than about 20 words, or with several polysyllabic words in close proximity? Not all sentences need to be short, but there must be a *good* reason for not breaking up a long sentence. Seek variety of word and sentence length.
- Are there any impersonal constructions (such as 'It is believed that... '; see page 35). Hint: use the 'Find' function of your word processor to find every 'It' and 'There'; some of course will be valid uses as pronouns. Above all eliminate any unnecessary clauses such as 'It can be argued that... ' or 'It should go without saying that... '.
- Are there any passive sentences (see page 40) and, if so, can they be eliminated?
- Have you used any jargon terminology (see page 37)? Are any terms vague?
- Double-check that each section deals only with the topic described in the words of the heading. Either change the wording of the heading or, more probably, add more headings.
- In some instances the clearest way of presenting information is by using 'bullets' (there are plenty of examples in this book, including this list). However, such lists should be checked to ensure that every item fits the wording of the introductory remark.

Essential feedback

Now put the text away for at least a fortnight and come back to it quite fresh. Go through everything once more. Then show it to at least three different people – preferably one who has detailed knowledge of similar topics and another who is a non-specialist but who is not shy about pointing out complex or ambiguous passages.

Chose people who are knowledgeable and likely to be frank. Friends and relatives may say it is great when it is anything but.

Schoolteachers are no longer reliable on grammar and have always been poor bets as critics of writing style. Editors of local papers may be able to help or recommend a colleague. Alternatively contact the Society of Freelance Editors and Proofreaders for recommendations. Their address is:

Society of Freelance Editors and Proofreaders
Mermaid House
1 Mermaid Court
London
SE1 1HR

telephone: 020 7403 5141
email: admin@sfep.org.uk
Web site: www.sfep.org.uk

Do not be tempted to argue with any feedback. You may have a clear idea of what you *intended* a remark to mean – but that does mean it cannot be read another way. Take note of all comments and then, in the cold light of another day, assess what changes are needed.

Under no circumstances be tempted to proceed to publication without either an experienced editor seeing the final draft, or having taken on board the suggestions of several well-informed people.

References

References are essential to any published history. Even the most popular of village history pamphlets should leave sufficient footprints to enable subsequent researchers to easily follow back to original sources.

However, my experience of editing local history books for publication is that few writers keep adequate notes on their sources. Initials of authors get 'lost', titles of frequently-cited works abbreviated or corrupted, names of publisher and dates of publication are erratically recorded and dates (for instance of newspapers) abbreviated inconsistently. All this will mean that extra time – all too often a lot of extra time – has to be found later to sort out the confusion. Much better to get it right in the first place!

For all published sources there are some basic 'essentials':

- The author (with first name or initials)
- The full *and correct* title of the work.
- The publisher (although this is less important for works over, say, 100 years old). Old fashioned practices of substituting place of publication for the publisher are most unhelpful.
- The year of publication. Where revised editions or facsimile reprints are involved then both the original and later publication details need stating.

- For articles in periodicals then the full and correct name of the article is needed, the title of the periodical, any issue and volume number, page numbers, plus of course the name of the author(s) – as ever, with first name or initials.

Non-published sources should be treated in the same manner but with a clear statement about the location of the document (with any reference number, if applicable e.g. county record offices assign accession numbers to their collections) or the date when 'personal communications' (usually abbreviated to 'pers. comm.') were received.

Ideally, each reference should cite a page number in the original source. Where articles in periodicals are cited, pagination should *always* be included. Unfortunately many researchers are not this thorough about keeping details such as page numbers, at least in the early stages of their work. With time it becomes exceptionally difficult to re-establish such details later. While keeping tabs on page numbers and the other minutiae of bibliographical details may initially seem like an unduly time-consuming chore, at a later stage you will realise that any time spent recording these details in the first place is usually much less than the time needed to re-establish such information later. There is a very simple moral to this paragraph – either start off with good habits or learn the hard way.

Footnotes and endnotes

Footnotes appear at the foot of the page, and endnotes appear either at the end of the chapter or at the end of the book. For convenience in this section I will refer to both as 'footnotes'.

You may have got used to reading books with copious footnotes, and may want to use them in your own writing to refer to sources or supplementary information. However most readers find footnotes unduly 'intimidating'. Unless you are writing *only* for an academic readership then avoid any form of footnoting. Brief remarks that are 'secondary' to the main text can appear in parentheses rather than being moved off into a footnote.

However the elimination of footnotes creates difficulties including bibliographical information. The Harvard system (see next section) provides a reasonably concise yet unambiguous solution. Most importantly, editing and redrafting text is much easier with the Harvard system than with traditional numbered footnotes.

Unfortunately some 'old school' humanities writers have a knee-jerk emotional reaction against the Harvard system, which they associate with scientific and technical writing. Frankly, take such emotional nonsense seriously only if you want to make life hard for yourself and your readers.

Worse still are writers who think that adding footnotes adds 'credibility' to their writing, even though they are writing for a popular readership. Far from adding credibility they are simply displaying all too clearly their unwillingness to write in an appropriate manner. No 'ifs'' 'buts', or 'maybes' – still less the arrogance of 'that remark doesn't apply to me' – in the final published version *never* use footnotes unless you writing only for academic readers.

Under no circumstances use Word's special footnote tool, except for initial drafts. It looks wonderful – but Microsoft have provided no way for this to be exported out to typesetting software. This means all such footnotes will have to be copy-and-pasted, and all the numbering will have to be manually reinstated – twice (once in the main text and again in the list of footnotes, without making any mistakes either time as these are very difficult to spot, and even more difficult to sort out). Unravelling Word's footnote function is a nightmare you will only want to experience once and, believe me, it's best never to go near there in the first place.

Harvard referencing system

With the Harvard system this book would be referred to in the main text as (Trubshaw 2005) – yes, including the round brackets. At the end of the book is a list of the full bibliographical details (see the next section for details of the format used).

Page references would be shown as (Trubshaw 2005: 16) or (Trubshaw 2005: 11–16) or (Trubshaw 2005: 3, 11–16, 55) – note *exactly* how the colon and comma are used. Multiple sources are separated by a semicolon thus: (Trubshaw 2005: 3; Smith 2001: 55)

Where the author is prolific it may be necessary to distinguish between (Trubshaw 2005a) and (Trubshaw 2005b). Multiple authors are cited as (Smith and Jones 2000) or (Smith *et al* 2002). It may also be necessary to distinguish between (A. Smith 2001) and (B. Smith 2001).

Preparing references for publication

Be warned. When editing it has taken as long for me to sort out the author's references as to edit the whole of the main text. Writers who are otherwise good at preparing their text may be sloppy about citing their sources or standardising abbreviations.

In general, minimise the use of full stops after abbreviations (e.g. 'PRO' rather than 'P.R.O.') and capital letters in subtitles (e.g. *A History of Anywhere: Some recent research* rather than *A History of Anywhere: Some Recent Research*).

When numbers are contracted (e.g. 1550–5) use an en-dash (' – ') not a hyphen (' - '). The quickest way to create an en-dash in Word is to type space, hyphen, space, any letter, space. Word will auto-correct the hyphen to an en-dash. Copy the en-dash (without the spaces) and paste where needed. Even better, learn how to set up Word's auto-correct function – it has lots of other good uses too! – and set this up to replace two consecutive hyphens with an en-dash (you'll need to create an en-dash then copy-and-paste it into the 'replace with' box). Once this is set up you can create an en-dash between numbers by simply typing two hyphens and the job's done!

Books should be cited thus:

> Smith, Alan, 1999, *A History of Anywhere: The Victorian era,* Littletown Publishing Co.

Note that the author's surname comes first, followed by the first name (or initials if the first name is not known), then the year of publication (in the case of revised editions, this is the year of the publication of the edition you are citing), the title and subtitle in italics, then the publisher. Pay particular attention to the use of commas, spaces and other punctuation. Ensure that there is *complete* consistency throughout the bibliography.

There are advantages in emphasising the authors' surnames in all capitals or in bold, e.g.:

> SMITH, Alan, 1999, *A History of Anywhere: The Victorian era,* Littletown Publishing Co.

or

> **Smith**, Alan, 1999, *A History of Anywhere: The Victorian era,* Littletown Publishing Co.

Multiple authors appear thus:

> Smith, A., and C.D. Jones, 1997, *How the Railways Changed Anywhere,* Littletown Publishing Co.

Note that only the first author's surname comes before their initials or surname. If you are using all capitals or bold then this reference would appear thus:

> SMITH, A., and C.D. JONES, 1997, *How the Railways Changed Anywhere,* Littletown Publishing Co.

> **Smith**, A., and C.D. **Jones**, 1997, *How the Railways Changed Anywhere,* Littletown Publishing Co.

Papers in anthologies should be shown with the title of the chapter or article in quotes and the volume title in italics:

> Smith, A.B., 1998, 'Anywhere in the sixteenth century', in C.D. Brown (ed.), *Everywhere and Anywhere,* Bigcity Press.

Papers or articles in periodicals should be shown similarly but with relevant information on volume and issue numbers and page references:

> Smith, A.B., 1999, 'Anywhere in 1550–55', in *Journal of Sixteenth Century Studies,* Vol.16, No.2, pp15–25.

Common practice in academic publications is to further abbreviate periodical references thus:

> Smith, A.B., 1999, 'Anywhere in 1550–55', in *J. of Sixteenth Century Studies*, 16, 2, 15–25.

However if writing for a non-academic readership this may not be sufficiently self-explanatory so the previous format is preferable.

Newspaper citations can normally be simplified to title and date (ensure consistency of abbreviation of dates):

> *Littletown Herald*, 2 Sept 1925.

For unpublished documents state where a copy is located:

> Smith, A.B., 1997, 'Mid-sixteenth century social transitions in Anywhere and environs', unpublished Ph.D. thesis, (University of Bigcity Library).

Unpublished historical documents are very similar but clear details of any document reference numbers should be given:

> Anywhere churchwardens' accounts for the mid-sixteenth century. Bigcity Record Office. Ref. 18/A/234/iii

Citing World Wide Web pages

References to information published on the Internet and World Wide Web begin with as much as possible of the information that would appear for a printed source e.g. author, title, name of Web site. Then state 'Retrieved on' and the date the information was downloaded as Web pages may change in content, move, or be removed from a site altogether. (For example, stories on newspaper Web sites are usually only temporary). Then comes the URL (i.e. Web site address). If at all possible copy-and-paste from the Web browser while this page is online to minimise the chance of typing errors. Do not put spaces or other punctuation in to create line breaks.

For example:

> Smith, Gavin, 1996, 'Recovering the lost religious place-names of England', *At the Edge* No.3, pp12–19. Retrieved 10 Jan 2005 from www.indigogroup.co.uk/edge/religpns.htm.

Citing emails

Emails direct from individuals should be cited as personal communication. Emails sent to email lists should be cited as:

Email from Jim Johnson, posted to ANSAX-L list on 2 Feb 2004.

Unfortunately someone can send an email disguised as someone else. Authors should *always* verify the source of emails before citing them as personal communications. Furthermore, many people regard their contributions to email lists as 'off the cuff' and may change their opinions later. If you intend quoting someone's email message then always check with the sender that they are happy for their opinion to be put into print (this will also confirm that they are, indeed, the authors of the message).

Abbreviations commonly used in references

Old fashioned references frequently use terms such as 'ibid.', 'op. cit.' and '*passim*'. Thankfully all but the most antiquated academic publishers have realised that these are impractical. One huge advantage of the Harvard system is that you no longer have to waste time going through pages and pages of footnotes trying to hunt down the details for an 'op. cit.'.

However, if for some reason you are not using the Harvard system (for example when writing articles which must conform to the house style of an academic-style journal) then they may be necessary. If you must use them, do so correctly:

ibid.

This is from the Latin *ibidem* meaning 'at the same place'. It is used only when a reference refers to the same work as the previous reference (although the page number may be different). Ibid. cannot be used after a different work has been cited – in this case you need to use op. cit. (see below). Ibid. is printed with a full stop after the 'd' to denote the abbreviation. It should *not* be italicised and the 'i' is capitalised only at the beginning of a sentence.

op. cit.

This is also Latin, from *opere citato,* meaning 'in the work quoted' and refers to a work which has been previously cited (but not immediately before). The author's name is given as well, and page-number (if applicable): Smith, op. cit. p155. Op. cit. is printed with a full stop after 'p' and 't' to denote the abbreviations; there is a space before 'c'. Op. cit. should *not* be italicised and the 'o' is capitalised only at the beginning of a sentence.

Be warned – using op. cit. may mean that the reader has to look back through hundreds of references to find the first citation. Many editors avoid the use of op. cit. entirely, perhaps by adopting an abbreviation for frequently-cited works. So James Wright *The History and Antiquities of the County of Rutland* could subsequently be cited as 'Wright *Rutland*'; or 'Wright *HACR*'; although if someone wants to know the publisher or dates of publication they will still have to laboriously track down the first citation.

passim

This is from the Latin meaning 'in every part'. It is used only where other references cite page numbers and appears instead of a page number when the majority of the work (book or article) cited is relevant to the reference.

Just to catch the unwary, there is no full stop after *passim* and it should be italicised; the 'p' is capitalised only at the beginning of a sentence.

Preparing for typesetting

Only when you (and as many other people who can be persuaded to comment on the final draft) feel that the words are as clear and concise as possible should you embark on the next editing step, which is to ensure consistency of 'presentation'.

Hierarchical headings

Books usually have chapters, probably sub-divided into sections. These sections may themselves be divided into sub-sections. All these *must* be ordered 'hierarchically'. Conventional type mark up is to code each of these types of headings as 'A' for chapter headings, 'B' for subheadings, 'C' for sub-subheadings and perhaps 'D' if a further sub-category is necessary. Under no circumstances can, say, a 'C' category heading follow directly under an 'A' heading – the hierarchy must be adhered to strictly.

Sometimes it will not be immediately obvious if, say, a 'B' or 'C' heading is required. These need to be thought through carefully and, if necessary, additional subheadings added elsewhere.

Traditionally such mark up was placed between the '<' and '>' characters. So this page would be marked up:

<A>PREPARING FOR TYPESETTING

Only when . . .

<B>Hierarchical headings

Books usually have chapters . . .

Unfortunately some typesetting software automatically converts mark up between '<' and '>' into formatting commands. And <B> or <b> usually converts all the following text into **bold** (and <I> or <i> converts the following text to *italic* which means using Roman numbering does not help either!). To avoid this try labelling the different level of headings <AA>, <BB> etc instead of simply <A>, <B> etc.

House style

There are a number of details of presentation which can be done either one way or another. What is important is that a book is consistent.

Publishers create what is called a 'house style' which determines usage.

The following points are based on house styles used by many UK publishers (American publishers have quite different house styles).

- Use single quotation marks; with doubles for quotes within quotes. No quotation marks around displayed extracts (i.e. quotations shown as a complete paragraph with bigger margins than the main text).

- Punctuation should be inside quotation marks if it belongs in the original, although final punctuation will be outside quotation marks if the quotation forms part of a sentence.

- Dates should be written consistently (e.g. 23 August 1998 *or* 23 Aug 1998; avoid 23rd, 25th etc). Decades should be the nineties *or* 1990s (without an apostrophe between the '0' and 's').

- With Old Style dates before 1752, when the year began on 25 March, then for dates between 1 January and 25 March use the form '1691/2' (N.B. *not* '1691–2' which denotes something quite different!).

- Centuries should be written in full i.e. nineteenth not 19th

- Contractions of numbers should be thus: 1–3; 1–20; 10–15; 1914–18 (*not* 1914–8); 10–31; 21–29; 101–9; 1974–78 (*not* 1974–8); 111–15 (*not* 111–5); 121–25; 128–45.

- Contractions of numbers use an en-dash (' – '), not a hyphen (' - '). (see page 46)

- Numbers higher than 10 should normally appear in figures except when used in general terms – e.g. about a hundred people – or for centuries – e.g. ninth century; nineteenth century.

- Four digit numbers and larger should have a comma (e.g. 1,000).

- Decimal points should appear at mid-figure level (e.g. 3·4 *not* 3.4)

- Percent should be spelt out in the text and the number preceding appear in figures. However the symbol (%) may be used in tables.

- 'Dashes' used for punctuation – like these – should be an en-dash (' – '), not a hyphen (' - ') and separated by spaces.

- Abbreviations consisting of capital letters should normally be expressed without full stops – PRO, MOD, GNP, CIA, IBM.
- Contractions ending with the same letter as the original word do not take a full stop – edn Mr Dr St – but where the last letter is not included do take a full stop – ed., ch. (although abbreviated units of measurement – mm kg lb – are correct and do not take a final 's' in the plural).
- Initial capitals are to be avoided, except to distinguish the specific from the general e.g. the Church (institution) and the church (building). Exceptions include Palaeolithic, Mesolithic, Neolithic, Bronze Age, Iron Age, Middle Ages (but normally 'medieval'), Gothic, Reformation, Renaissance, Enlightenment, etc.
- Hyphenation should be minimal but above all consistent.
- Spelling must be standardised to British rather than American forms. '-ise' rather than '-ize' is to be generally preferred although consistency is essential (except for quotations).
- Archaisms such as 'whilst' and 'amongst' should be replaced with 'while' and 'among'.
- Full stops should normally be omitted after headings and subheadings.
- Commas should be omitted before the final 'and' or 'or' in lists unless essential for clarity. Commas should normally be omitted after adverbial phrases or conjunctions especially when they begin a sentence – 'At last... '; 'During the summer... '.
- Square brackets are used only for editorial notes or interpolations in quotations. Round brackets (parentheses) should be used in all other instances.
- Ellipsis – use [...] (including the square brackets) for the omission of long passages in quoted text. Use '**...** ' (N.B. no space before and a single space after) for shorter omissions. For example, 'The end of this sentence and the whole of the next sentence have been omitted [...] However this sentence has just been shortened... '
- Chapters should be numbered in Arabic and referred to in the text as Chapter 1 (note upper case 'C').
- Figures and illustrations should normally be unnumbered.

Correct use of abbreviations and hyphenation can be found in *The Oxford Dictionary for Writers and Editors.* This is an essential reference book for any 'sub editor'.

Note: Direct quotations should *not* be changed to conform to 'house style'.

Proof reading

Some people spot errors in printed text as if they were flashing neon signs. Other people (myself included) seem to miss most of them.

Although spell checking software helps there are still plenty of errors which can be missed:

- Literals (a correctly-spelt word but not the correct word).
- Incorrect punctuation.
- Grammatical errors.
- Proper names incorrectly or inconsistently spelt.
- Inconsistent use of abbreviations or date formats.
- Inconsistent citing of bibliographical information and other references.
- Inconsistent typography

So far as I can tell, proof reading is something you are either 'born good at' or start out badly and never get to be really good. Unless you are excellent at spotting errors, or know somebody who is, then use a professional proof reader. Suitable contacts can be provided by the Society of Freelance Editors and Proofreaders

Society of Freelance Editors and Proofreaders
Mermaid House
1 Mermaid Court
London
SE1 1HR

telephone: 020 7403 5141
email: admin@sfep.org.uk
Web site: www.sfep.org.uk

If you are excellent at spotting mistakes but new to proof reading then the best advice is to read through the proofs several times, each time looking for just one type of mistake or inconsistency. If you are proof reading your own work (exceedingly risky!) then try to put the proofs aside for a week in between proof reading sessions, so you come back to them with 'fresh eyes'.

Professional proof readers use a standard system of symbols to mark up errors which are described in British Standard BS 5261.

Keep doing it

There are two parts to writing – what you are writing about and how you write about it. The first is down to research and inspiration, and the latter owes more to craftsmanship and experience. Assuming you have something to write about – even if the inspiration about the best way of approaching the subject is a bit elusive – then the best way of getting better at writing is simply to do more of it.

No matter how modest the scope of your writing projects, always aim to get a balance of narrative, description and analysis (see page 30) and keep asking:

- Who and what is this information for?
- Where and when do the readers need to know it?
- Are you informing, persuading, or both?

As you come back to drafts to revise them then pay increasing attention to the other aspects of writing 'craftsmanship' outlined in this chapter. But such details are secondary to setting your ideas out in a suitable style and with appropriate analysis. No one is born with ability to write well any more than any one could set off and win a marathon race without plenty of training – but keep practising and what once seemed impossibly difficult will begin to seem just a part of your normal routine.

Further reading

Historical research

History: What and why, Beverley Southgate, Routledge, 1996
Computing for Historians, Evan Mawdsley and Thomas Munck, Manchester University Press, 1993
Ordnance Survey Maps: A Concise Guide for Historians, Richard Oliver, Charles Close Society, 1993

Oral history

Sounding Boards: Oral Testimony and the Local Historian, David Marcombe, University of Nottingham, 1995
Interviewing Elderly Relatives, Eve McLaughlin, Federation of Family History Societies, 1985 (2nd edn)
The Myths We Live By, Paul Thompson and Raphael Samuel, Routledge, 1990
Oral Tradition as History, Jan Vansina, University of Wisconsin Press, 1985
The Oral History Reader, edited by Rob Perks and Alistair Thomson, Routledge 1998
Storied Lives: The cultural politics of self-understanding, G.E. Rosenwald and R.L. Ochberg, Yale University Press, 1992

Landscape history

Interpreting the Landscape, Michael Aston, Batsford 1985
The Making of the English Landscape, W.G. Hoskins and Christopher Taylor, Hodder and Stoughton, revised edition 1988
Historic Landscape Analysis: Deciphering the countryside, Stephen Rippon, Council for British Archaeology, 2004
Shaping Medieval Landscapes: Settlement, society, environment, Tom Williamson, Windgather Press, 2003

Writing style

Writing Local History, David Dymond, Phillimore, 1988 (2nd edn)
The Complete Plain Words, Ernest Gowers, HMSO, 1994 (revised edn)
The Oxford Guide to English Usage, Oxford UP, 1994
Cassell English Usage, Tim Storries and James Matson, Cassell, 1991
Fowler's Modern English Usage, H.W. Fowler, Oxford Univeristy Press, revised edition 2004
A Concise Dictionary of Correct English, B.A. Phythian, Guild Publishing, 1993
Troublesome Words, Bill Bryson, Penguin, 3rd edition 2002
Penguin Guide to Punctuation, R.L. Trask, Penguin, 2004
BBC News Style Guide. Download from www.bbctraining.com/pdfs/newsstyleguide.pdf

Editing

Editing Records for Publication, R.F. Hunnisett, British Records Association 1977
Basic Editing (2 vols), Nicola Harris, The Publishing Training Centre 1991
The Chicago Manual of Style, University of Chicago, 2004.
Copy-Editing, Judith Butcher, Cambridge University Press, 1992 (3rd edn)
Hart's Rules for Compositors and Readers, Oxford University Press, 1983 (39th edn)
The Oxford Dictionary for Writers and Editors, Oxford University Press, revised edition 2002
The Oxford Guide to Style, Oxford UP 2002
[*The Oxford Dictionary for Writers and Editors* and *The Oxford Guide to Style* are available as a combined volume titled the *Oxford Style Manual,* Oxford University Press, 2003.]

Chapter Two

LEGAL MATTERS

There are relatively few legal matters relating to publishing in Britain. The most important are copyright, moral rights of the authors, plagiarism, 'passing off' and libel (local and family history books are rarely blasphemous or obscene).

This section cannot offer detailed advice, not least because laws and legal practice are subject to change. *If the following remarks cause any concern then take professional advice.* The aim of this section is to provide some indication of the issues involved as these will usually need to be considered at a fairly early stage in the writing process.

For a broad overview of all legal matters relating to publishing read *Publishing Law* by Hugh Jones and Christopher Benson (Routledge, 2nd edn 2002).

Copyright

Copyright legislation is intended to protect a variety of so-called 'intellectual rights' and the resulting complexity does not make life easy for publishers. However the general principles are easy to understand.

There is one golden rule that applies to copyright – it can only be assigned in writing, never verbally. So written agreements are essential and these need to be kept together in a safe place.

In general, the copyright of any text (be it a book, short article, poem, play script or whatever) and any illustration (drawing, chart or photograph) remains with the author or artist until 70 years after that person's death. Where authorship is shared, copyright persists until 70 years after the death of the last surviving author. Note that copyright persists in perpetuity when the publisher is part of Oxford or Cambridge University Press or the material is Crown copyright.

Another key exception to normal copyright rules relates to Ordnance Survey maps (see pages 65 to 67). Other exceptions arise where the copyright has been sold or transferred. Sheet music, sound recordings, films and videos are also subject to copyright. Copyright protection is automatic when the material is published, although copyright holders are usually named in the prelim pages (see page 126).

Obtaining permission to reproduce previously published material

This summary can only touch on the more important points. If you are considering incorporating other people's work which is likely to be still in copyright then detailed help and practical advice is at hand if you obtain a copy of *Buying and Clearing Rights* by Richard McCracken and Madeleine Gilbart (Blueprint 1995).

Customary practice is for short quotations (except when from poems) to be used without permission, so long as the source is identified and no more than 250 words in total are quoted from the same book. Note that quoting another text (even short sections) without using quote marks and identifying the source is plagiarism. For legal and ethical reasons, don't do it! (This is another reason to keep close control of sources – see page 44 – so that you do not inadvertently borrow exact phrases.) However, so long as you do not use the same words then a paraphrase of the source is acceptable (there is no copyright on ideas, only on their 'execution'), although be wary of infringing moral rights (see page 67).

Seek permission from the original publisher for:

- all illustrations, including charts and diagrams;
- when quoting more than 250 words from the same book or article;
- when there is more than 125 words in any one quotation;
- when the quotation is more than 10 percent of the total length of the original;
- any quote, however short, from poems and song lyrics.

The current addresses of publishers can be found in the writers' yearbooks (almost always on the shelves of local libraries). The publisher will probably not own the copyright but should be able to tell you how to contact the relevant copyright owner.

When requesting permission, the copyright holder will need to know:

- the proposed title for your publication
- the author
- the expected print run and format (paperback etc.)
- expected cover price

- where the book will be sold (typically UK-only for most local history books)
- most importantly, exact details of what you want to reproduce.

For typical local history print runs fees are rarely requested, except for illustrations and poems, unless the quotations really are substantial. In my experience county record offices and local museums used to be happy to accept a complimentary copy of the publication instead of a fee. Unfortunately many museums have now subcontracted 'rights management' to outside organisations that have only one aim – to make as much money as possible out of selling rights. However, if you consider the requested fee to be unreasonable then try to negotiate. For photographs expect to pay for the cost of producing a print or slide, even though this usually is only on loan.

Reproduction fees for use on CD-ROMs and Web sites are usually much greater than for specialist print-based publications.

Getting permissions can be time consuming, so under no circumstances leave it until the last minute. The people you request permission from will not necessarily respond promptly and, rather than grant permission, may ask you to contact the current copyright owner. While some copyright clearances will happen within a few weeks, some are going to take a few months. Expect real difficulties finding out when an obscure author or artist died, and seemingly never-ending difficulties establishing current owners of the transferred copyright.

If the publisher seems to have 'disappeared' then some detective work is needed. WATCH (Writers, Artists and their Copyright Holders) is a database project set up by USA and UK universities to help track copyright owners, alive or dead. The database is available on the Internet at www.watch-file.com; there is also an excellent fact sheet on this Website.

If this fails then you will need to track down the copyright owner's will. There is detailed advice on this at www.booktrust.org.uk/copyright.htm

However, one of the many frustrations of the 1988 copyright laws is that there is no way to seek permission if the copyright owner cannot be traced. The realistic answer is to do everything possible to trace the copyright owner (and keep records of what steps you took) so that if, after publication, the copyright owners do contact you then they cannot claim you have been negligent.

Bear in mind you cannot make a statement to the effect of 'All reasonable steps have been taken to contact current copyright holders' unless indeed you can prove that such steps have been taken – and a court of law is quite likely to regard 'reasonable steps' as much more time-consuming and expensive than you consider 'reasonable'. For example, they will expect you to have placed an advert in *The Times* or *Times Literary Supplement* (or a more relevant publication) requesting the copyright holder to make contact.

Copyright and previously unpublished photographs and memoirs

Local and family history publications frequently make use of old photographs and even sections of old diaries and memoirs. Invariably these become increasingly interesting as the years roll on. But copyright persists for 70 years after death which raises the problem of obtaining copyright clearance from someone who is dead, or more accurately, obtaining permission from their estate. An old photograph taken in the 1930s by someone who died in the 1980s will still be copyright until 2050. The problem is that the descendants of that person may not be easily traced. If their spouse is still alive then they can assign copyright. But otherwise the rights will have passed down (probably unbeknown!) to the person's children. Tracing these may be difficult and, assuming you contact one of them, you need to be assured they are acting with the full agreement of their siblings.

Another problem is with portraits taken by photographic studios. Since the change in law in 1988 the copyright always remains with the photographer. For photographs taken before this date the photographer probably retained copyright (the crucial factor is who paid for the film on which they were taken – and studios are able to make the rather nonsensical claim that the film was not paid for by the client).

If you publish copyright material without prior approval then at any future time the copyright owner could claim a reproduction fee from you. For relatively specialist printed publications and CD-ROMs this would reasonably be between £50 and £100 (unless used in colour or for the cover, each of which could reasonably double the fees). However for Web use the fees would start at around £100 per image, and could be much more for substantial sections of text.

In practice local history publishers may need to make informed decisions about how much effort to put into tracing copyright holders before deciding to risk publishing and maybe having to pay up later. The reality is that many copyright owners are happy for old photographs to be used in exchange for a free copy of the publication, but this cannot – and must not – be assumed.

The best way of avoiding such problems is to make sure copyright in old photographs, oral history recordings, and the like are assigned while the person is still alive. And bear in mind that copyright can *never* be assigned verbally but only in writing. See pages 12 to 14 for details of assigning copyright.

Copyright and oral history

With oral history the copyright situation becomes even more complex as separate rights exist for

- the sound recording
- the transcript
- any edited version(s) of the transcribed words

Copyright for the recording and the 'verbatim' transcript both belong to the speaker, unless transferred *in writing* (see pages 12 to 14).

Note that copies of sound recordings cannot be made, even for archival purposes (such as deposition in a local record office), without written permission from the speaker.

Photographs taken inside buildings

Another odd situation arises with photographs taken in semi-public places such as churches. This is a grey area I have encountered when publishing photographs of medieval carvings. The law is clear enough – photographs of a work of art in a public place (such as a sculpture in a public park) can be reproduced without infringing the rights of the sculptor or the owner of the sculpture. In contrast, any work of art that is not in a public place – and that includes works that are in museums, churches and anywhere owned by the National Trust or English Heritage – can only be reproduced with the permission of the owner and the artist (or their estate if they have died within the last 70 years).

This means that if I take a photograph of an old gargoyle on the outside of a church tower while standing on the churchyard path (i.e. a public place) then I can publish that photograph without requiring any permission. However if I take a photograph of an old carving *inside* the church then I need the permission of its owner. In the Church of England the vicar or rector technically owns the church, but pedantically this is not the case if they are a priest-in-charge, where the diocese is the owner. Nevertheless, if the photograph(s) you want to publish are all taken in one church then contact the parish clergy, whatever their exact title, for permission. If you want to reproduce photographs taken inside several churches in the same diocese then the first approach would best be to the Diocesan Office. The response may vary. One midlands diocese offered me 'blanket' approval to reproduce my photographs of medieval carvings without the need to approach the parish clergy direct, while the adjoining diocese insisted that I contact all the relevant clergy direct.

Note that being given permission to *take* photographs is not the same as being given permission to *reproduce* them. Even if you have paid to take photographs (as is often the case in cathedrals) you most certainly will not have permission to reproduce them in any way without paying a further fee.

There are other permissions that may need clearing too. If you photograph, say, a memorial in a church to someone who died in the twentieth century check whether the artist who made that memorial is still alive or died less than seventy years ago. If this is the case then you will need their (or their executor's) permission before reproducing their work.

Works of art important enough to be in a museum will often attract large reproduction fees, particularly if used on CD-ROMs or Web sites. Note that even if the artist died more than 70 years ago the museum or gallery who owns the artwork will have rights in reproducing any photographs of it, and such fees are regarded as an important source of income.

Copyright should be assigned sooner rather than later

Historical items such as photographs and diaries collected from 'senior citizens' and older family members are often an important outcome of any research. Consider how frustrating it would be if, when you are ready to publish, some of these people have died and the copyright is now owned by their various descendants. Not too bad if you have kept in touch with their family, but a potential nightmare if not. And even if you have kept in touch with some of the family, how can be sure that any one person is acting with the agreement of other family members who may have equally inherited (knowingly or otherwise) the rights?

To avoid problems tracing copyright holders and obtaining approval to reproduce at some future date, there are many benefits from getting the copyright 'transferred' (more correctly 'assigned') to you. This is especially important for photographs, dairies, letters, memoirs and recordings of interviews, even if you are not entirely sure if or how much you may want to publish.

Assignment of copyright needs to be in writing and signed by the copyright owner. If the copyright owner wishes to make limitations on use or access then the wording may include suitable conditions. At the time this may seem rather cumbersome, but will save the risk of considerable trouble later.

See page 13 for a form devised for the 'Memories of Nottinghamshire' project which visits older residents to scan photographs into a laptop computer then record the person's reminiscences.

The work that you are writing and publishing will also remain in copyright for 70 years after your death. Members of local history groups who write or compile books on behalf of the group should consider assigning their copyright to the group so that no problems arise keeping the work in print after their death, or for record offices to make copies available to researchers. (See page 210 for a more detailed discussion of the rights of jointly produced projects.)

Commissioned illustrations

Commissioning cover illustrations and designs, drawings, maps and photographs requires that the artist assigns copyright to you. This can only be done in writing. On the next few pages is a copy of the agreement used by Heart of Albion, which in turn is based on *Clark's Publishing Agreements* edited by Lynette Owen (Butterworths 6th edn 2002).

Initially you may be surprised at how long this document is – 'Its just a picture' we're asking for! However reading through this agreement should alert you to a number of scenarios that need to be 'firmed up' in writing if future misunderstandings are not to arise.

Clearly the references to licensed editions are unlikely to apply to local history works – although Heart of Albion has been approached for translation rights for some very specialist titles, so just about anything is possible – and the VAT clause may well be unlikely to apply to specialist publishers (although professional illustrators and photographers may be registered for VAT).

If the image or photograph could potentially be sold elsewhere then you may have to relax the paragraph about the 'sole and exclusive right and licence' to a license to reproduce in the specific publication – but clearly there should be a corresponding reduction in fee as well!

AN AGREEMENT

This agreement is between Robert Nigel Trubshaw, trading as Heart of Albion Press (referred to as 'HOAP'), and [*illustrator*] of [*address*] (referred to as 'the illustrator', which expression includes the author's executors and assigns) whereby it is mutually agreed as follows concerning the illustrator's [*artwork/transparencies/photographs*] (referred to as 'the artwork') for a work at present entitled [*title of work*] (referred to as 'the work' or 'the publication').

The illustrator shall provide 'the artwork' as described in the Schedule to this agreement in a form suitable for reproduction and subject to the approval of the Publishers (which approval shall not be unreasonably withheld).

The illustrator shall provide roughs not later than [*date*] and the finished Artwork not later than [*date*].

The illustrator hereby warrants to the HOAP and their assigns and licensees that [*he/she*] has full power to make this agreement, that [*he/she*] is the sole creator of the artwork and is the owner of the rights herein granted, that the artwork is original to [*he/she*] and has not previously been published, that the artwork is in no way whatever a violation or an infringement of any existing copyright or licence, and that it contains nothing obscene, libellous or defamatory. The illustrator will indemnify and keep the HOAP indemnified against all actions, suits, proceedings, claims, demands, damages and costs (including any legal costs or expenses properly incurred and any compensation costs and disbursements paid by HOAP on the advice of their legal advisers to compromise or settle any claim) occasioned to HOAP in consequence of any breach of this warranty or arising out of any claim alleging that the artwork constitutes in any way a breach of this warranty. HOAP reserves the right to insist that the illustrator alters the artwork in such a way as may appear to them appropriate for the purpose of removing any feature which may be considered objectionable or likely to be actionable by law, but any such alteration or removal shall be without prejudice to and shall not affect the illustrator's liability under this warranty and indemnity.

All warranties and indemnities herein contained shall survive the termination of this Agreement.

Pages 62 to 65: *An example of an agreement for commissioned illustrations.*

In consideration of the payments hereinafter mentioned the illustrator hereby grants to HOAP the sole and exclusive right and licence to produce, publish and themselves further to license the artwork or any part of it in any and all forms and media for the legal term of copyright and any and all extensions, renewals and revivals thereof throughout the world.

The illustrator shall permit HOAP free of charge to use the artwork to promote the work in catalogues, advertisements and other promotional material in any form.

While proper care will be taken of the artwork, HOAP shall not be responsible for any loss or damage to it while it is in their possession or in the course of production or in transit.

Should the artwork contain a recognisable likeness of any person the illustrator undertakes to explain to such person the use to which the artwork will be put and to obtain from each such person a form of release and to deliver the same to HOAP in a form satisfactory to them.

HOAP shall pay to the illustrator a fee of [*amount]* payable as to [*name*] on signature of this Agreement, [*amount*] on delivery and approval of roughs of the Artwork and [*amount*] on delivery and approval of finished Artwork as provided for in Clauses 1 and 2 hereof.

HOAP shall further pay to the illustrator a proportion to be mutually agreed of any net sums received in respect of the artwork sub-licensed by them to a third party for reproduction in volume form or in newspapers or magazines or otherwise.

Should HOAP for any reason cancel the commission, they shall pay to the illustrator a cancellation fee to be agreed and proportional to the degree of completion. HOAP shall have no rights in any artwork so cancelled.

The illustrator's name shall be printed either on the title page of the work or prominently on the half-title or the reverse of the title page at the discretion of HOAP. HOAP shall use their best endeavours to ensure that [*he/she*] is given full acknowledgement in any edition of the work sub-licensed to a third party.

The illustrator shall retain ownership of and copyright in the artwork and HOAP shall print the following statements on the reverse of the title page of the work: 'Illustrations © [name of illustrator]' and 'The moral rights of the author and illustrator(s) have been asserted.' HOAP will include in any contract with any licensee an undertaking that the same assertion of copyright and moral rights appear in every edition published or further licensed.

The illustrator on written request from HOAP undertakes to give consent or to waive in writing the right to object to derogatory treatment of the artwork as provided for in s. 80 of the Copyright, Designs and Patents Act 1988 when such consent or waiver is an essential condition of the exercise of any of the rights granted to HOAP under this agreement.

HOAP shall send to the Illustrator on publication [*three*] complimentary copies of the work. The illustrator shall have the right to purchase at normal trade terms further copies for personal use but not for resale. The illustrator shall receive [*one*] complimentary copy of any sub-licensed edition of the work which includes the artwork on receipt by HOAP from the sub-licensed publishers of their edition of the work.

If at any time HOAP allow the work to become out of print and not be available in any edition and if HOAP return to the author of the text all rights granted to them under the terms of the agreement between them and the author then HOAP shall at the same time return to the illustrator all rights in the artwork granted under this agreement without prejudice to all rights in respect of any contracts or negotiations properly entered into by them with any third party prior to the date of such reversion.

Should HOAP fail to fulfil or comply with any of the conditions accepted by HOAP in this agreement within 30 days' notice of such failure from the illustrator, or if a manager, receiver, or other encumbrancer takes possession of or is appointed over, the whole or any substantial part of HOAP's assets, or if HOAP enter into any arrangement or composition with or for the benefit of their creditors (including any voluntary arrangement under the Insolvency Act 1986), or if a petition is presented or a meeting convened for the purposes of considering a resolution for the making of an administrative order, the winding up or dissolution of the Publishers (other than voluntary liquidation for the purpose of reconstruction) then, in any of the foregoing events, this agreement shall thereupon terminate and all rights granted under this agreement shall revert to the illustrator, without prejudice to all rights of HOAP in respect of any contracts or negotiations properly entered into with any third party prior to the date of such termination and without prejudice to any monies already paid or then due to the illustrator from HOAP.

All monies accruing to the illustrator under this agreement shall be exclusive of Value Added Tax (VAT). The Publishers shall be notified of any change in the illustrator's VAT status, including any alteration to the illustrator's VAT registration number.

If both the illustrator and HOAP are at any time registered for the purposes of VAT then HOAP shall, after notification of the illustrator's VAT registration number, add VAT to payments made to the illustrator in accordance with statutory regulations.

In the event of any dispute which cannot be resolved between the illustrator and HOAP then in the first instance the matter shall be referred to the Informal Disputes Arbitration of the Publishers Association. In any event any disputes shall be resolved in accordance with English legislation, irrespective of the nationality or place of residence of the author. Both parties hereto submit and agree to the jurisdiction of the English courts.

This agreement is the entire and only agreement between the author and HOAP concerning this publication. Any prior agreements, arrangements and understandings (whether written or oral) are superseded by this agreement. No addition to or modification of any provision in this agreement shall be binding upon either the author or HOAP unless it is agreed by both parties in writing.

SIGNED BY:

For Heart of Albion Press by R.N. Trubshaw:

Date:

The illustrator:

Name in block letters:

Date:

Schedule

The Artwork referred to in the agreement shall consist of:

	A [*jacket/cover (front only/wrap-around)*] for printing in full colour
	[*number*] illustrations in full colour
	[*number*] illustrations in black and white
Medium:	[*e.g. 600 dpi TIFF file on CD-ROM*]
Method of reproduction:	[*e.g. digital printing*]
Size/proportion:	[*e.g. approx A5 size – and be more specific if you know exact details of the proportion*]

Copyright and maps

The Ordnance Survey (OS) strictly controls the copyright of the maps it issues (and of other map publishers who licence their data) and takes a close interest in the activities of local history publishers. Unlike other copyright items, OS maps remain in copyright for 50 years from the end of the calendar year in which they are issued. Redrawing an OS map does *not* get around their copyright.

The Copyright and Legal Affairs department of the OS in Southampton issue guidance leaflets, which should be read before applying for permission. The following information is taken from the OS's Web site in July 2004 (check that it is still current advice by visiting www.ordnancesurvey.co.uk or telephoning 023 8030 5030).

OS maps remain in copyright for 50 years from the end of the year in which the map was first published. So a map dated 1962 will go out of copyright on December 31 2002. Any reproduction of a OS map still in copyright in a newsletter, booklet, book,

CD-ROM or Web site requires an OS Publishing Licence or OS Paper Map Copying Licence (contact the OS advisors on the above phone number for further details).

The OS has a complex fee arrangement but, at 2002 rates, the cost of reproducing part of an OS map still in copyright at up to A5 size is **4.5p per copy**; the cost of reproducing a map redrawn from a copyright OS map is **1p per copy**. The equivalent costs for reproductions between A5 and A4 size is **9p** and **3p** respectively.

Clearly the reproduction of more than one or two OS maps will add significantly to the cost of each copy of the publication.

Unlike other forms of illustrations, simply redrawing an OS map does not 'get around' copyright, unless the new drawing is derived from an out of copyright map (see below).

At the time of writing the OS Web site does not offer clear advice on the costs of reproducing their maps on Web sites, although on the basis of the print reproduction fees then Web site usage is likely to be prohibitively expensive. Telephone the Ordnance Survey on the above phone number to discuss.

Alternatively link to online map services such as www.multimap.com.

Reproduction of OS maps more than 50 years old

With OS maps more than 50 years old you do not need permission but the OS still ask for the following caption: 'Reproduced from the... [year of publication] Ordnance Survey map' followed by the scale, the sheet number and the edition.

Reproducing maps not published by the OS

Note that maps issued by organisations other than OS remain in copyright for 70 years from date of issue.

The law becomes more difficult to interpret about *copies* of non-OS maps held in record offices or other archives. If an obscure map (say an estate plan) has never previously been published, then the copyright will run for 70 years from first publication (which may be your book!). This will apply whether you are working from the original map or a previously unpublished copy. Bear in mind owning a copy does not mean you own the copyright; this is equally true if the original is probably lost and/or the legitimate copyright owners are unknown. Copies made by record offices and similar archives of maps may have an ambiguous status; at the least check with the archive staff before assuming that copyright is not being breached.

Record offices and the like may also impose contractual limitations on the publication of copies of material in their archives. These are not the same as copyright but may pose similar limitations on legitimate publication.

Publication rights

The 1998 Copyright, Designs and Patents Act added two new rights to British law (although similar rights had long existed in some other countries). The first means that any person who 'communicates to the public' any previously unpublished work anywhere in the EU acquires a right known as the 'publication right'.

The scope of 'publication' is wide and includes not only any paper-based or electronic publication but also public exhibitions.

This publication right is akin to copyright, except that it expires after 25 years from the date of first publication. The person publishing acquires it whether they want it or not. So when you organise a display about village history and include an old photograph you (and not the owner of the photograph or the person who owns the copyright to the photograph – who may not be same person) acquire the publication rights for that photograph.

Publication rights in local history and family history photographs are unlikely to be valuable. But make sure that they are not acquired 'inadvertently' by other people who want to use your photographs for books, Web sites or exhibitions by requesting a written waiver.

Moral rights

The second right created in British law in 1988 is 'moral rights'. Since then the creators of copyright material (whether text, illustrations, photographs, lyrics, music, sound recordings, film or video) have a right to be identified as 'authors'. This mostly means that if the work is quoted in print or broadcast then (a) their work needs to be credited to them; (b) their work cannot be subjected to 'derogatory treatment' such as editing, adapting or otherwise altering the meaning or sense. For paper-based publications a simple statement in the prelim pages (see page 125) is sufficient to assert moral rights; equivalent statements can be included in the 'small print' of Web sites (see page 208).

Passing off

This is a thoroughly ambiguous area of the law, but usually easy for local history publishers to avoid. 'Passing off' is where you give the impression that your work is by another, even though copyright (or trade marks) have not been infringed. So books with titles such as *James Bond gets His Girl* or *The Teletubbies Come to Town* would quickly be subject to law suits. Likewise an illustration that looked too much like, say, a Walt Disney character (even if the illustration is original and the character's name is different) is likely to end up costing a lot of money. Even calling yourself, say, Oxford Unitary Press, might well result in Oxford University Press briefing their solicitors for an expensive court case. Indeed, any major organisation with a strong 'brand name' will usually sue first and ask questions later if it considers there is any infringement (and expect their opinions to be much less open-minded than yours!).

Libel

Historical sources can be very candid about individuals. Such 'revelations' can make interesting reading, but care needs to be taken to avoid statements that 'bring into disrepute' or could be considered a breach of confidence. Every effort should be made to check that the more 'sensational' stories are, indeed, true. Individuals who are still alive should be contacted before publication and ask to sign a 'waiver'. If serious allegations are made (and 'serious' should be interpreted from the perspective of the subject) then a libel lawyer must be consulted, even if there is good evidence to support the remarks.

Web sites have more potential for libel problems than printed publications – see page 211 for a further discussion of this specific issue.

Final thoughts

The 1998 Copyright, Designs and Patents Act was designed to protect the rights of those who own 'intellectual property'. It was not designed to make the life of publishers easy and, in many instances (such as tracing current copyright owners nearly 70 years after the death of an author or artist), this law can be regarded as totally unworkable. However there is little prospect of this badly drafted legislation being improved so use this chapter as a guide to the pitfalls that need to be negotiated.

This chapter does not attempt to provide detailed advice on legal matters. Read the first three titles in the 'further reading' list below for more specific information. Bear in mind that laws and legal practice are subject to change. *If any remarks in this chapter suggest your publication may cause any concern then take professional advice.*

Further reading

Cassell Handbook of Copyright in British Publishing Practice, J.M. Cavendish and K. Pool, Continuum, 1993

Copyright Made Easier Raymond A. Wall, Aslib, 2000 (3rd edn)

A User's Guide to Copyright, Michael F. Flint, Butterworth, 2000 (5th edn)

Copyright, Ethics and Oral History, Alan Ward, The Oral History Society, 1995

Chapter Three

PREPARING ILLUSTRATIONS

In the last few years changes in technology have made it much easier – and cheaper – to include photographs and other illustrations in local history publications. Improvements in digital printing have meant that this technique has become the best way of producing books under about 700 copies (which is the sort of print run associated with most local history titles).

This chapter provides some specific advice on preparing drawings and photographs for printed reproduction and for use on Web sites. It begins with some definitions of the jargon, then looks at ways of scanning images. The main section is about optimising pictures and the chapter concludes with advice on specific topics such as maps and family trees.

Understanding the jargon

Illustrations for traditional printing

From a traditional printing point-of-view there are two types of illustration – 'line art' and 'half-tones'.

Line art is drawn with solid black lines (although these may be close enough to provide 'cross-hatch' shading) and requires no special preparation by the printer and therefore incurs no extra cost.

Half-tones are images where subtle shades of grey (or colour) need to be reproduced using a pattern of fine dots.

Strictly, 'half-tone' refers to the final printed image and the plate used to print from. Artwork that needs to be reproduced by half-tones is often known as 'continuous tone'. To keep things a little simpler, in this book the term 'half-tone' will usually be used to mean both the final image *and* the associated artwork.

Typical half-tones are photographs (black and white or colour) and 'line and wash' drawings. Traditionally the printer prepared each half-tone specially which added

Top: *Example of line art (Beeby church and well from John Nichol's* History and Antiquities of the County of Leicester).

Centre: *Example of a half-tone (Little Stretton church, Leicestershire).*

Right: *Enlargement of part of a half-tone of the same photograph.*

around £5 for each black and white half-tone to the preparation costs. This quickly made specialist heavily-illustrated books prohibitively expensive. Thankfully all printers now accept all the pages of a book – text and illustrations – as PDF files, and these files can be produced on any computer with suitable software. This means that the time and effort needed to prepare illustrations rests with the publisher rather than the printer.

If the printer is using digital printing techniques then illustrations that look good on screen should print successfully. In any event, digital printing allows accurate proof copies to be made; if the proofs reveal any problems with the images then improvements can be made easily before the main print run is started. However some special tricks and skills are needed to prepare photographs for traditional offset litho printing – see page 89.

Illustrations for digital printing

There are effectively no special requirements regarding preparing either black and white or colour images for digital printing apart from the usual rules for reproduction:

- Adjust the gamma to avoid shadow areas blocking up.
- Adjust the contrast to achieve consistent images that are neither too contrasty or too flat.
- With colour images optimise the saturation to give a slightly 'bright' image.

Anything reproduced with less than 300 dots per inch (dpi) is likely to appear slightly 'soft' or even 'jaggy'. Aim for 600 dpi but use 1200 dpi if possible.

Pages 78 to 89 provide further details of optimising photographs for digital printing.

Illustrations for Web sites and CD-ROMs

In many respects images for Web sites are different to images for printing. Colour is normal and resolution is rarely an issue. Compressing file sizes is key to Web sites, although irrelevant for CD-ROMs. File formats are different for electronic publications.

This chapter offers basic advice on preparing images for electronic publications, and in Chapter 7 there is a section on the more sophisticated use of images on Web sites and CD-ROMs.

Software for optimising images

Among professionals the software synonymous with editing images is Adobe's Photoshop. A stripped-down version, known as Photoshop Elements is often supplied with scanners and digital cameras. Unfortunately the tools most necessary for optimising images for printed reproduction – such as histogram adjustment –

have been disabled in Photoshop Elements, preventing it from being of any use for anyone wanted to prepare images for publication.

If you are a Mac user your only choice seems to be to spend £500 on the full version of Photoshop. Thankfully PC users who do not want to spend that sort of money on a single item of software have a much more sensible alternative: JASC Paint Shop Pro. At the time of writing this is available for about £75. There is other photo-editing software available for PCs but, like Photoshop Elements, these do not have the 'bells and whistles' needed for preparing images to a professional standard.

The examples and screen shots in this chapter are from Paint Shop Pro version 7, although there are equivalent tools in Photoshop and (allowing for the changes to the interface) in later versions of Paint Shop Pro.

Scanning illustrations

As with all computer peripherals, technology continues to improve. And, as with most other things in life, with scanners you roughly get what you pay for. While bottom of the range scanners may be adequate for putting photos of pets onto family Web sites, they are not capable of the more subtle quality needed for effective printed reproduction. If you are only going to scan a few images then muddle by with whatever is to hand. But if you are likely to be preparing more than a dozen or so images for publication then (at the time of writing) expect to pay about £130 for the right level of quality. The leading monthly computer magazines review scanners so look out for an issue with comparative surveys.

Do not be seduced by the option for adapting a flatbed scanner to scan transparencies and negatives as the quality is greatly inferior to specialist film and slide scanners. Notably, shadow detail in transparencies will tend to be blocked and highlight detail in negatives will be burnt out – whereas a transparency scanned on a proper transparency scanner should have masses of 'invisible' detail in the shadow areas, which can be brought out when the image is digitally optimised.

All scans should be saved in TIFF format (use any of the available compression techniques, although the LZW compression option is considered slightly better than others). Always save as RGB format, never CMYK format (see page 102 for details of RGB and CMYK formats).

Never use JPG format for saving scans and other images. Although JPG files take up less hard disc space than TIFF files, this is achieved by throwing away detail. Such losses may not be too apparent on screen but may affect the quality which can be achieved when printed. More crucially, if any editing is done to a JPG image and it is saved again as a JPG then losses increase significantly. JPG format has only one use – compressing edited versions of images so they are a suitable file size for publishing on Web pages and CD-ROMs (see page 89).

While it may seem overly cautious, experience soon confirms that original scans (and images from digital cameras too) should be kept in a folder clearly labelled 'master files' and backed up promptly. 'Working copies' of these files should then be copied into a different folder.

Scanning line art

Many illustrations in out-of-copyright books from the nineteenth and early twentieth centuries are line art which can be readily scanned. Although line art by definition should only contain pure black and pure white, in practice line art in books (or which has been photocopied) needs to be scanned in as if it was a black and white photograph so that it can be optimised for further reproduction (see pages 76 to 78).

Line art should usually be scanned in at a resolution that equates to at least 600 dpi *reproduced size*. So scanning in an image 6" x 4" which will be reproduced 3" x 2" requires the scan to be at 300 (or more) dpi. Scanning at a higher resolution than needed is preferable, assuming your computer has sufficient memory – high-resolution scans can easily exceed 50 Mbytes.

If the image will only be used on screen for Web sites or CD-ROMs then 300 dpi scanning resolution will be sufficient.

Scanning photographic prints

When scanning from photographs if at all possible work from glossy prints. If you have a choice avoid prints that have little contrast (such as those taken under grey skies) and, at the other extreme, avoid prints where the lighting is too harsh (such as reflections from camera flash or shooting into the sun). Although graphics software can 'tweak' contrast, it cannot make an image suitable for reproduction from the proverbial pig's ear.

When the original is in colour, but the printing will be only black and white, still scan in colour and convert to 'grey scale' later when optimising.

Scanning photographic slides and negatives

Sometimes your originals will be on colour transparency slides or only the negatives are available. As already noted on the previous page, some flat-bed scanners have adapters for scanning slides and negatives. These sometimes produce tolerably good results (more likely if the photographs are on a larger format film than 35 mm) but do check carefully that the shadow areas have not 'blocked up'. Slides that are underexposed scan badly by this method.

Dedicated 35mm slide (or 'film') scanners are available. Unfortunately the cheaper ones are no better at dealing with shadows and highlights than transparency adapters on flat bed scanners. Units costing upwards from £300 are excellent, even for the dark areas. But their cost may be prohibitive unless considerable numbers of slides to be scanned.

The most cost-effective option for a moderate number of slides is to take the slides to a shop specialising in photographic developing and printing and pay to have them scanned onto a CD-ROM.

When scanning slides select 1200 to 2400 dpi resolution. The latter will create files which, uncompressed, are about 40 Mbytes (compare this to digital cameras which, at the time of writing, create up to 8 Mbyte files). If the slide will be reproduced without much cropping then 1200 dpi resolution will be quite adequate for all but the largest full page reproduction, and far bigger than anything needed for on-screen display.

Scanning existing half-tones

When a photograph or similar continuous-tone image has been reproduced in a book or magazine (watch out for copyright!) it will have been converted to half-tone. This means that when scanned you will see the screen effect; this can cause a 'jazzing' effect – known correctly as a 'moiré pattern' – as this clashes with the pixels on your computer monitor. A similar (but different!) jazzing effect will be created if the image is reproduced digitally or by offset litho.

Above: *Screen shot of the Moiré Pattern Removal tool in Paint Shop Pro.*

Right: *The half-tone from page 70 after using the Moiré Pattern Removal tool.*

Such previously-printed images need to be 'tweaked' before being printed again or being uploaded to the Web as otherwise conspicuous moiré patterns will form. See page 85 for details of how to eliminate the problem.

Scanning from photocopies

Scanning line art from photocopies usually works well, although some cleaning up is often necessary (see overleaf). However photocopies of continuous tone images (such as photographs) can present serious problems. Treat them as especially challenging photographs.

If you have plenty of experience with graphics software then you may be able to scan as half-tones and carefully 'tweak' brightness and control to get a tolerable half-tone (see page 86). However this will never reproduce particularly well. Make sure such images are only used very small, and never more than about 60 mm wide or high.

This problem is especially common with local history researchers who have taken photocopies in record offices and the like. The only real answer is to obtain permission from the record office (or wherever) to revisit with a professional photographer. He can use a copy stand, with necessary lights, and re-photograph the relevant images on high contrast black and white film such as Ilford Pan F (120 format is best but professional photographers can produce adequate results with 35 mm format or with high-specification digital cameras).

Record offices may be able to arrange for such services to be provided but this is likely to work out expensive.

All this sounds very troublesome but is well worth the effort. The last thing you want is to have duff-looking images scattered through your book. Where certain images are particularly important to your text, or will be reproduced more-or-less full-page, then it is the only way.

Digital photographs

Digital cameras have come of age and higher specification models are good substitutes for 35 mm SLR cameras. Those offering 4 megapixel or more images are ideal for images to be used in printed publications, CD-ROMs and Web sites. The only constraint is that such images are barely big enough for printing larger than about A5 size (do not be fooled by inkjet printers that cleverly interpolate small files to make them look acceptable when printed at less than 300 dpi resolution), so be wary of using digital images for the cover of books, unless the image is much less than full page.

When choosing a digital camera look out for models which offer a lens with a wide angle equivalent to 28 mm focal length on a 35 mm camera and with at least a 5:1 zoom (10:1 would be much better). You will need enough memory cards to take up to 100 high-resolution images and at least one spare rechargeable battery – make sure you take into account the cost of these essential 'extras' before deciding which model is the best value.

Once you have transferred digital photographs always keep the original file tucked away somewhere safe, and backed up (see pages 3 and 212 for discussions of archiving data). Work on copies of the original files – and these copies should always be saved as TIFF format, even if the digital camera creates JPG files. Images which have been saved as JPGs easily degrade when saved again in JPG format.

Optimising line art

The trick is to scan line art as a greyscale image (i.e. as if it is a black and white photograph). Save the original scan then, using a copy of the file, use the histogram tool to make the white background whiter, and the black lines blacker.

This traction engine is reproduced from an unedited scan made from a record office photocopy and shows the typical problems associated with line art from old periodicals – an uneven grey background and text showing through from the reverse.

In the improved version the 'High' has been brought down to 221 to brighten the white background; the Gamma has been increased to 1.20 to open up the shadow details; and the 'Low' brought up to 20 to give good solid blacks. Finally the 'Midtones compress' (better thought of as the 'contrast' option) has been set to '–8' to increase the contrast. Then the unwanted text and assorted black specks were painted out using the standard paintbrush tool.

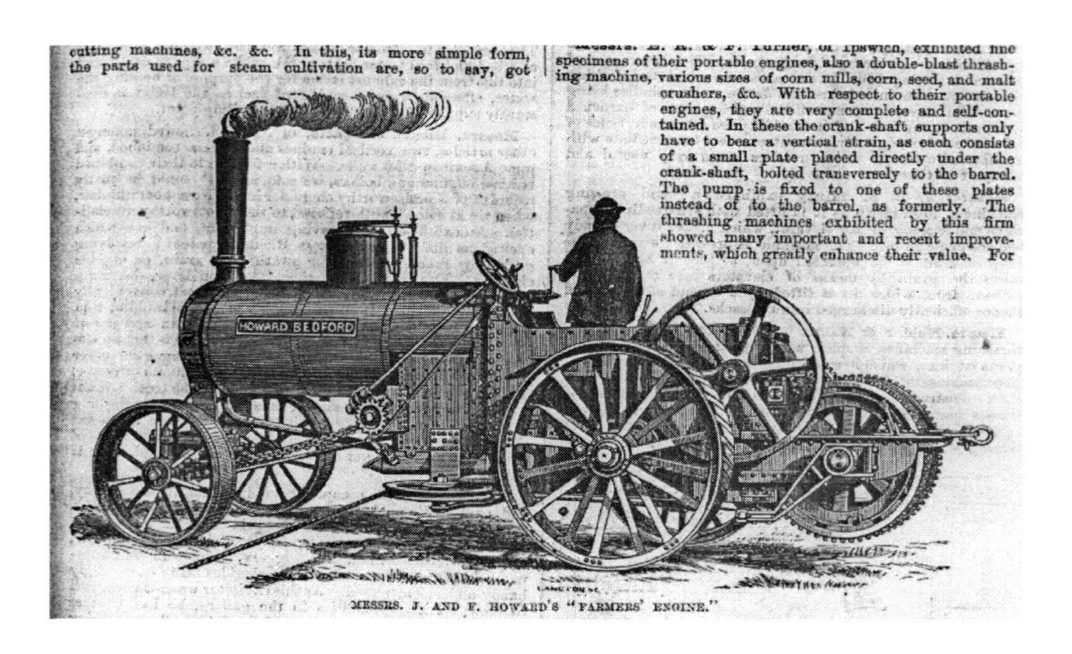

cutting machines, &c. &c. In this, its more simple form, the parts used for steam cultivation are, so to say, got

specimens of their portable engines, also a double-blast thrashing machine, various sizes of corn mills, corn, seed, and malt crushers, &c. With respect to their portable engines, they are very complete and self-contained. In these the crank-shaft supports only have to bear a vertical strain, as each consists of a small plate placed directly under the crank-shaft, bolted transversely to the barrel. The pump is fixed to one of these plates instead of to the barrel, as formerly. The thrashing machines exhibited by this firm showed many important and recent improvements, which greatly enhance their value. For

MESSRS. J. AND F. HOWARD'S "FARMERS' ENGINE."

Grey-scale scan from the Implement and Machinery Review *of 1876.*
Reproduced by kind permission of John Hamilton.

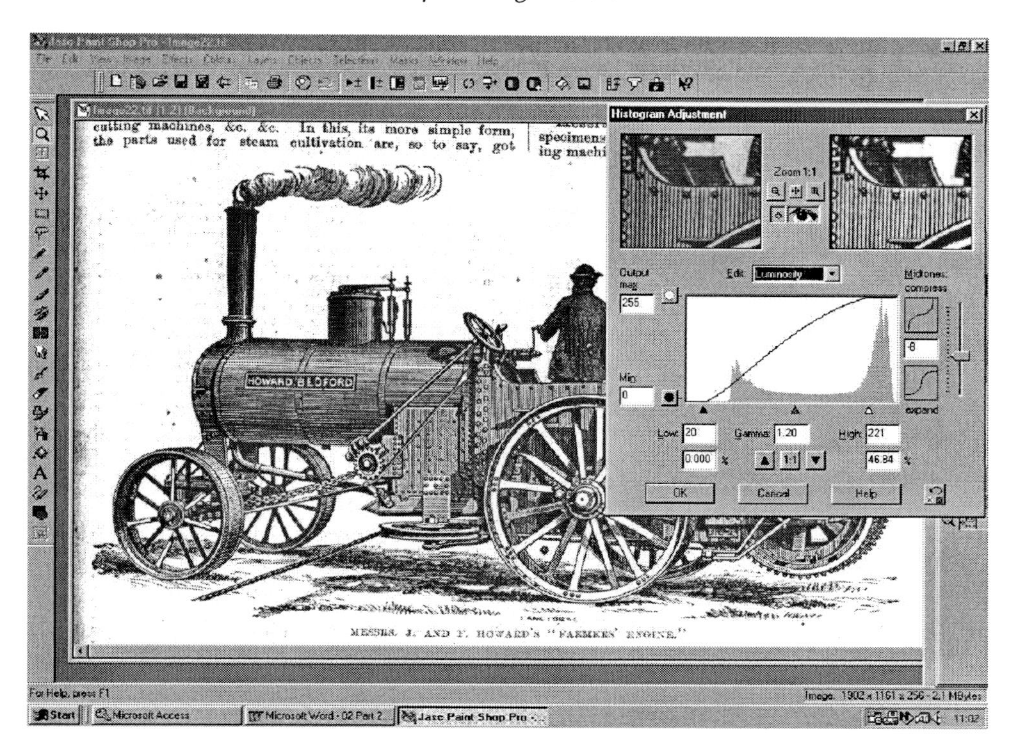

Above: *The Histogram Adjustment tool allows for some immediate improvements.*

Below: *The image as optimised for reproduction in* Glad for God. *Reproduced by kind permission of John Hamilton.*

Maps, plans and such like may have text written on them. Often erasing the text and replacing it with newly-typeset wording is preferable. Resist the temptation to add the text in Paint Shop Pro or Photoshop – you will get *much* better results by doing this later in the DTP software.

Optimising photographs

Firstly, any problems caused by scanning – especially poor contrast or white backgrounds going grey – or defects in the photograph need to be corrected. So tall buildings which appear to be leaning backwards because of perspective effects can be brought upright (see page 83). Likewise unwanted telegraph wires, litter, even parked cars can be removed. 'Red eye' in portraits too can be corrected. If necessary featureless skies can be replaced with a graduated 'overcast' effect, or clouds 'imported'.

Likewise any damage to old images can be digitally 'repaired'. Fading, 'foxing' (light brown stains), dirt marks, creases, missing corners and so forth can usually be dealt with quite well.

If you have scanned in a colour photograph but intend to reproduce it in black and white then convert to 'greyscale' before trying to optimise the image in any way. (You may well want to use 'Save as' so that you still retain the colour version for future use, perhaps on a Web site.)

With all scans I strongly recommend that you use 'Save as' so that the original scan – warts and all – is always available to go back to if some 'improvement' proves to be rather too heavy handed.

Using the Histogram Adjustment tool

Considerable improvements are often possible by using the Histogram Adjustment tool. The interface looks somewhat unfriendly but if you take things in the correct order then you have complete control over the image.

First of see how much the shadow detail can be opened up by increasing the value of the gamma (do not worry if this makes the shadowy parts of the image look lacking in contrast). Once the shadows have been unblocked as much as possible then adjust contrast (Mid-tones Compress).

Opposite is a typical old family photograph, rather faded and lacking in contrast, together with a version after using the Histogram Adjustment tool.

Removing damage and 'clutter'

Paint Shop Pro and its rivals all have a 'clone' tool. This is one of the most effective ways of enhancing photographs, such as taking out spots, scratches and creases. If the 'hardness' is set to between 50 and 80 then changes blend in much more easily. More subtle changes may be easier if the 'opacity' is reduced to 50 to 80.

Top: *A typical family snap shot. Note the lack of solid shadows and bright whites.*
Middle: *Using PaintShop Pro's histogram tool.*
Bottom: *The same photograph optimised with histogram tool.*
Reproduced by kind permission of Joan Shaw.

You may also want to use the 'soften' and 'smudge' tools (in PSP 8 these are hidden in the submenu of the 'dodge' tool which is next to the clone tool icon). Both these tools can be rather savage so use with a hardness of under 50 and an opacity of 30 to 50. Watch out for overdoing them and losing any texture or 'grain' in the image.

The same photograph after use of the clone, soften and smudge tools.
Reproduced by kind permission of Joan Shaw.

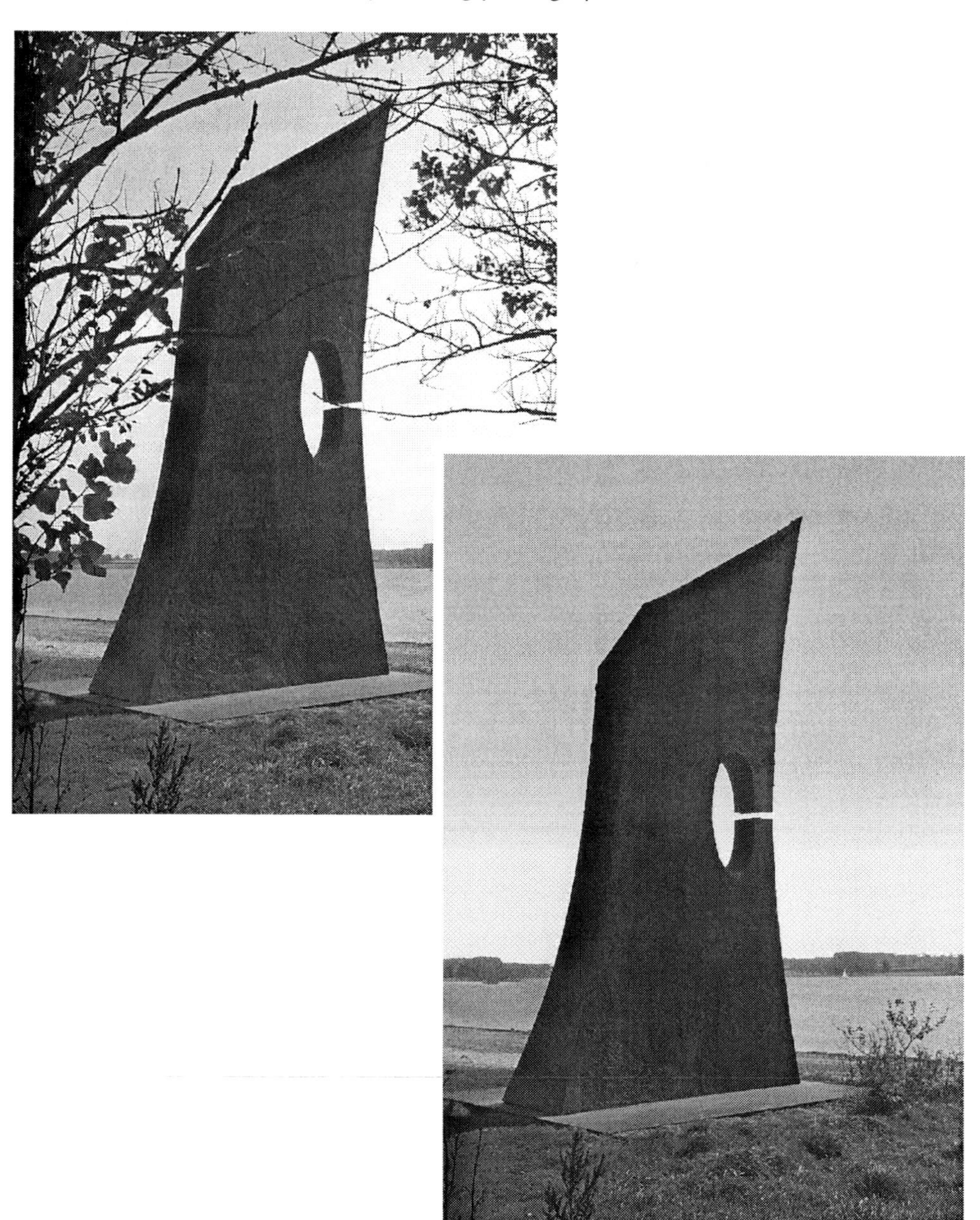

Top: *A large sculpture on the edge of a small wood, by the shore of Rutland Water.*

Bottom: *The same photograph after digitally 'pruning' the trees. The sky was recreated by using the colour selector ('dropper') tool to select the foreground colour from the horizon and the background colour from the top of the image to create a graduated fill between these two shades of grey, then using the 'Fill' tool to replace the original sky.*

Above: *These two photographs of a medieval hermitage now used as a farmhouse show that quite minor 'tweaks' can improve the overall impression. Notable digital enhancements are the removal of the plastic container in front of the left-hand window, removing the open bonnet of the car on the right, and ironing out the dent on the boot. All this was achieved with the clone tool.*

Opposite top: *The typical problem of photographing church towers – by pointing the camera upwards the building appears to be leaning backwards.*

Opposite middle: *Using the vertical perspective correction tool in Paint Shop Pro version 7 (the tool operates in a different way in version 8). Note that this tool requires plenty of space between the building and the edge of the photograph to allow for cropping off the 'wedges' created by the perspective correction.*

Opposite bottom: *The same photograph after correcting the vertical perspective, rotating to the left by 1^0, cropping, then optimising using the Histogram Adjustment tool.*

Correcting 'leaning' buildings

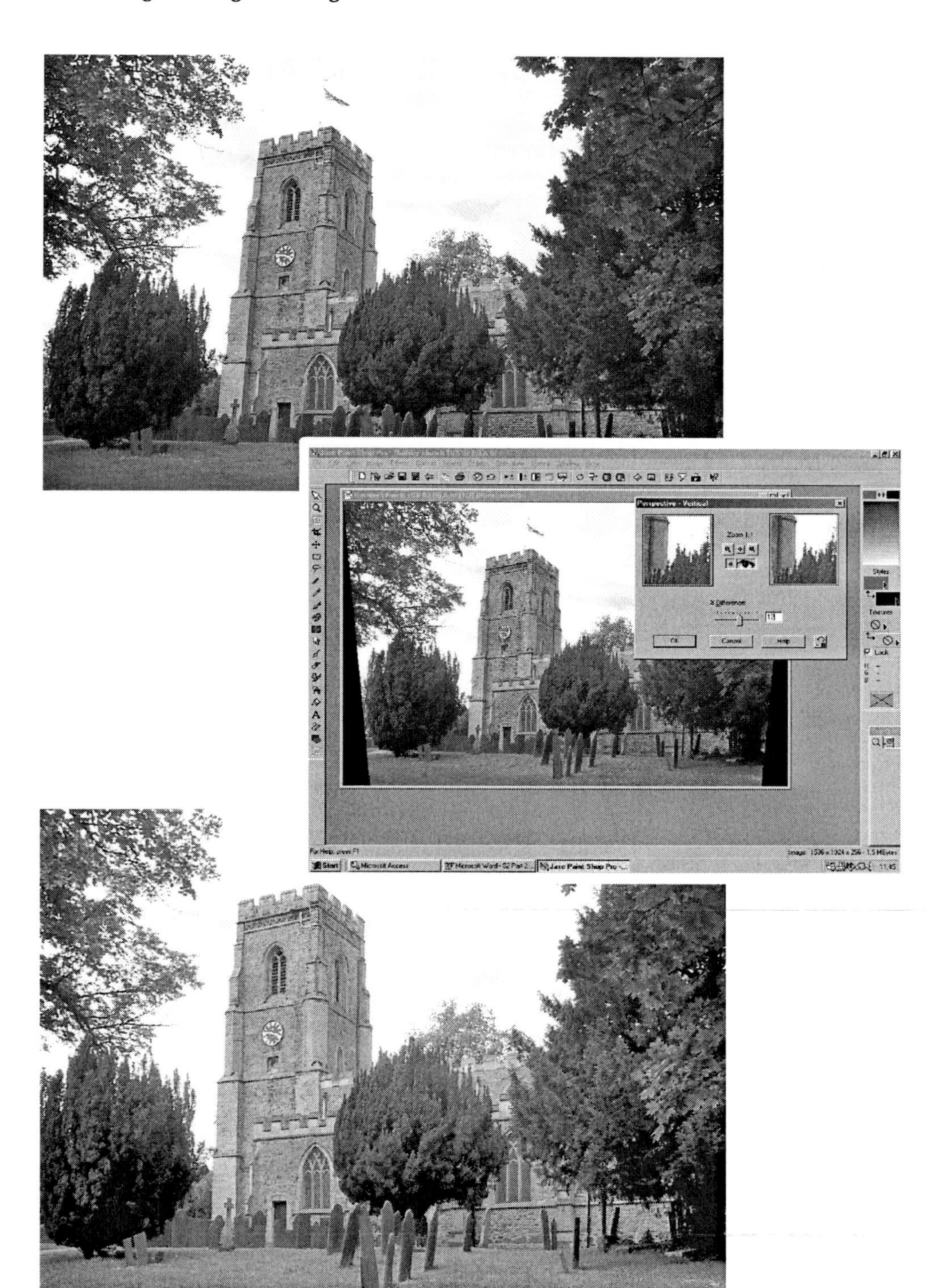

Sharpening

If the image is a bit blurry then use the oddly-named Unsharp Mask tool (the strange name is a carry-over from an old fangled darkroom trick). Depending on the size of the image start with a Radius of 1 and 4 (fine tune with decimal increments) and Strength of 50 to 100; Clipping (Threshold in Photoshop) of between 3 and 10 is usually sufficient to prevent sharpening in undetailed areas.

Note that sharpening cannot rescue a noticeably blurred photograph – it can only add a small amount of extra 'crispness'.

Above left: *A detail of a photograph of a medieval pack horse bridge. The photograph was taken with a hand-held camera and shows slight signs of blurring.*

Above right: *The same detail after applying the Unsharp Mask.*

Dealing with previously printed photographs

Assuming you are not infringing anyone's copyright, or have permission, then you may want to reproduce images from newspapers, magazines and books. These will have printed as 'half tones' and after scanning you may well see curious banding effects on the computer screen. These come and go as the magnification of the screen image is changed. The technical name for them is 'moiré patterns'.

If you try to print such images – either by offset or digital techniques – then such moiré patterns will be created on the printed pages. If you include such images on Web sites or CD-ROMs then similar problems will arise.

However Paint Shop Pro and Photoshop have a moiré removal tool. First of all increase the view size to 1:1 and select a 'characteristic' part of the image. In Paint Shop Pro version 7 go to Effects/Enhance Photo/Moiré Pattern Removal. In Paint Shop Pro version 8 this tool is hidden under Adjust/Add-Remove Noise/Moiré Pattern Removal. Depending on the size of the image then start with a value of 3 to 6 in 'Fine detail' and a value of 2 to 4 in 'Remove bands' (use the smaller values for lower resolution images). Select a value which just removes the dots without making the image look blurred.

After using the Moiré Pattern Removal tool click on the 'Sharpen' tool. If this kind of works but is not ideal then try the 'Unsharp Mask' tool, varying the parameters to get the best results. However some images that have been subjected to Moiré Pattern Removal do not benefit from any sort of sharpening. See pages 70 and 74 for examples of a scanned half-tone before and after Moiré pattern removal.

Enhancing photocopied photographs

One of the problems for local historians is with images that are only available as photocopies. Some of these will be from newspapers and other printed sources so you will need to sort out the moiré patterns (see previous section). Do this before trying to improve the image in other ways.

Go to the Histogram Adjustment tool and see how much the shadow detail can be opened up by increasing the value of the gamma (don't worry if this makes the shadow parts of the image look lacking in contrast). Once the shadows have been unblocked as much as possible then adjust contrast (Mid-tones Compress). You may need to bring the 'High' value on the right down to 245 or less to make a white background appear 'clean'. If the darkest blacks look a little washed out then increase the 'Low' to between 3 and 10. Tricky images may need different parts of the image being optimised in a different way to other parts; see the next section for using the Selection tool. See overleaf for an example of optimising a photocopied photograph.

Optimising photographs taken by flash

Photographs taken by flash may be rather too contrasty, or suffer from uneven exposure. You may need to use the selection tool to adjust one part of the image –

Above: *A rather contrasty photocopy with poor shadow detail.*

Below: *Although still a long way from being a good photograph, the Histogram Adjustment tool has opened up the shadows slightly and added some brightness to the highlights, without totally washing them out.*

Reproduced by kind permission of Joan Shaw.

for example, a person in the foreground – differently to the background. Use the selection tool set to either 'Point-to-point' or 'Smart edge' and finish the selection with a right mouse click to 'close' the selection. Then go Selections/Modify/Feather tool and create a feather edge of between 3 and 6 pixels. Now go to the contrast tools and optimise the selected part of the image. Then go to 'Selections/Invert' and adjust the contrast for the rest of the image. Be prepared to have a few goes at selecting exactly the part of the image and changing the width of the feather edge.

Optimising colour photographs

Colour photographs will be required for Web sites, CD-ROMs, book covers and other paper-based publications that use digital colour copying.

Optimising photographs

In general all the tips for preparing black and white illustrations also apply to colour photographs. Predictably there are a few more 'tricks' that are helpful.

Don't be deceived by your screen

Always bear in mind that what looks good on your monitor may not look the same on other people's screens. TFT flat screens, especially older ones and those on lap tops, produce a much more limited range of colours than 'old fashioned' cathode ray monitors. The main weaknesses is that greens are poorly differentiated, although blues and reds are more limited too.

In addition Apple Macs screens are set up slightly differently to PC screens, so there is an inevitable difference. This will be most noticeable with dark images and the shadow areas of 'normal' pictures. So you need to take your 'tweaked' files to lots of friends who have a wide range of ages and specifications of computers to check that what you think looks good really does.

Optimising colour prints

The most common colour photographs are the ubiquitous prints, usually 6" x 4" or a little larger. A flatbed scanner will scan these adequately. However by the very nature of being a print, the contrast range is not is high as a computer monitor can generate. And, because such photographs are rarely taken in bright sunshine, there may be a rather 'unsaturated' look to the colours.

Paint Shop Pro and Photoshop can readily 'optimise' these images. Indeed Paint Shop Pro's tools for 'Auto-enhance Contrast' and 'Auto-enhance Saturation' are quite likely to do a good job. Note that both these tools have a limited number of preset options – be prepared to try a few variations before deciding that the default 'mid-range' options really are the best. I find it best to optimise the contrast before moving on to the saturation.

However if the shadow details are rather blocked then do not use these tools, but head instead for the Histogram Adjustment tool and start by increasing the value of the gamma. Depending on how good the scanner is you may be able to bring out considerable shadow detail without generating spurious banding. Then adjust the contrast ('Mid-range Compression' on the right-hand side). After using the histogram adjustment switch to the Auto-enhance Saturation tool.

Some old photographs will have started to fade. This means the contrast needs to be increased. However the dyes that provide the different colours will have faded at different rates. Usually the yellow fades first (giving a green cast), then the red. The blue dyes are most resistant to fading. Use the Colours/Adjust/Red-Green-Blue tool to add some red and a little less green (say +8 red and +4 green). Be prepared to spend some time fine-tuning the colour correction. The trick is *never* to try to change all three colours – keep one of them set to '0' – otherwise one change is simply trying to cancel another and the image will lighten or darken with no benefit to the intended result.

Even if the print has not faded it may well be worth adding +4 or +6 red to a photograph, especially if it was taken on a cloudy day. For really grey looking pictures try reducing the blue by –2 or –4 as well as increasing the red.

However if a photograph is already too red – as it might be if taken at sunset or sunrise – then you may want to produce a more natural effect by reducing the red slightly.

My experience is that all colour prints will look a little bit brighter and 'attractive' after some simple adjustments. Even the most faded or discoloured prints will improve significantly, although probably cannot be made to look as good as an image scanned from a much better quality print.

Optimising colour slides

Slides are more contrasty than prints. Unlike prints, slides are usually taken on better cameras and by photographers who have a better idea of how to get saturated colours. Nevertheless, gentle use of the contrast and saturation tools can produce a better effect.

Assuming that slides have been scanned on a professional slide scanner you should also be able to increase to gamma to open up shadow areas quite dramatically. However slides scanned on adapted flatbed scanners will probably not allow the same options for increasing the gamma; indeed the shadows may be blocked even more when slides are scanned this way.

Slides are still prone to fading and even more likely to suffer from colour casts, so fine adjustments to the red-green-blue balance will often be beneficial.

Optimising digital photographs

These are least likely to need changes, unless taken by flash (see above). Photographs taken on grey days will benefit to an increase in the red and, if taken in really murky weather, a small decrease to the blue.

Optimising images for printing

Finally, the image needs to be optimised for reproduction. With printed publications this means getting the right balance of brightness and contrast, without the shadow areas blocking up or the highlights burning out. The 'Histogram Adjustment' tool may at first sight look formidable but it is an excellent way of optimising images.

One of the tricks of optimising the tonal range of images is to always start by adjusting the gamma. Increasing the gamma to 1.20 or 1.30 often brings out the detail from the shadow areas, although with very dark or underexposed images a bigger increase in gamma will be needed. Do not worry if the rest of the image starts to look 'faded' – that will be corrected later. Just concentrate on adjusting the gamma to get the best out of the shadow detail.

Next use the 'Midtones compress' to increase the contrast to say –5 or –7. For rather 'flat' images the setting may need to increase to –12 or –15, exceptionally to the extreme of the range. Aim for a picture that looks on the light side but not so much so that the highlights have washed out. A further tweak on the gamma may be needed. Increasing the 'Low' to 3 or 5 may help to get solid blacks, although revert to '0' if the shadows start to block up. Try reducing the 'High' to 240 or 245 to see if this makes the highlights brighter, but revert to 255 if the highlights look washed out.

For digital printing or any sort of colour printing the 'Output max' and the 'Output min' should *always* be 255 and 0 respectively. However if you intend to reproduce a black and white image using offet litho then these *must* be set to 235 and 15 respectively. The result will look a little 'washed out' and 'grey' on screen but this adjustment is *essential* to overcome so-called 'dot gain' in the printing process.

Optimising images for Web pages and CD-ROMs

For electronic reproduction the same ways of improving images and using the Histogram Adjustment tool apply. However colour images also need the saturation optimising. Paint Shop Pro has an 'Auto-enhance Saturation' tool which offers sufficient control for most purposes, although there is a separate tool for manually adjusting Hue/Saturation/Lightness. Aim for a *slightly* bright appearance.

The next step is to resize *a copy* of the image to the number of pixels needed for the Web page or CD-ROM. Make sure you are viewing the image on screen at 1:1 size. Then select the Sharpen tool. Sometimes the result looks too 'jaggy' but usually this gives the smaller image a suitable boost. If areas of the image without too much detail are looking too 'grainy' then use the Unsharp Mask tool. For low resolution images for on screen viewing the Radius will probably need to between 0 and 1 with Strength of 50 to 100; Clipping (Threshold in Photoshop) of between 3 and 10 is usually sufficient to prevent sharpening in undetailed areas. Over-sharpening will create white fringes or haloes around details – undo and select less aggressive sharpening parameters.

After all the tweaking has been done, go to Paint Shop Pro's 'File' menu, select 'Export' then 'JPEG Optimizer' (if you use this tool often then it worth customising the toolbars so the relevant icon is only one click away). Photoshop's equivalent is under 'File' then 'Save for Web'. Try different compression levels to assess how much the file size can be reduced without creating obvious problems. The places where JPEG compression usually shows first is in areas of similar tone, such as skies, or where there is important fine detail, such as text.

If you are planning on including several images on a Web page then they should be under 20 Kbytes each. Only if there will be one image on a Web page can the file size creep above the 50 Kbyte level. (File size is usually not a problem for CD-ROMs so a JPEG compression of 5 to 10 can normally be used.)

If you are struggling to keep the necessary amount of detail within a realistic file size then the easiest option will be to make the image slightly smaller – even a reduction from, say, 800 to 700 pixels wide will reduce the file size by about a third. However *never* resize an image that has already been resized, especially if it has also been

The photograph reproduced on page 70 saved as a JPG file with excessive compression.

sharpened! Go back to the original larger file and resize that to the new dimensions (this is why three paragraphs back I said resize *a copy* of the image...) then sharpen, assuming this helps.

JPEG is especially tricky at compressing line art. Here the better option is to use GIF format rather than JPEG. If appropriate, reduce the number of colours in the image to 16 before selecting Paint Shop Pro's 'GIF Optimiser' tool (or the corresponding part of Photoshop's 'Save to Web' tool).

Commissioning illustrations and photographs

If original illustrations are not available, or cannot be used because the copyright owner cannot be traced (see page 58) then specially commissioned drawings or photographs will be needed.

If at all possible use an artist or photographer who is used to preparing material for printing. Many people have been to art classes and may, indeed, be good at pencil sketches, watercolours, and the like. However they may have no previous experience of seeing their work reproduced in print. Likewise, photographs need to be well composed and 'crisp', but without deep shadows or washed out highlights. Someone who has considerable experience of taking photographs to a commercial standard will produce images considerably better than someone who simply points a digital camera in roughly the right direction.

The problem with local history groups is that someone who may not be aware of the skills really needed for appropriate illustrations or photographs volunteers their assistance, making it difficult to refuse their offer without causing offence. Always respond to such offers somewhat cautiously (unless you have every reason to believe that they have considerable experience of providing illustrations or photographs for reproduction, in which case don't let them get away!).

See pages 62 to 65 for a draft agreement which must be signed by any artist or photographer commissioned to provide illustrations.

Charts

Graphs (also known as line charts), bar (or column) charts and pie charts are often especially useful for local historians. Usually charts can be produced as line-art, either by hand then scanning or by using vector graphic software. Some people find it easier to roughly sketch a chart on graph paper, then scan it in. By adding a new layer to the image the original sketch can be used as a template for a crisper digitally-produced version. When everything has been redrawn the layer containing the original scan can be deleted, leaving only the improved version. With charts be careful not to use overly-subtle dot patterns to distinguish different parts of the data – these may not reproduce sufficiently clearly.

There are at least 14 different types of charts, and many variations. All local libraries have books about how to prepare and use graphs and charts. Make sure you know which type of chart 'goes with' specific types of data. Do not fall for the novice's mistake of using graphs when bar charts are needed, or using bar charts when pie charts would be more effective. 3-D column charts can *sometimes* be helpful but make sure they are as simple and clear as possible.

Population information derived from census returns is ideally suited to graphical presentation, as the examples overleaf show.

Spreadsheet software (such as Excel) will generate most types of chart and the manuals provide guidance on which type of chart is most appropriate to specific types of data. Unfortunately it can be difficult to adjust the fine details of such spreadsheet charts in a way which fits exactly with what is required for book illustrations. Be prepared to redraw the charts using software specifically intended for drawing.

Never assume that charts are self-explanatory. The caption *must* explain or summarise the significance of the data.

Maps

Maps are especially tricky for the inexperienced to produce to a satisfactory standard. Try contacting a local university with a geography department and ask if they can put in contact with any freelance cartographers.

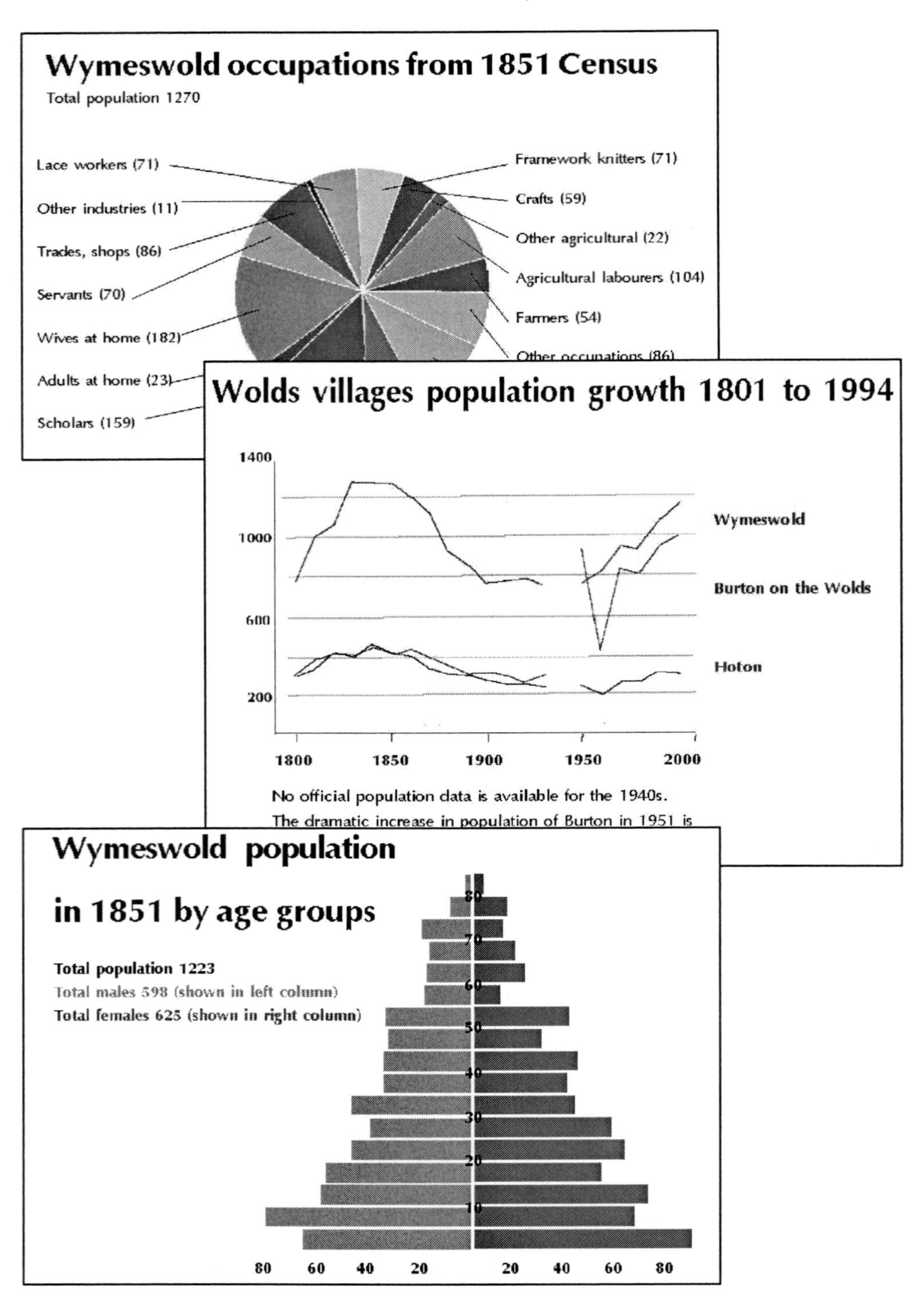

Examples of graph, bar chart and pie chart, based on Alec Moretti's analysis of census data for Wymeswold.; originals in colour.

If you want some professional tips on preparing maps then get hold of *The Complete Guide to Digital Illustration* by Steve Caplin and Adam Banks (Ilex 2003). Unlike most similar how-do-it books this has a section specifically on maps.

There are two possible ways of preparing maps for reproduction. One is to learn to use vector graphic software (Xara X; CorelDraw; Adobe Illustrator; Macromedia Freehand; etc). However these have fairly steep learning curves and, frustratingly, do not necessarily export out reliably so, when the carefully prepared images are loaded into DTP software, there are glitches that cannot be corrected. This may mean that the image has to printed out at the highest resolution possible (at least twice the

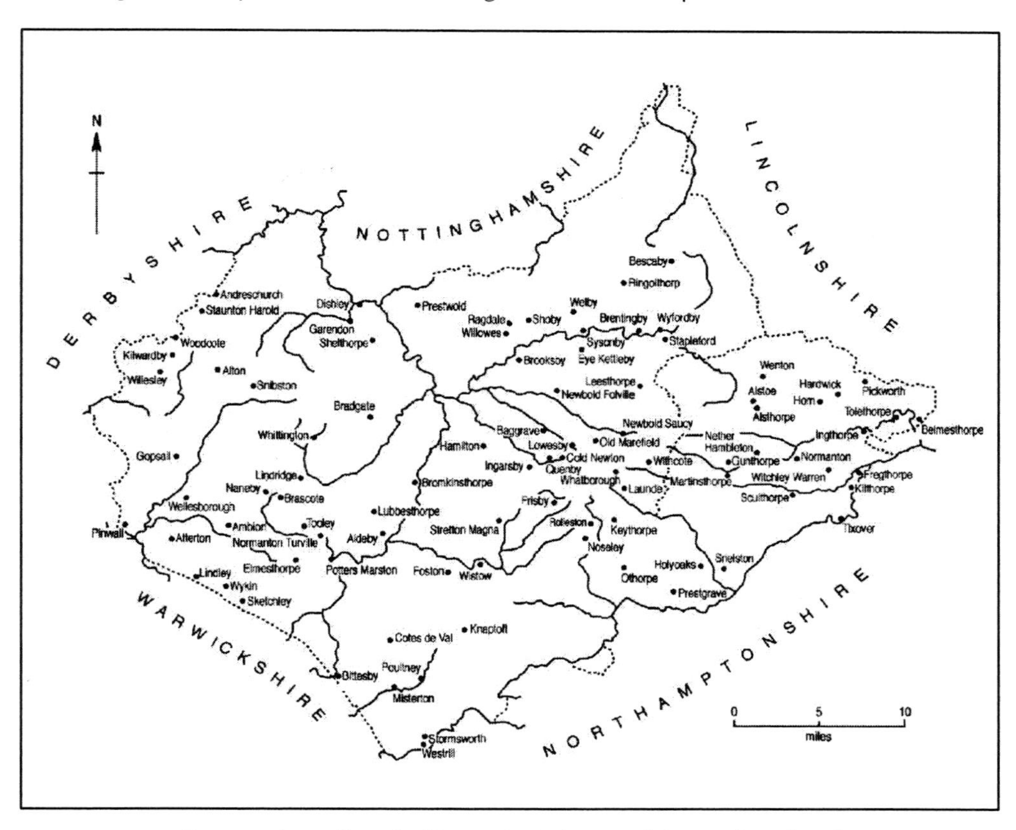

Deserted medieval villages in Leicestershire and Rutland.

Map prepared by Anne Tarver for Jill Bourne's Understanding Leicestershire and Rutland Place-Names *(Heart of Albion 2003); reproduced by kind permission of Anne Tarver.*

This was produced in Macromedia Freehand, printed out at twice final size at 600 dpi, then scanned in and the brightness and contrast enhanced to produce a 'clean' white background and solid black lines and text. However the text has not reproduced as crisply as it would have been if only this had been added in the DTP software.

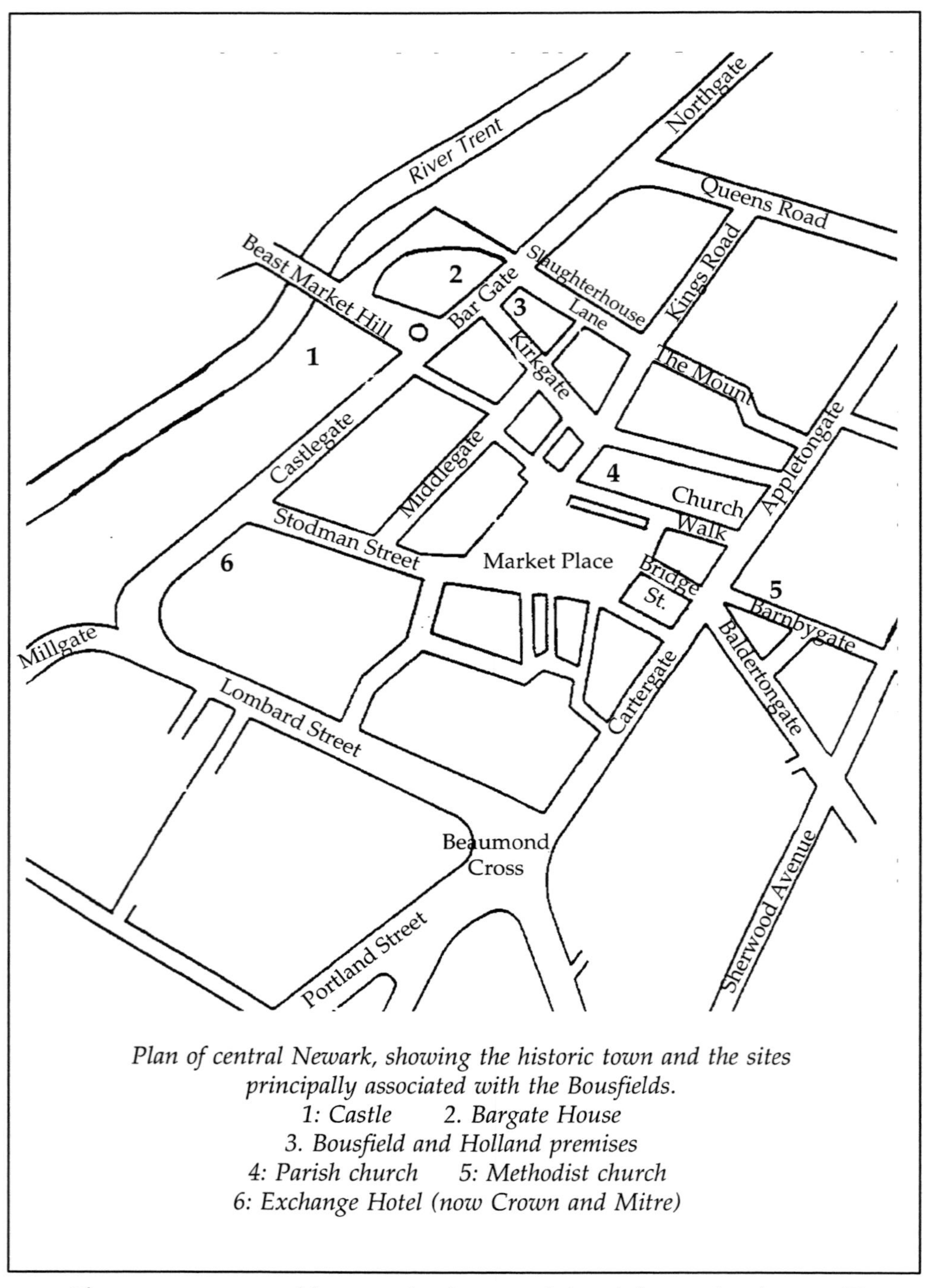

Plan of central Newark, showing the historic town and the sites principally associated with the Bousfields.
1: Castle 2. Bargate House
3. Bousfield and Holland premises
4: Parish church 5: Methodist church
6: Exchange Hotel (now Crown and Mitre)

The map was created by scanning in a rough hand-drawn sketch map. The lines were cleaned up and the original text removed. This image was imported into the DTP software where the text was added. Reproduced from Glad for God *by kind permission of John Hamilton.*

resolution required for the final printing), scanned, cleaned up and then imported into the DTP software as an image (see caption to the map on page 93).

The 'failsafe' and less technically tricky way is to draw the lines (but none of the text) on paper, scan into Paint Shop Pro or PhotoShop and then clean up the scan. Import this image of the lines into the DTP software and add the text, putting each section of text into its own box. If necessary the text boxes can be rotated. See street map of Newark, opposite, for an example.

Remember that maps should usually have a north point and a scale.

Above all remember that any map which derives in any way from Ordnance Survey maps – even ones out of copyright – must comply with the relevant copyright statements. Maps redrawn from Ordnance Survey maps which are still in copyright will require a fee to be reproduction fee to be paid to the Ordnance Survey (see pages 65 and 66 for details of Ordnance Survey copyright and reproduction fees).

Family trees

If your publication needs one or more family trees then, apart from preparing complex maps, this may prove to be one of the trickiest tasks. Experience helps a little, but the major challenge is fitting the necessary information onto the relatively small space of a page (or even a pair of facing pages).

Family history software generates trees, but not in a manner which can be prepared for publication. Attempting to scan in family trees printed by other software does not help as the small text will reproduce with jagged edges.

There are two possible solutions. One is to learn to use vector graphic software (see previous section on maps); as noted these are tricky to learn and do not necessarily export out reliably.

The only solution which can be made to work reliably is to work directly in the DTP software, putting each section of text into its own box, then creating empty text boxes with a border down one side only for each of the lines. By switching off the 'snap to guides' option these boxes can be positioned accurately. This is tedious work and, in the later stages, a relatively small change can mean moving much of the previous work.

Because the text in family trees invariable needs to be kept small, use an easily read face (such as Arial) – even if this is not used for the rest of the book. Regard 8 pt as the smallest which can be read and use 9 pt or 10 pt if there is room. Keep to the same font size for the whole family tree. The spacing between lines ('leading') should be about 2 pt. You will find it much easier to work if the paragraph style is set for no indents, no space above or below. (See Chapter 6 for more information on all aspects of typesetting.)

You are probably already familiar with the conventions of abbreviations for family trees. An equals sign (' = ') denotes marriage. Be sure to consistently abbreviate

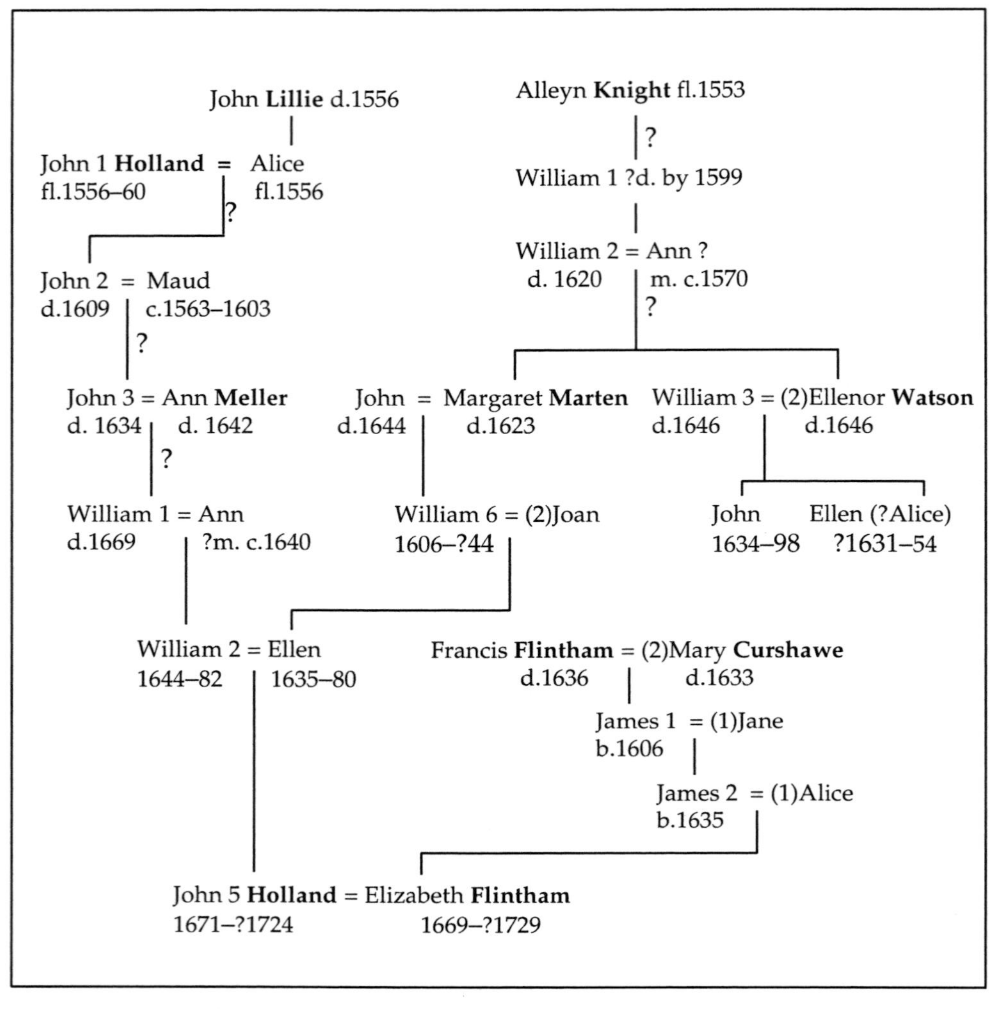

A fairly simple family tree typeset using the DTP software.
Reproduced from Glad for God *by kind permission of John Hamilton.*

You may find it easier to turn such pedigrees on their side, so the oldest ancestors are on the left and the youngest on the right, rather than running top to bottom as shown here.

'baptised' (usually 'bap') and 'buried' (usually 'bur') in a way that does not become confused with 'born' (usually 'b'). Decide whether or not such abbreviations will be followed by a full stop – and be consistent! You may want to use 'circa' (always abbreviated to 'c' or 'c.') for 'approximately' as it takes up less space than 'approx.'.

The abbreviation 'd.s.p.' derives from the Latin *decessit sine prole* and means 'died without issue' but this rather old school term can be replaced by 'w/i' or such like, so long as there is an explanation of this abbreviation somewhere on the same page.

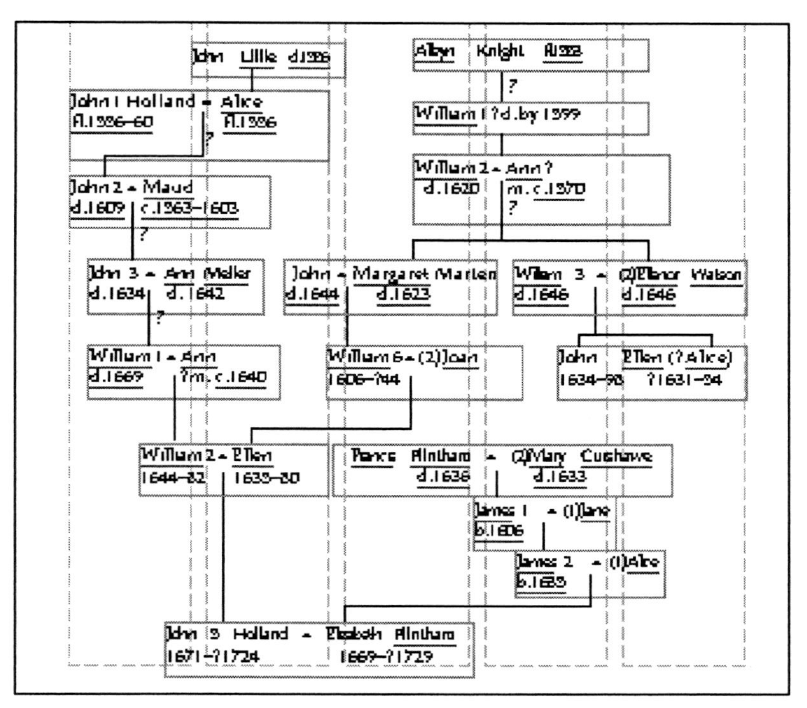

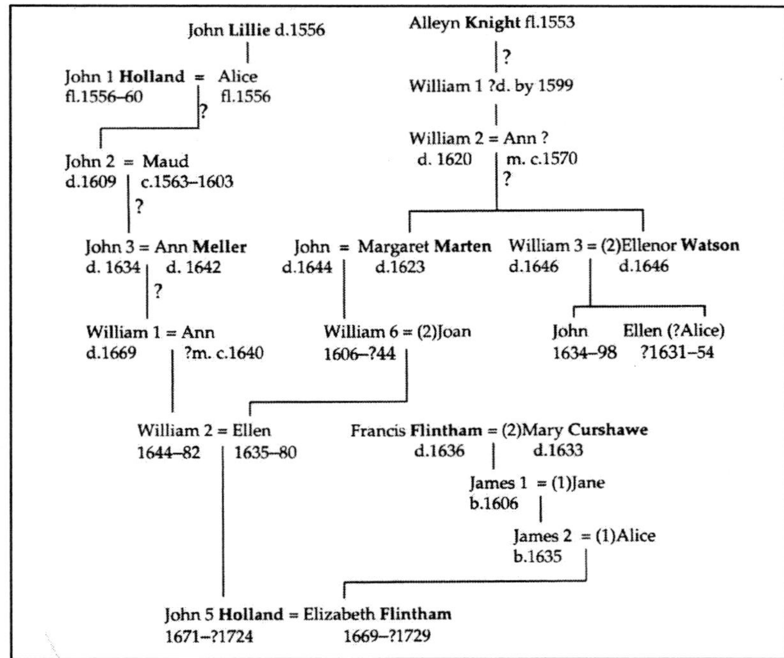

Top: *Screen grab of the same family tree being prepared in the DTP software.*

Above: *The same family tree scanned in from a good quality print out.*

With Old Style dates before 1752, when the year began on 25 March, then for dates between 1 January and 25 March use the form '1691/2' (N.B. *not* '1691–2' which denotes something quite different!).

Creating family trees for Web sites and CD-ROMs may require a different approach; this is discussed on page 199.

Captions

Every illustration in a publication should have a caption that explains its significance, provides key information (e.g. names of people in photographs) and perhaps information relating to copyright.

Often captions can be quite brief but, as with books that comprise mostly of old photographs, the writing of captions can become an 'art form' of its own. Think how many times you have opened a book and simply flicked through reading the captions to decide whether or not to buy or read it. The best captions manage to convey the necessary information concisely while telling a mini-story, or raising curiosity about the more extensive discussion in the main text.

So a caption reading 'Mr and Mrs Smith outside their house in the late 1930s, showing some of the original outbuildings' may be true. But it is much less informative than 'Mr and Mrs Smith outside "Hilltop House" shortly before it was requisitioned by the RAF at the start of the Second World War. To the right is part of the stable block demolished in the 1950s.'

With old illustrations an indication of the original source is customary. With specially-commissioned illustrations a credit for the artist or photographer is appropriate. Where permission has been given for reproduction (for instance, by a museum or county record office) then the caption should include the *correct* wording (many organisations request a very specific wording).

However, an appendix providing a cross-referenced list about sources and copyright may be more appropriate – although some copyright holders may insist on their permission statement being printed alongside the illustration.

Where most of the illustrations are by one person (especially if that person is the author) then a general statement in the prelim pages to the effect of 'All illustrations are by the author except where stated' is entirely sufficient (see pages 126 and 127 for more details). Remember that copyright is automatic (see page 56) and does not need to be asserted, so there is nothing more amateurish than a book full of illustrations where each one is captioned 'Copyright of the author'.

How many figures or illustrations (photos, drawings, charts, maps, etc) and tables there are (and whether or not they fit neatly near the text they relate to) partly determines whether they need to be numbered in the book. However there is little advantage from using figure numbers except when frequent cross-referencing is needed, as 'see photograph on page xx' is only slightly more cumbersome than 'see fig. yy'.

Marking up illustrations

Whether or not illustrations are numbered in the book they need to be given a unique name or number before the typesetting stages. Such naming need have nothing to do with the sequence in which they appear in the text. Traditionally captions for illustrations are supplied as a separate list to the main text of a book. However, I find that typesetting is easier if the reference number of the illustration and the text for its caption are included in the main text at approximately the correct position.

To make this stand out from the main text include a row of ******* characters before and after the illustration details. In the following example the words 'Pic 32a' will be deleted from the final text.

> *****************
> Pic 32a
> The interior of Anywhere church photographed before the restoration of 1892. Courtesy of Oldtime Photographs Ltd.
> *****************

Final thoughts

Whether or not an illustration says as much as a thousand words is a moot point, but preparing illustrations for reproduction may require as much attention to detail as carefully crafting a thousand words.

This chapter is intended to help novices make useful improvements to images, if only by drawing attention to what can or should be corrected. The nature of the software means that descriptions of how to make changes are often read in a complex way, although with just a little practice these techniques become second nature.

As with writing, the best way of getting better is to keep practising. With regular use the Histogram Adjustment Tool will seem the most intuitive way to optimise a image, not the intimidating multi-headed monster that it seems at first acquaintance.

However the subtleties of optimising images for reproduction can only be achieved by building up experience of what works – and what doesn't work! – when printed. Unfortunately experience of producing colour prints on inkjet printers counts for little when preparing images for digital printing. Getting a feel for the levels of contrast, brightness and shadow detail (gamma) which print up well is something that only comes from experience.

Thankfully digital printing allows for affordable one-off 'proof copies' that are exactly the same as the final print run, so a final check is possible, allowing for any final tweaks and changes to be made. This is a wonderful advantage over traditional off-set litho and makes the publishing of books based around old photographs much less of a risky activity. I can only recommend that you develop the necessary skills and take full adavantge!

Chapter 4

THINKING ABOUT PRINTING

There are three relevant printing processes: photocopying, digital printing, and offset litho. Each has its strengths and weaknesses, especially regarding illustrations. And, predictably enough, each has different costs.

There are also different ways of binding – stapled booklets, paperbacks and hardbacks. These will be considered later in this section.

Once you have decided what options there are for printing your publication then you can ask for quotes to compare the different options – and the costs of different printing companies. However this means getting to grips with some of the jargon of the printing trade. By the end of this chapter you will be thinking like a printer.

Photocopying

For newsletters and magazines with a limited circulation (as is often the case with village history periodicals) then photocopying and stapling has been the usual option. Unfortunately photocopying usually copes badly with photographs and other half-tone illustrations (see page 69).

Some employers may be willing to partly or completely subsidise the costs of photocopying for employees who are involved in 'not for profit' spare time activities (although do ask relevant management first rather than try to sneak several hundred pages through in a lunch break!). But the real disadvantage may be the time taken to collate and staple the pages, especially when the print run gets to around a hundred copies. The modest costs of a long-reach stapler enable A3 or A4 sheets to be centre-stapled then folded down to A4 or A5, making a much more attractive publication than one where A4 sheets are edge stapled. But remember that for this to be an option then the total number of pages *must* be divisible by four!

Even where 'subsidised' copying on office photocopiers is not possible, every town has one or more High Street 'copy shops' that operate with standard charges. These will also collate and staple for a modest extra cost. The machines in such copy shops will use A3 paper, so plan for the total number of pages being a multiple of four and ask for centre stapling. They will be able to offer (a usually rather limited) range of fairly thin coloured card that should be suitable for covers (see page 151 for suggestions about cover design). Unfortunately thicker card can easily cause very expensive damage to photocopying machines.

Digital printing

Higher specification 'photocopiers', such as those found in High Street copyshops and larger offices, also print direct from computer files. Later in this book such 'digital printing' will be discussed in more detail. Unlike photocopying, digital printing will produce excellent photographs (assuming they have been suitably prepared – see Chapter 4). This makes such printing ideal for all short run publications.

However not all digital printing machines are capable of copying onto thick card, so check what 'weight' of card is available for use.

Short-run book printers now make extensive use of even more sophisticated digital printing equipment. Digital printing of books means that very short print runs are feasible. So only the minimum needed to be printed initially, followed by reprints when stocks get low.

Digital colour printing

Digital colour printing is also available. At the time of writing this book (2004) the cost is between 15p and 50p per A4 side, making the use of extensive colour rather prohibitive. However within the next few years costs will no doubt drop, making short-run colour publications an affordable option. Until digital colour printing is more affordable colour illustrations are best avoided. If they are necessary then include them on consecutive pages which can be printed separately and then incorporated with the rest of the book at the binding stage.

Covers of digitally printed books

Be wary of digitally printed covers (in colour or black only) as these will probably not be laminated. This is partly a limitation of the equipment (lamination is not an integral part of digital printing) and partly because the pigments used for digital printing, especially colour ones, cause bubbling with conventional laminating processes. Without laminating the slightest scuff mark and fingerprint (especially on dark coloured backgrounds) will show. Bookshops will understandably refuse to take copies with such defects to the covers – and copies on their shelves will soon look tatty. There can also be problems with getting crisp folds on the spine of digitally printed covers. The reason is because the relatively small size of most digital printers means that card needs to be fed 'cross grain' (yes, card does have a 'grain' – although it is not visible – and this affects the way it folds and creases).

Until digital colour printing becomes more cost effective full colour covers remain a compromise. The approach adopted by Heart of Albion and many other specialist publishers is to use offset litho (see next section) for the covers. The initial costs of printing plates for the cover are high but the 'run on' costs of extra copies are low – think in terms of around 15 pence for each extra cover. This means printing the maximum number of covers likely to be required (say 1,000 or 1,500) but only printing and binding say 200 or 300 books initially. The remaining covers are kept flat, clean and dry for use when a reprint – perhaps of only 50 or 100 copies at a time – is required. This has two major advantages. Firstly you are only paying for books that are likely to be sold within a few months (the cost of the 'spare' covers being less than 10 percent of the cost of the total cost of each copy). Secondly, and this may be the even bigger advantage, you do not have to store a large number of books.

All short run book printers are able to print covers by offset litho. They usually subcontract this to a suitable specialist printer, but there is little or no advantage for you to seek out and approach such suppliers direct.

As you may have guessed, the covers of this book has been printed using offset litho then laminated, with the inside pages by digital printing.

Offset litho

Once the print run gets to at least 700 to 1,000 copies then digital printing may not be so cost-effective. Offset litho requires every page to be printed from a 'plate'. The plates can either be made of plastic (confusingly, often referred to as 'paper plates') or metal. Metal plates give better quality and are usually needed for half-tones such as photographs. 'Paper' plates have a limited life (although usually more than adequate for the print runs associated with local history) and, unlike metal plates, cannot be kept for reprints. Predictably, metal plates are more expensive than 'paper' plates. The cost of the plates, even 'paper' plates, is a substantial proportion of the cost of offset litho printing.

While offset litho may be ideal for the initial print run of, say, 800 copies what happens if you need a small reprint? Assuming you are unlikely to sell another 800 copies, using offset litho for a 100 or 200 copy reprint will not be cost effective. The answer is to plan ahead. Print extra covers (see the previous section on digitial printing) as these could be used for a *digital* reprint. The only problem would be for a heavily illustrated book, as the preparation of half-tone illustrations for offset litho is slightly different than that needed for digital printing. But, so long as this is planned in advance all the illustrations can be redone fairly quickly.

Offset litho colour printing

Colour produced by offset litho can produce very different results to images seen on a computer screen or printed by inkjet or digital colour. This is because offset litho colour printing uses four coloured inks – cyan, magenta, yellow and black (referred to as 'CMYK'). Adding tints of these colours to each other produces a wide spectrum of colours; the more ink that is added the *darker* the colour. However computer monitors use three colours of light – red, green and blue (known as RGB) – to get fintermediate colours. Here the more light that is added the *lighter* the colour. Not only are these two very different ways of achieving a wide range of colours, but the range of colours and shades possible with mixing light is greater than that possible with mixing inks on paper.

Furthermore monitors need to be accurately calibrated if colour critical files need to be prepared. Bear in mind that flat screen monitors and lap tops show colours differently to cathode ray monitors (for example, greens may be poorly differentiated).

In practice the specialist plate makers used by printers should be able to adjust for the differences between an RGB computer file and the need to produce CMYK plates. However yellows and pale orange shades often come out weaker.

When you place an order with a printer (see page 157) be sure to state State 'Proofs must be submitted before binding'. This will give you a chance to pick up major problems with cover printing before they are made into books.

Binding

To be able to get quotes for printing you have to decide how you want the publication to be bound.

Different types of binding

There are three main ways of binding books and booklets.

Hardback

Hardback binding is also known in the trade as 'case bound' or 'cloth bound'. It is the most expensive but most attractive and durable type of binding. The pages can be glued or, more usually, 'sewn in ligatures'.

The spine needs to be hot-foil blocked with the title and (usually) author and imprint name. Most hardbacks come with a dust jacket, usually in full colour. Alternatively the colour 'jacket' can be glued to the card (this is typical for children's books).

Attractive end papers add an appropriate 'touch of class' for a modest cost increase over plain end papers.

Paperback

Most paperbacks are simply glued (known in the trade as 'perfect bound'). Some binders offer paperbacks with sewn ligatures, which (although more expensive) is recommended as this makes for a stronger and longer-lasting book. Paperback binding needs at least 64 pages to form a spine (and even then it may be only about 4 mm thick).

Some printers are happy to include coloured end papers in paperbacks. This provides a good 'first impression' when people initially open the book. See page 107 for further details.

Stapled booklets

What you and I call stapling the printing trade refers to as 'saddle stitched' or just 'stitched' – not to be confused with books that are 'sewn in ligatures' using thread.

Stapling is by far the cheapest method of binding but has several disadvantages:

- The number of pages is limited (anything over 60 sides looks unattractively 'plump' and 80 sides is about the top limit physically).
- There is no spine to attract the attention of browsers in bookshops.
- Stapled booklets look less professional alongside 'real books'.
- Staples may rust, ruining unsold stock.

Other types of binding

There are some specialised techniques for short-run publishing (such as comb, wire and spiral binding and so-called thermal binding) but these are less suitable for books that will be sold in bookshops as there is no 'spine' and they all look very amateurish. Wire binding has some advantages for manuals that need to be opened flat; although local history books rarely need to be used in this way.

Learn the lingo

When talking to printers, be prepared to discuss binding in terms of 'case bound', 'perfect bound' and 'stitched'. However, to make life easier for readers of this book I will use the terms 'hardback', 'paperback' and 'stapled' as these are more familiar to the non-specialist.

Which type of binding to use?

The big advantage of both hardback and paperback books, compared to other types of binding, is that they provide a 'spine', along which the title and, usually, the author's name can be boldly printed.

In contrast, booklets on bookshop shelves simply get lost, with no text to catch the eye. And the reality of the book trade is that shelf space is always at a premium, meaning that only a few books (usually the current best sellers) can be displayed 'face out'. Few booksellers place local history publications 'face out' – and if your book is the exception then this should always be greatly appreciated!

Hardback binding is still a labour-intensive craft industry and costs more than paperback binding (although not as much as the retail price differences between hardback and paperback editions would suggest). Unfortunately most local history titles are barely viable as paperbacks, so the additional cost of hardback binding is usually prohibitive.

However there is no reason for not learning the skills of book binding and, time permitting, doing your own hardback binding. A useful book to help you get started is *Domestic Bookbinding* by Jean Dark, published by Pixie Inc www.pixie-inc.demon.co.uk; also helpful are *The Thames and Hudson Manual of Bookbinding* by Arthur W. Johnson (T&H 1978) and *The Craft of Bookbinding: A practical handbook* by Eric Burdelt (David and Charles 1975) and *The Complete Book of Bookbinding* Josep Cambras, Lark Books 2004.

If books are sewn in ligatures then the same print run can be bound in hardback or paperback format. Many 'real publishers' bind a few hundred copies as hardbacks (which will be sold mostly to libraries) and bind the rest as paperbacks. With major publishers the tradition is to produce a hardback edition initially and, if it sells well, follow up with a paperback edition about twelve months later. If the hardback has not sold well then over-stock copies are 'remaindered' at a price similar to a paperback edition. Local history publishing rarely benefits from this approach, however.

The rest of this chapter will mostly assume you are produced a stapled booklet or paperback book, as these are the types of publications most commonly produced by local and family historians.

Page sizes

Printers are generally an obliging sort and will print books to whatever strange size you want. However their presses and paper suppliers are designed to work with some traditional sizes. If you go for an 'in between' page size you may find you are paying as much as for the next standard size and for a lot of trimmed-off paper ending up in the recycling bin.

In Chapter 6 the pros and cons of different page sizes and layouts are discussed in detail.

Estimating the number of pages

A key factor in the cost of printing is, predictably, the number of pages. How many pages there are in the manuscript is not an accurate indication of how many pages there will be in the book as the number of words per page could change substantially. The only way to know exactly how many pages there will be in a book is to typeset it (see Chapter 6). But clearly there is not a lot of point typesetting a book until you have decided whether the costs are viable. This 'Catch 22' situation is endemic to publishing so the following 'rules of thumb' may help.

First of all estimate the number of words in the text (not forgetting end notes, references and bibliographical details). Most word processing software can give accurate word counts, otherwise count up the words on a 'typical' page and multiply by the number of pages. If the text is not yet fully written then some inspired guesses are necessary!

Do not forget to allow 6 to 15 sides for prelim pages (see page 125) and, if expected, a foreword and index. Allow at least 3 pages of indices for each 100 pages of main text – less if there are many pictures and more if many different people are mentioned (as is often the case in family history books).

Next, count up the number of illustrations, and get a 'feel' for the approximate size that they will be printed at e.g. full page, half page, or smaller.

If you will be supplying the printer with camera-ready-copy rather than PDF files (see page 155) then also count up how many photographs and other half-tones (see page 69) there will be (line art does not have any effect on printer's quotes).

To get to a total page count, the following 'typical' figures may be helpful.

- A5 pages have about 350 words on a page full of text.
- A4 pages have about 550 words on a page with one or two columns of text.
- A4 format magazines with three columns of (fairly small size) print may have between 600 and 700 words per page.

Unless illustrations will be full page then assume that each illustration will average at half a page for A5 format or a third of a page for A4 format.

While the above 'rules of thumb' will never be exact they should be sufficiently close to enable reasonably accurate estimates.

Know your sixteen times table

With offset litho books are usually printed on large presses which print many pages at the same time. For books with pages that are A5 (or its old Imperial counterpart, known variously as Demi 8vo or Demy Octavo, i.e. 8½" by 5½") then usually 16 pages are printed at a time. This means that the total number of pages in your book needs to be *exactly* divisible by 16. If you are just a few pages short then some adverts or blank pages can be included. But it can be very frustrating if you just go 1 or 2 pages into the next 16. This could result in a significant increase in costs if it means the difference between, say, an 80 and 96 page book.

One of the real advantages of digital printing is that pages are typically printed in pairs or four-up, so the 'divide by 16' problem disappears.

Paper types

There are many different types of paper used by printers. Some are smooth ('bond') and some are textured ('wove'). Some are glossy ('coated') and some are 'matt' – and some are in between (usually called 'silk').

Coated (glossy) paper is excellent for reproducing half-tones but costs more than uncoated paper. However few if any digital printing machines will work with coated papers. Coated paper is also unsuited for some types of perfect binding.

Some wove papers can be difficult when reproducing half-tones – take your printer's advice rather than insist on using something you like the look of.

Paper comes in different thicknesses or 'weights' (usually described in grams per square meter or 'gsm', often referred to as just 'grams'). Typical office photocopier paper is 80 gsm. Company letterheads often use 100 or 120 gsm paper.

Unfortunately weight is not directly related to thickness, so one type of 100 gsm paper may be thicker than another type. 'Wove' papers tend to feel thicker than 'bond' papers with the same gsm. Coated papers tend to be thinner than the same weight of non-coated papers.

This book is on 100 gsm laser pre-print paper.

Be careful with 80 gsm papers (especially coated types) as solid blacks on one side of the paper may be too clearly visible on the other side. This is known as 'show through' and would be a problem if you have strong line-art 'back to back' on the same leaf of paper. Heavier papers reduce show through but cost more.

Some local history books look especially attractive on 'tinted' paper – usually various shades of cream and ivory. Tinted paper usually costs more than basic white, but not always. Stronger tints and 'marbled' papers are available but this would be unusual for books or booklets and these papers tend to be much more expensive than white paper.

Many printers will have their favourite papers that are known to work well with their presses, and for which they probably get advantageous prices. They will provide samples for you to see and feel. Unless there are very good reasons otherwise, go along with suggestions the printer makes for paper types. This applies especially to digital printing which works best with a restricted range of papers.

End papers

One nice touch which adds greatly to the appearance of a paperback book but does not cost very much is to include an 'end paper' between the cover and the half-title page, and a matching end paper between the last page and the back cover. These end papers are usually 'exotic' tinted, marbled or 'flecked' papers – your printer or book binder will be able to provide samples and suggestions.

As noted on page 125 the first prelim page is used by libraries for the renewal date form and an end paper at the front of a book is a useful alternative to a half-title page.

Note that the largest digital printing companies may not be able to offer the option for end papers, although in my experience this is not a problem for smaller printers.

Types of card for covers

Your printer will advise on the card (or 'board' – but, in the printing trade, never 'cardboard') for paperback covers.

Weight tends to be between 210 and 250 gsm. (The cover for this book was printed on 240 gsm Trucard.)

With booklets you may be considering black-only on tinted card (see page 151). Such tinted card is expensive and not all photocopiers and digital printers work with thicker types. If the printer needs to buy in card specially he will be paying a premium for a small order. Card usually comes in packs of 500 sheets so if you order 300 copies you may be (unknowingly!) charged for 500 sheets of card. So the cheapest option is to use what the printer has in stock.

Laminating covers

To avoid the covers of paperbacks (and the dust jackets of hardbacks) getting scuffed and grubby – either while being read or, more importantly, while on display in bookshops – the cover or the dust jacket should be laminated. In the printing trade this always means applying a very thin varnish, not the thick 'encapsulation' offered by, say, High Street copy shops.

Historically laminating always produced a gloss effect but, in recent years, matt laminating has gained popularity. This is more because of it becoming a 'fad' among trendy graphics designers. In practice matt laminated covers scuff almost as much as unlaminated covers so, frankly, why bother paying for matt lamination?

For large print runs gloss and matt effects can be mixed (the covers of mass market paperbacks often provide good examples) but this is unlikely to be cost-effective for short runs.

Gloss lamination improves the appearance of photographs, especially with solid blacks and other strong designs. While lamination adds to the cost, the improvement in appearance and durability almost always makes this worthwhile.

The cover of this book has been gloss laminated.

Estimating sales

Before you can get a quote from printers you need to have a realistic idea of how many copies you will sell. Some publications, such as periodicals produced by societies, are produced mostly for circulation to paid up members. Indeed, the publication may be a major reason for subscribing to the society. This means that the number of copies required is usually fairly easy to estimate, allowing for some additional sales to 'outsiders' and as back issues.

However, usually estimating sales is far more tricky. Local history publications, by definition, have a rather limited market. Family history publications are typically even more limited.

Forget any thoughts about selling thousands of copies. At best you will have regional appeal (but rarely more than one or two counties). You may have written about aspects of the history of a major city – but do not assume that more than a small percentage of the population will be interested enough to want to buy a copy. The best 'market penetration' is usually achieved with village history booklets, especially when the village has a close sense of community and many middle class residents. But such villages rarely exceed 1,500 households, so again the total sales will probably be under 1,000 copies. Low-cost 'guide books', especially when related to specific aspects of a region or county, can be excellent sellers, but this format is not suitable for all local history topics.

Except in 'tourist rich' areas (where there is usually plenty of competition from other publishers) most local history publications sell between 300 and 1,000 copies – but *only if the price is right* and considerable effort is put into the selling and marketing; see Chapter 8). Suitably promoted village histories sell quite well if priced at under £5 (which probably means a modest A5 stapled booklet of about 48 pages).

Information about towns, cities or aspects of county history may sell quite well if the content has wide appeal, the presentation is excellent and the price kept under £7. However, to keep the costs down, this means a book of about 100 pages maximum.

As the cover price goes up, so sales drop off. Once the magical £9.99 price barrier is passed then the drop off is dramatic (although within a few years even quite modest paperbacks will often cost a tenner, so a new 'watershed' may slowly develop at, say, £12.99 or £14.99.

At the time of writing a 250-plus page book, with a cover price of £15 and £20, may sell no more than 100 to 200 copies, no matter how well researched and produced. Often the subject can be broken down so a series of smaller books or booklets selling for under £7 can be successfully published, rather than one major 'opus' with an off-putting price.

However how do you know what cover price to charge if you have no idea how much the book will cost to print? To break out of this vicious circle you first need to get some quotes from suitable printers.

Getting a quote

Print runs and 'run ons'

Ask the printer for a quote based on the *minimum* print run you require and for the 'run on cost per 100'.

So, asking for the cost for a '300 run plus run on' will, for instance, give a quote of, say, £900 for the first 300 plus £180 per 100 run on.

The £900 in this example covers

- the setting up costs (whether for offset litho or digital printing)
- the costs of the paper for 300 copies
- the machine time needed to print the first 300 copies
- the cost of binding the first 300 copies

The 'run on' cost of £180 covers only the cost of the paper, machine time and binding for each additional 100 copies.

As the name implies, such 'run ons' *must* be produced at the same time as the original 300 copies, otherwise some or all of the setting up costs will be incurred again.

So, if I decided to accept this quote and go for a run of 500 copies, I would be charged £1,260 (£900 + £180 + £180).

Extra covers

If you are asking for covers printed by offset litho (whether or not the pages of the book are printed by offset or digitally) then – especially if the cover is in full colour – the cost of the plates for the cover and setting up the machine will be a substantial part of the total quote for a fairly short run. However the run-on cost for more covers at the time of writing is in the region of just 15p.

This means you should ask for a run on cost for *covers only.*

Making the best of digital printing by printing extra covers

Assuming you can reasonably expect to sell no more than 500 copies initially, and no more than 1,000 copies if you do very well, but you want an impressive-looking book then a combination of offset printing for the colour cover and digital printing for the pages is probably the most cost effective overall approach. This approach is the one most used by specialist short run book printers.

While the offset litho is an expensive process, all the cost is incurred to print the first cover. After that, as noted above, the cost per copy is fairly small (perhaps 15p per cover). If you print 500 covers initially and then need another few hundred later the cost will be much greater than printing 800 or 1,000 covers in the first place.

However the set up costs for digital printing are comparatively low (especially if the printer is supplied with PDF files). More importantly, if more copies are needed later then the printer can just go back to the same files he used previously, without any significant repeat set up costs. Assuming you have not selected some obscure type of paper then this means the printer should be able to do a reprint for little more than the original run on costs.

So, the trick used by many specialist publishers is to print enough covers to meet all but the most unexpected *maximum* sales, but only print and bind enough books to meet the *minimum* sales expectations. For example. from experience I know that a fairly specialist book about Leicestershire will probably sell about 250 copies in the first year. A further 50 copies or so will go out as 'freebies' for reviews and gifts. This means I am reasonably certain of needing 300 copies within a year. However there is a chance I might need two to three times this number within a few years. I also know I need about 50 flat covers for promotional purposes. My best approach is therefore to print at least 900 covers but to only print up 300 books initially.

This has two benefits. Firstly, the amount of cash tied up in unsold books is kept to a minimum. Secondly, the amount of space needed to store unsold books is also reduced.

Unless there are good reasons to believe that an initial print run of over 700 copies is realistic (in which offset litho for the pages of the book is probably the cheaper option) then use digital printing and keep the print run short. And, even if you do use offset litho for the inside of the book, it may well be worth printing plenty more covers initially.

Who to ask for a quote

Only a small proportion of printers are interested in printing books. And not all book printers are interested in short runs.

One way to find out who to approach is to look in the prelims pages of books that are similar in specification to what you want. Make an intelligent guess as to the probable print run – you are unlikely to be wanting the same runs as a major player in the paperback publishing industry. Web searches will probably give contact information for the company; otherwise go to your local library and consult a trade directory such as Kompass.

Another way is to use an online print quotation service such as Dotgain. At the time of writing this is a free service and can be accessed at ww.dotgain.co.uk

When approaching digital short-run printers ask about their printing equipment's resolution. 600 dpi is acceptable for text and will produce photographs reasonably well. But you will need 1200 dpi or better if you have lots of photos.

Heart of Albion has experience of using three short run printers. All can offer offset litho and sophisticated digital printing:

Antony Rowe Ltd
Bumper's Farm
Chippenham
Wiltshire
SN14 6LH

telephone: 01249 659705

Rowe are by far the biggest company in the UK doing short-run printing. However, I prefer the more personal service of their smaller rivals.

Intype London Ltd
Units 3/4
Elm Grove Industrial Estate
Wimbledon
SW19 4HE

telephone: 020 8947 7863
fax: 020 8947 3652

Booksprint
New Barn
Milverton Road
Wellington
TA21 0QJ

telephone: 01823 665338

(This book has been printed by Booksprint.)

How to find a suitable offset litho printer

'High Street' copy shops may have small (A3 size) offset litho presses suitable for single-colour or two-colour work. However prices are usually at least twice as much as for specialist book printers and rather too often the expertise of the operators can leave much to be desired. Test out your local outfit but do not spend serious money with them unless you are confident that they are offering good value and acceptable quality.

Bigger printers will have much larger printing presses, mostly set up to run four (or more) colours simultaneously. However good offset litho printers who are willing to consider print runs under 10,000 or so are rare, and even fewer offer competitive prices. Finding them is never easy. Frustratingly many 'unsuitable' printers will offer to quote as there is plenty of subcontracting in the printing trade. This means the company you are dealing with takes the order but, unknown to you, another company does the actual printing. This means that (a) if the work is not up to standard you will find it difficult to get things put right; (b) probably you will be paying more for your printing than if you went to the subcontractor direct!

There are three better options to find printers. First, when you are in bookshops, make a point of looking at the imprint page (see page 126) of other local history books and see if the name of the printer is given. With luck this should 'short circuit' many of the difficulties in tracking down suitable companies.

The second option is to use Internet search engines to locate UK-based specialist book printers. Telephone their sales departments (they are unlikely to respond to emails) and tell them in as much detail as possible the sort of printing you want (especially the sort of quantities) and see how they react. Be sure to ask if they have done similar work (especially the sort of print runs you want) before. If they have relevant experience and seem reasonably interested, rather than merely going through the motions, ask them to quote (see page 115). Always ask printers to quote for exactly the same specification otherwise you will be unable to make meaningful comparisons.

Heart of Albion has not printed books by offset litho for some years. Several companies are well-known for short runs; the following also specialise in case bound ('hardback') binding as well as paperbacks.

Woolnough Bookbinding Ltd
Express Works
Church Street
Irthlingborough
Northamptonshire
NN9 5SE

telephone: 01933 654200
fax: 01933 654201

(Despite their company name they are both printers and binders.)

Cromwell Press Ltd
Aintree Avenue
White Horse Business Park
Trowbridge
Wiltshire
BA14 0XB

telephone: 01225 711400
fax: 01225 711429

Ebenezer Baylis & Son Ltd
The Trinity Press
London Road
Worcester
WR5 2JH

telephone: 01905 357979
fax: 01905 354919

Please note that this is only a small number of the many book printers in the UK. There are other printers who specialise in longer runs (e.g. several thousand copies). You should request quotes from any other printers who you think will meet your requirements.

The final option is to contact the British Printing Industries Federation (BPIF) and ask for their list of book and journal printers. Clearly this is not a complete list of all such printers because it only includes members of the Federation and therefore some of the small specialist companies may not appear. BPIF are at:

British Printing Industries Federation
11 Bedford Row
London
WC1R 4DX

telephone: 0870 240 4085
website: www.britishprint.com

The difference in prices that come back from printers will be surprising – at least a two-to-one range and maybe even a three-to-one ratio between the cheapest and most expensive. However a good proportion of printers will not come back to you at all, at least without several reminders.

If you find someone who seems reliable and offers realistic prices then if at all possible, try to visit their premises and have a look around to get a feel for how well they run their activities.

Finding a booklet printer

With booklets the range of specialist suppliers is fairly limited. While all local High Street copy shops will be capable of producing booklets, they will probably charge about twice as much as a specialist booklet printer. In recent years Heart of Albion has had few requirements for booklets and used only one company that specialises in booklet printing:

Doppler Press
5 Wates Way
Brentwood
Essex
CM15 9TB

telephone: 01277 224632
fax: 01277 223453

However you may also want to contact:

Catford Print Centre
PO Box 563
Catford
London
SE6 4PY

telephone: 020 8695 0101
fax: 020 8695 0566

Juma Printing and Publishing
1st Floor, Trafalgar Works
44 Wellington Street
Sheffield
S1 4HD

telephone: 0114 272 0915
fax: 0114 278 6550

At the time of writing Juma only accept camera-ready copy or TIFF files, but not PDF files, which will add to the cost if you have any half-tones.

How to ask for a quote

Printers will prepare quotes on request and, so long as none of the details change (and the order is placed within a few weeks of the quote) they will stick to the original quote *unless the information was wrong or the specification was changed by the customer*. This means the more specific (and accurate) you are when asking for a quote the less room for manoeuvre the printer will have when making out the final invoice.

To be able to quote accurately a printer needs to know:

- The page size (A4, A5, etc.)
- The number of pages (N.B. always in multiples of 4 for stapled booklets, and usually multiples of 8 or 16 for offset litho)
- Type of paper
- Type of binding
- Whether end papers are required
- How the artwork will be supplied (e.g. as PDF files or camera-ready copy – see page 155)
- Number of half-tones, if you are supplying as camera-ready copy (not applicable if you are supplying as PDF files)
- Number of colours to be used for cover (see page 151)
- Whether or not cover will be laminated (strongly recommended except for booklets; see page 108)
- How many copies you want
- How many extra flat covers should be 'run on'
- Where the books are to be delivered to

For comparison purposes send *exactly* the same specification to all companies, even if this means that a short-list of two or three companies need to requote when the final details (e.g. number of pages) are confirmed.

Note that, at the time of writing, VAT on books is zero-rated.

Calculating the cover price

Unless the publication will be heavily subsidised then the expected sales must cover the costs of preparing, printing and promoting the publication. The following paragraphs offer some help in trying to balance costs and cover price.

Estimating costs

Costs fall into four broad areas: royalties, preparation, printing and promotion.

Royalties and other fees

Do the contributors (authors, illustrators, photographers, etc.) to the publication expect paying? Will this be a one-off 'flat fee' or will royalties need to be paid on each copy sold?

In local history many authors and contributors are willing to waive royalties, or to accept a modest 'flat fee'. Some are willing to accept one or more complimentary copies of the publication instead of any payment. However, some authors and (when they have made a major contribution to a publication) some illustrators will expect royalties.

Expect to agree between 5 to 10 percent of the cover price as royalties. If several people expect royalties then ensure the total royalties do not exceed 10 percent. (Royalties on electronic publications such as CD-ROMs and ebooks work in a different way.)

Conventionally, books are considered sold (for the purposes of royalty payments) when the shop has been supplied and invoiced – even though payment may follow some time later! Major publishers usually pay royalties quarterly but, unless sales reach substantial levels, calculating and paying royalties on a six-monthly basis is more practical. Indeed, once a book has been out for a year or more and sales have slowed down, once a year may be quite appropriate for royalties. 'Real' publishers typically only pay royalties if more than £50 has accrued since the previous royalty payment.

No matter how well everyone involved knows each other and agrees verbally, always ensure that any financial deals are confirmed before deciding on a cover price and, equally importantly, put it in writing *before publication.*

For short-run publications such as local history contributors rarely expect or receive an 'advance' on royalties. However, if such advances are paid then ensure they are understood to be advances on royalties!

Preparation costs

These include:

- any 'up front' payments to authors, illustrators and photographers
- all fees for reproduction rights
- typesetting
- cover design
- proof reading
- indexing

Printing costs

At first glance these can be calculated fairly accurately from quotes (not forgetting delivery charges). However estimating the print run required for most local history publications is usually little more than a wild guess, so until someone sticks their neck out and says 'this is how many will be printed' then the cost per copy can fluctuate greatly.

Promotion costs

These include:

- printing press releases and similar promotional leaflets
- postage and stationery for press releases and promotional leaflets
- packaging and postage for review and complimentary copies
- costs of a launch event
- advertising and/or mail shots
- telephone costs
- travel costs for visiting bookshops
- display material for launches, book signings and other promotional events

In many cases these can only be estimated in advance. When you have totalled up the estimates add at least 20 percent to allow for unexpected costs.

Estimating total costs

Even if an exact estimate of costs is impossible, try to estimate the minimum costs (e.g. lowest print run, minimal promotion costs) and maximum costs (longer print run, more comprehensive promotion).

Converting costs to cover price

Take your estimate of costs and convert to a cost-per-copy. If appropriate, work with both your minimum and maximum cost estimates.

Multiply the cost-per-copy by **4** if royalties will be paid and by **3.5** if all costs are 'up front'. You are now looking at a *minimum* cover price for a publication to be sold via shops (although publications with a 'known' circulation, such as periodicals produced for society members, require a different approach – see below).

Why multiply by 3.5 or 4?

Bear in mind that shops will want at least 33 percent discount – and post free (see page 242). Also, not every copy printed will be sold. At least 30 copies are likely to be sent out free for reviews and another 10 to 20 as complimentary copies to contributors. A few copies (hopefully no more than 1 or 2 percent) may have printing defects.

Unless storage conditions are ideal then a few copies will damaged 'in storage' (e.g. paperback covers get folded and creased). And, more importantly, are you really sure that every copy you print will actually be sold?

An imaginary example

As an example, if I expect to pay the printer £940 for the first 500 copies and spend £260 on preparation and promotional costs (this is a low-budget title!) I will have a total cost of £1,200. This gives a cost-per-copy of £2.40. There are no royalties so multiplying by 3.5 makes the estimated cover price £8.40. I would probably round this up to £8.50 or even £8.95.

Let us follow what has happened to my 500 'imaginary' books after a year. My estimate of promotion costs was too low, especially as I printed a leaflet and paid to have it circulated with a national magazine read by family history researchers. I now reckon this book really cost me nearer to £1,500 rather than the £1,200 estimate. However sales have been about what I expected:

- 50 complimentary copies went out for reviews, etc. (the cost of posting these was included in the estimated costs).
- 100 copies were sold by mail order at full cover price.
- 150 copies were sold to shops at 35 percent discount.

- 15 copies had printing defects and I managed to spill coffee on another 5 while making up an order.

- After the first year's sales, 180 are still sitting on the shelf unsold.

I decided on a cover price of £8.50, despite being tempted to round down the cover price to £7.95 in the hope of a few extra sales. However, quick calculations showed that to offset the reduction in cover price I would need to sell 25 more at full cover price or (because of trade discounts) 40 more copies through shops – this seemed unlikely.

Mail order sales generated £850 income (the customers paid for post and packing). The sale to shops generated invoices of £828.75, after the 35 percent discount. Although I delivered to local shops, the cost of postage and packaging for other trade orders came to about £130. Then there were the costs of posting statements and a few phone calls chasing late payments. Unfortunately, two shops have still not paid after nearly a year. So I've only made about £650 on shop sales. The total of mail order sales and shop sales comes to £1,500.

So I've just broken even – and there are still 180 copies left to sell, although sales have now slowed down and I doubt if they will all go, at least not for two or three years.

When not to use 3.5 or 4 times cost per copy

'Real' publishers who need to also meet other overheads (such as staff costs) as well as paying royalties to authors use a ratio of between **5** and **7** times cost-per-copy when calculating cover prices.

However cover prices can be closer to the cost-per-copy if:

- You really are sure that most copies will be sold (such as a society periodical sent to all members).

- When only a very small proportion will be sold in shops.

- When sponsorship means that possible losses are not a problem.

A few moments 'doodling' with numbers on the back of an envelope (or using spreadsheet software if you prefer) should enable cover prices to be calculated for a variety of 'best case' and 'worst case' scenarios.

To print the price on the cover or not?

Generally the price of the book should be included on the back cover. However if, as suggested previously in this chapter, you decide to print extra covers for later reprints then there is a possible problem, especially if you have kept the cover price close to the print costs.

Most books sell quickly initially but then sales slow down. This means that reprints, while they may sell eventually, will take time to cover their costs. Also reprint runs may be shorter than the initial runs, increasing the cost-per-copy. Indeed if more than a year or so has passed since the original printing then paper costs may have increased. This may mean that a higher cover price is needed for copies sold a year or two after publication.

If the reprints use covers printed initially, and these covers have the price printed on them, then you will need to use small sticky labels to mark them with the new price. This is rather tedious and does not look too attractive, although it is a method used by many 'real' publishers.

Summing up

This chapter has been about making a series of guesses:

- estimating how many pages there will be in the finished book
- what the total costs will be
- how many copies are likely to be sold
- estimating the cost per copy
- setting a cover price that will not put off too many purchasers

While there is no way this can ever be an exact science, by bearing in mind the various tricks and rules of thumb in this chapter you should at least be able to make it an intelligent guess.

Chapter Five

BECOMING A PUBLISHER

Choosing an imprint name

The first thing necessary to become a publisher is to choose a suitable name under which to publish. This is also one of the most important decisions.

Local history societies may wish to publish under the name of their society. 'Self-publishers' should avoid something too obviously self-referential (so Alan Smith should avoid publishing as Alan Smith Books or even as AS Books). Subject to the usual 'legal and decent' restrictions you can choose any name you like. Be especially aware of 'passing off' (see page 67) especially if part or all of your proposed name is similar to an existing publisher. Trade directories in your local library should be consulted, together with a search on the World Wide Web, to check that your ideas are as original as you first thought.

Give considerable thought to the best option. Try 'brainstorming' ideas with friends and keeping lists, even of the duff suggestions, as they may inspire a better idea a few days later. Once you have adopted your 'brand name' it will acquire a life of its own and will become increasingly difficult to change or 'disown'.

Designing a logo

A logo or symbol (pedantically, a 'colophon') is not essential but, if you do adopt one, it is essential that it is professionally designed. Too many small publishers betray their 'home spun' status with amateurish logos. Owning a graphics software program is not the same as being trained as a designer – and logo design is one area of graphics design where professional training really counts. What you think looks natty may look dreadfully tacky to most other people.

Because the colophon usually appears in a prominent position on the spine, cover and title page (see page 125) it helps to create that all-important first impression. In my experience of looking at a large number of publications by local history groups and enthusiasts, the logo most conspicuously creates a poor initial perception.

There is a special requirement for publisher's logos – ideally it should be suited for reproducing on the narrow spine of a book, so square and upright-oblong shapes are much to be preferred to more horizontal designs.

ISBN and ISSN numbers

Once you have finally decided on a name to publish under (but not before!) then you can contact the Standard Book Numbering Agency for a series of ISBNs. These are the 'International Standard Book Numbers' that uniquely identify each book, booklet, CD-ROM or other publication.

Note that periodicals (whether annual, quarterly, monthly, weekly or daily) have an ISSN (International Standard Serial Number); the publisher should decide if an ISBN is also needed. Anything which is to be sold in bookshops will benefit from an ISBN so yearbooks (such as transactions and journals) would be best having both ISSN and ISBN numbers, whereas magazine format publications have just an ISSN. There is just one seemingly daft technicality to watch out for – you cannot have both ISBNs and ISSNs if more than one issue of a publication appears in any one year.

The ISBN number always changes for revised editions (only reprints with no significant changes and the same cover design can reuse the original ISBN).

The same ISSN is used for *all* issues of the same periodical. The ISBN number always changes. So the 2006 *Transactions of the Anycounty Historical Society* would have the *same* ISSN as the 2005 (and 2004, and 2003 . . .) *Transactions* – but each year's volume would have a *different* ISBN.

To obtain ISBNs phone or write to:

UK International Standard Book Numbering Agency
3rd Floor
Midas House
62 Goldsworth Road
Woking
Surrey
GU21 6LQ

telephone: 01870 777 8712
fax: 0870 777 8714
email: isbn@nielsenbookdata.co.uk

ISSNs for periodicals are issued by:

ISSN Agency
British Library
National Bibliographical Services
Boston Spa
Wetherby
West Yorkshire
LS23 7BQ

telephone: 01937 546959

At the time of writing ISSNs are free but the standard charge for up to 10 ISBNs is £75 (including VAT); should you have more ambitious plans then the cost for 100 ISBNs is £140 (including VAT).

To ISBN or not to ISBN?

Charging £75 for a piece of paper with a list of ten numbers is clearly a shameless rip off (they used to be supplied free of charge until about 1999). For a one-off modest booklet then the costs of obtaining an ISBN number may be a substantial part of the total costs.

So what are the disadvantages of not having an ISBN? There is no problem selling books direct and by mail order without ISBNs. Most local bookshops will cope (perhaps with a little grumbling) with selling titles without ISBNs. The first real problem is that your publication will not appear on the book trade databases, so shops cannot reorder except direct from you (which relies on them keeping your contact details safely – a very improbable scenario). Neither can someone walk into any bookshop in the country and order your title. Nor will it be sold by online booksellers such as Amazon.co.uk (and this can be especially beneficial to sales of titles of interest to family historians, who can be anywhere around the world). Neither will it automatically get briefly mentioned in trade periodicals, such as *The Bookseller*, routinely used by librarians purchasing for loan stocks.

These problems may not be relevant for exceptionally specialist titles, or for CD-ROMs (which tend to sell only in specialist shops or by direct contact with the purchaser). In these cases a simple Web page giving details of how to obtain by direct mail order should be picked up by anyone entering relevant details into a search engine. However for other types of publication the benefits of having an ISBN probably outweigh the costs, especially if there is any chance that some of the nine 'left over' ISBNs will be used one day for further publications or revised editions.

If you have purchased 10 ISBNs then the first eight digits are unique to you, followed by one digit issued by yourself for each title or edition, then finally a computer-generated 'check digit'.

From ISBNs to EAN-13s

However by January 2007 the book trade will have dropped eight digit ISBNs in favour of thirteen digit EAN-13 numbers. These are already used for bar coding all products, including books. Don't panic – the change is a fairly subtle one. Existing ISBNs will be prefixed by 978 (and, in future, 979). As a result the check digit at the end also changes. So ISBN 1 872883 70 2 changes to EAN-13 number 978 187 2883 70 0. Likewise ISBN 1 972883 71 0 becomes EAN-13 number 978 1872 883 71 7. See also the bar code on the back of this book for an example.

Helpfully the software that generates barcodes takes ISBN numbers and automatically generates EAN-13 numbers – see page 153 for details. So, assuming you have an ISBN number and have downloaded barcode software, then creating an EAN-13 number is effectively automatic.

The title

Deciding on the title of a book is perhaps the most crucial decision you will have to make in publishing. Without doubt the right title can make an indifferent book into a best seller, whereas the wrong title can consign excellent work to obscurity.

Titles must grab – and hold – attention. They must be both succinct and informative. Successful titles are concise; every word does a useful job.

Subtitles are, of course, used to add more description.

Bookshops and libraries can search for 'key words' in the titles and subtitles. Make a list of the most important words that describe the contents of your book. How many of these can you incorporate in a succinct and 'snappy' title and subtitle?

As an example of how keyword seaches in bookshops can help sales, an early Heart of Albion publication was called *Good Gargoyle Guide: Medieval church carvings in Leicestershire and Rutland.* After some time I was receiving orders from people living a long way from the Midlands. Eventually I was able to find out that the reason was because there was a GCSE Art exam with the option to design a gargoyle – and this booklet was the only suitable title that was showing up on bookshop searches.

When the first edition of *Good Gargoyle Guide* went out of print I intentionally produced a 'sequel' which could easily be printed on demand and called this *Gargoyles and Grotesque Carvings of Leicestershire and Rutland.* Although I never organised any publicity for this, not even a single review copy, it still sold over 250 copies, apparently all as a result of people going into bookshops and asking for something on gargoyles.

Eventually I prepared a second edition of the original *Good Gargoyle Guide* book for sale in Leicestershire and Rutland – although by then the GCSE exam board seemed to have dropped the option to design a gargoyle.

Write down *all* the ideas you have for titles, even ones which seem 'daft'. Ask everyone you meet to suggest ideas and write down their suggestions. Keep coming back to this list and take each suggestion as the starting point for 'brainstorming'. After a while try out a 'short list' of ideas on friends and see what improvements they suggest. Keep trying to make the title 'punchier', shorter, more descriptive.

I suggest you cast an eye along your bookshelves and consider which titles work best. Try to think of alternative titles for a few books. Can you do better than the publishers?

What about the title of this book? Could it be shorter? Does the word 'successfully' at the end add an appropriate emphasis or detract by making the title too long?

Prelims

'Prelim pages' are the preliminary pages at the beginning of a book (numbered in lower-case Roman i.e. i, ii, iii). However the numbers are not always printed on every prelim page.

Note that in books odd-numbered pages are always on the right (recto) and even-numbered pages on the left (verso).

Do not include the covers (inside or outside) in the page numbering.

Prelim pages have a fairly predictable sequence.

Most books (but few booklets) have a **half-title** for the first prelim (i.e. page i). The half-title page usually contains the title of the book and maybe the name of the author, but *not* the publishers name or logo. This may seem wasteful but bear in mind that libraries usually obliterate this page with renewal date forms (although see 'end papers' on page 107 for an alternative solution).

The verso of the half-title (page ii) may be left blank, or could include details of other titles in the same series, or the author's previous publications, or maybe just a brief statement of the scope of the book.

The **title page** (always either page i or page iii) should contain all the following information:

- Title
- Subtitle (if any)
- Author(s) or editor(s)
- Perhaps information about illustrator(s) or (exceptionally for local history books!) the translator
- Publisher's name or imprint
- Perhaps the publisher's logo

The place of publication is traditionally stated on the title page, but this is now uncommon. Some publishers include the year of publication on the title page.

The verso of the title page (either page ii or page iv) is known variously as the **imprint page, title verso** or **copyright page**. It contains all the legal and 'formal' details, such as:

- Full name and address of publisher
- Date of first publication (together with details of any reprints or new editions, if appropriate)
- Copyright notice(s) (see below)
- 'Rights notice(s)' (see below)
- ISBN (see page 122)
- British Library Cataloguing-in-Publication Data (CIP) statement (see below)
- The country in which the book is *printed* (this is a legal requirement)
- The printer's name and, usually, address.

If you send Advance Information (see page 220) *at least three months before publication date* to Bibliographic Data Services (see page 217) this entitles you to put *exactly* the following words on the imprint page:

British Library Cataloguing-in-Publication Data
A catalogue record for this book is available from the British Library

I suggest you turn to page vi of this book to see how these look in practice and compare to the imprint pages on any other books you have handy.

Copyright notices

Copyright is automatic on publication but stating details is helpful.

Typical statements range from something simple:

© Text and illustrations copyright A.B. Smith 2005

to more complex variations along the lines of:

© Text copyright C.D. Brown 2005
© Illustrations (except where indicated) copyright E. Black 2005
© Maps copyright F. Jones 2005

When a new edition (but *not* a reprint) appears, the copyright is extended thus:

© Text copyright A.B. Smith 1998, 2003

When the author is deceased the format may be:

© Text copyright the estate of A.B. Smith 2004

The copyright of edited works can become complicated but the following combination usually suffices:

© Text and illustrations copyright individual contributors 2004

Rights notices

There are two rights notices that may be needed (see pages 67 for details of moral rights). The first may simply state:

The moral rights of the author have been asserted.

or:

The moral rights of the author and illustrators have been asserted.

Some publishers extend this with reference to the Copyright, Designs and Patents Act 1998 but this is not essential.

Most books also have a statement reserving all rights in the work, although this is not a legal necessity. Heart of Albion titles simply state 'All rights reserved' although many publishers have much lengthier statements. Try to avoid plagiarising such remarks exactly however.

Other prelim pages

Should you decide to include a **frontispiece** illustration then this normally on a left-hand page facing the title page. The page *before* the frontispiece is either blank or repeats the half-title page.

After the imprint page you may want a **dedication** or **epigram.**

Next come the **acknowledgements**. The problem with acknowledgements is remembering to include everyone who has helped you. The trick is to keep a record of who is due a 'mention' as you are working. The wording can be sorted out later but at least no one who is due thanks should get left out.

The acknowledgements may conclude with details of copyright owners and permissions for photographs, use of text extracts, and such like. However if these are extensive these can form their own section probably headed **permissions.** Lists of permissions could alternatively be included at the end of the book.

After this come the **contents pages** (although these cannot be completed until the remainder of the book has been typeset). The contents pages of books should list chapter headings, subheadings and sub-subheadings, with the correct page number for each.

For booklets contents pages are usually simpler and rarely exceed one page. However, if the booklet is not indexed (see page 147) then the contents page(s) *must* include subheading information as well as chapter headings.

The contents pages may be followed by a **list of illustrations** (which may also contain acknowledgements for reproduction rights, if they have not appeared in the acknowledgements) and, maybe, a **preface** and/or **foreword**.

Prefaces and forewords are usually included in the numbering of the prelims (i.e. in lower case Roman). However, an **introduction** will start on page 1 (i.e. the first page numbered in Arabic numerals).

A **foreword** is written by someone other than the author. Only spell it as 'forward' or 'forword' if you want your book to appear to have been published by utter twerps (quite a few do...).

A **preface** is usually written by the author or editor and typically provides a 'context' for the book (especially when this 'context' is not mentioned in the main text), rather than an outline of what it contains. For example, where the author of the main text is deceased then the preface may outline how the work was prepared for publication and any difficulties incurred.

An **introduction** is usually more substantial than a preface and less personal, and may be essential to the understanding of the subject matter.

The benefits of a foreword

There is usually only one reason for asking someone to write a foreword – it helps sell the book. Forewords should be written by someone who potential buyers will know and respect. They are usually established writers that the author has got to know, probably while researching the book.

Requests for a foreword should be made cautiously. Be prepared to 'back off' if a positive response seems elusive. Understandably, people may be unwilling to endorse a book unless they are entirely happy that it will be well-produced. But, at the same time, they may wish to avoid the risk of offending by refusing because of subjective doubts.

If you get even a provisional 'Yes' from someone approached to write a foreword then under no circumstances approach anyone else! You can not have two forewords and you risk offending someone influential if you have to say you do not want their foreword after all. Regard the offer of a foreword from someone influential as a bit of a coup and, without being sycophantic, make sure that this contribution is acknowledged with a letter of sincere appreciation.

Endorsements

An alternative to a foreword is to ask a 'famous name' (or two or three not-quite-so-famous names) to write a brief endorsement for the cover of your book.

Send a draft of the manuscript and a polite letter asking if they would consider writing a short endorsement. With luck, you will receive a suitably eulogistic paragraph.

However, unless this paragraph is exceptionally short, you will probably not use all of it. Be prepared to take out the 'best bit' but be sure to show where words have been deleted by inserting '... ' (note that this is 'dot-dot-dot-space' not 'space-dot-space-dot-space-dot-space').

Be very careful not to distort the original meaning. An endorsement which reads 'This book has some interesting information and, in places, is excellent' should *not* be changed to 'This book... is excellent'. The reality is that most people who write endorsements will have intentionally worded their sentences in such a way that such distortions are not easy.

If you are in any doubt as to whether or not your edited version of the original endorsement is acceptable, then contact the person and ask him/her to confirm that the shortened version is acceptable.

Make sure to graciously thank everyone who contributes an endorsement and make sure they receive a signed copy and/or are invited to the launch.

Sponsorship and advertising

If your publication features a local business that is still trading then they may well be willing to meet some or all the print costs, perhaps in exchange for an advertisement. If you are writing about a town where there are one or two large businesses, they may be willing to offer some sponsorship even if they are not prominently featured. With large organisations telephone and ask if they have a public relations department; if they don't ask for the managing director's secretary – she will either advise you on the best way of making a formal request or pass you on to the right person.

It is always worth asking – the worst that can happen is the company say 'No', and they will always do so politely! For example, a local history annual journal which I help to put together included an article about the restoration of the stained glass windows in one of the village churches. The company restoring the windows offered to sponsor the publication costs. In exchange for an advertisement (which conveniently fitted onto the otherwise blank back cover) the local history society received enough money to comfortably meet most of the print costs of the journal.

Financial matters

By the time you are ready to sell books (especially if mail order sales from magazine reviews and such like will make up even a small part of your 'outlets') make sure you have a bank or building society account in the name you will be publishing under. There is little point in asking people to send cheques made out in your personal name as this information may not be printed in reviews and you will end up returning a lot of cheques.

Shop around for the best deals as many banks and building societies want to charge for clearing cheques when the account is not a personal 'current account'. It should be fairly straightforward to open a 'trading as' (T/A) cheque book account (e.g. R.N. Trubshaw T/A Heart of Albion Press), although there may be limits on how many cheques you can write or clear without incurring charges.

Choose a bank that is located where you regularly shop and/or where there is easy parking. If a reasonable number of mail order sales are expected then you will be making frequent trips to the Post Office. Setting up an Alliance Leicester account will mean you can post books and pay in cheques without queuing twice.

Local history groups may already have a bank account. However it may be tricky to get all cheques correctly made out to the name of the account if the imprint name is subtly (or substantially) different. Few reviewers will add the crucial information 'cheques must be paid out to xxxxxx'. There are few worse chores than wasting time and postage sending lots of cheques back for correction.

Credit cards

Unless you already run a business that takes credit cards you may find it difficult to set up such facilities – there's a real Catch 22 mentality to the relevant UK banks. The annual fees exceed £100, on top of which a transaction fee of 3 to 5 percent is levied. This makes merchant credit card facilities prohibitive for small businesses.

Only if you can reasonably expect many hundreds of pounds worth of business by Internet sales would it be worth setting up a merchant credit card account at an early stage.

PayPal

If someone insists on paying by credit card (and overseas customers may have few other choices) then set up an account with www.paypal.com . Such an account will allow customers to pay using their credit card. Overseas customers get billed in their local currency and you get payment from PayPal in Sterling. There is a small fee levied by PayPal but this is a small price to pay for the convenience of such easy international payments.

VAT

Printing and selling books in the UK is currently zero-rated for VAT (although from time to time the EU threatens to change this). Unless your annual turnover is likely to exceed the statutory limit (£70,000 in 2004) there is little point in even trying to register for VAT, as the 'VAT man' will resist attempts by small organisations to register. In any event, the cost of keeping accounts to the standard required by the 'VAT man' is prohibitive for small organisations.

Keep records

However, even if not VAT registered, do keep accurate records of *all* expenses and income.

Apart from all the big bills like printing, packaging and postage, remember to keep a note of all the mileage driven while liaising with authors, illustrators, proofreader, indexer and printer. You will be surprised how these mount up, and they can be all offset against income and reduce tax liability. Keep a note of the miles incurred selling to shops and retain relevant car parking tickets (parking fines, however, cannot be offset against income!).

If publishing is part of a group's activities then the Treasurer will be able to reconcile financial matters associated with publishing as part of the overall annual statement.

If you are a one-man part-time publisher then your promotional activities could also make the Income Tax Inspector aware of your new-found income. Rarely will the tax man allow loss-making part-time publishing activities to be set off against PAYE on a 'day job' but a correctly prepared statement of accounts (especially when prepared by a professional accountant) avoids unnecessary hassles with HM Inspector of Taxes. Any competent accountant can, for a moderate fee, compile annual accounts that correctly offset income generated against expenses. Allowable expenses include 'capital equipment' (such as computers and cameras), 'overheads' (such as heating and telephone costs) and 'research costs' (which can include purchase of relevant books, subscriptions to specialist magazines, travel costs, etc). Once all such allowable expenses are correctly taken into consideration few small publishing activities are sufficiently profitable to be liable for any significant tax.

Final thought

And that is really about all there is to 'becoming a publisher'. At least the 'setting up' part is easy, even if there is plenty more hard work before you actually have a book to sell!

Chapter Six

DESIGNING AND TYPESETTING BOOKS

The development of software for 'desk top publishing' (DTP) over the last fifteen years has enabled many people to produce professional-looking typesetting using nothing more than a computer and a good printer.

Unfortunately it has also enabled a much larger number of people to produce very unprofessional publications. Bear in mind that a good proportion of the book-buying public has artistic or graphic skills. What may look good to a novice DTP user may be deemed 'visually illiterate' by would-be purchasers.

Designing books and producing attractive typesetting requires skill and, although many of these skills can be learnt, like all skills there are real benefits from experience. Professionally-trained book designers provide many advantages. Unfortunately professional designer's fees may add substantially to the costs of producing a book.

Also be aware that there is a distinction (although plenty of overlap in functions) between designers and typesetters. Professional typesetters too often produce 'safe but boring' page designs unless given clear instructions by a graphic designer. On the other hand not all graphic designers have experience of the finer details of designing books and/or deem their idiosyncratic designs more 'creative' than conventions. The moral is always to ask to see samples of previous work and only commission designers who you feel really understand your requirements.

To avoid being caught in the middle if a printer is unable to sort out any technical problems with the files sent by a designer then it is safest (although not necessarily cheapest) to ask the designer to provide a 'design and print' package. In other words the designer selects the printer and is therefore responsible for making sure everything comes together successfully. From my experience there are usually at least some hiccups when a printer has to work from files sent by a designer with the printer has not previously worked. Unless you have built up some experience of such situations this is probably a scenario that is best avoided from the outset.

A small number of organisations offer what may be termed 'design and print' packages for short run publications. I have no experience of locating or using such services however because Heart of Albion is one of that small number. Indeed I will be pleased to quote for anyone who considers that designing, typesetting and printing are parts of the writing and publishing process that they would prefer to subcontract.

The rest of this chapter is for all those who do not want to subcontract in this way.

Thinking like a designer

The limited budgets for most local history and family history books mean that DIY typesetting with DTP software is the only affordable option. There are a large number of conventions and 'tricks' to professional-looking book design, mostly referred to by arcane terminology. This chapter aims to raise awareness of the more important aspects of book design and typesetting without necessarily going into the nth degree of detail.

DTP software

Most professional designers and typesetters use Apple Mac computers. Quark Xpress is the most commonly used, along with the rather elderly Adobe Pagemaker and its replacement Adobe InDesign. All these programs are available in PC versions as well.

They all have two major problems – price and seriously unfriendly interfaces. At the time of writing Amazon.co.uk is offering PC versions of Quark Xpress for £799, InDesign for £670 and Pagemaker at £225 (and if £225 seems like a bargain, bear in mind it is effectively obsolete software).

I accept that Quark and InDesign are capable of some very clever tricks that may help when doing fancy designs for mass circulation magazines or commercial brochures, but they are a long way removed from the requirements of short run book design. And readers of this book presumably cannot afford to spend more on one item of software than is necessary to buy a well-specified PC.

If you intend to use a Mac for DTP then buy InDesign, plus a user-friendly instruction book, and a large supply of aspirin and/or whisky to deal with the headaches and frustrations of trying to learn how to use software with such a wilfully difficult interface. Don't say you haven't been warned...

However if you have a PC obtain a copy of Serif PagePlus for £20 (and look out for fully functioning 'demo' versions on computer magazine cover discs). The low price is deceptive – this is a powerful and generally well-designed program that does everything that you are likely to need to do when typesetting books. At the time of publication version 10 had just appeared and the new features include a number of aids specifically intended for book publication.

In contrast to PagePlus, Microsoft's DTP software – unimaginatively just called 'Publisher' – costs £99 and buries a basically easy-to-use interface under a blizzard of wizards and walkthroughs. To add to the frustration, these wizards offer design templates which are too dull to be used. If you already have a copy of Microsoft Publisher and have learnt to use it then by all means carry on. Otherwise PagePlus is the better option.

You may be tempted to go for the budget option of trying to make your word processing software, such as Word, into an effective tool for typesetting books. However Word makes it tricky – indeed seriously frustrating – to control the exact placement of text and pictures. And there is no in-built support for exporting to PDF format (see page 155). If you are only producing a short A4 magazine for running off on the office laser printer then Word may be the easiest option. But for smaller page sizes – which usually means tighter control of layout – and for longer publications then I strongly suggest learning PagePlus.

You may be wondering which software was used to typeset this book. Over the years I have had the opportunity to briefly use both Pagemaker and Quark and found the interfaces for commonly-used tasks slow me down substantially (even after I have begun to learn my way around). I made a serious attempt to learn InDesign and after two days was still thoroughly frustrated by the inability to find basic features and functions. So I have remained with the software I started using in 1989. This was before Windows 3.0, although the software was upgraded (and repeatedly changed name) until 1999, by which time it was known as Greenstreet Publisher. It is now obsolete but I have stuck with it partly because I know it all too well and, more importantly, because I need to access files and templates that have built up over fifteen years. There are a few aspects of the interface that are easier to use than PagePlus and few of the extra features of PagePlus are helpful to me.

If I was starting out today I would certainly use PagePlus. All the examples in this chapter will be based on PagePlus. Apologies to Mac users but, for what you paid for Quark or InDesign you could have bought both a well-specified PC and a copy of PagePlus.

First steps with DTP

The first step to learning about book design and typesetting is to look closely and critically at the books you have around. Try to decide why the text of some books is easier to read than others (some clues will be given later in this chapter), and why some look more attractive than others. Bear in mind that good typesetting does not draw attention to itself – it makes the book attractive and easy to read but does not shout 'clever' or 'trendy'.

The next step is to use your DTP software is to try to copy as accurately as possible the page layout of books that 'look good'. Ideally you should 'borrow' design ideas from books with broadly similar readership to your assumed readers. So, when typesetting local history books, I would not borrow ideas from a magazine aimed at teenagers!

With typesetting it is the detail that matters. So you should be aiming to fit exactly the same words onto the page (this will mean that you have matched font face, font size and 'leading' – see page 142) as well as matching the size of margins and 'gutters' (see page 134).

However to really understand book design you need to think through a number of inter-linked aspects described in the next sections of this chapter.

Page design

There is more to page design than deciding how big the page should be. Nevertheless the size of the page is an important decision. Most books are produced in 'portrait format' (and the following remarks assume this is the case) but 'landscape format' (with the spine or staples on the shortest side) may be more suited to some publications.

Paper sizes

A5 (210 by 148 mm) allows for attractive pages of text, but is rather limited if there are a lot of photographs. Full-page 'portrait format' illustrations work well in A5 format, but 'landscape format' illustrations must be placed sideways to use the full page, which looks decidedly old fashioned. Landscape format books work well for illustrations fitting across the width of an A5 page but portrait format illustrations used under full size leave awkward spaces for the text to flow around.

A4 is twice the area of A5 at 297 by 210 mm and is the ubiquitous page size for letters and photocopiers. Frankly it is a very difficult size for book design (see overleaf), although worth considering for magazines and similar periodicals.

There is another metric size known as **B5**. This measures 257 by 182 mm which puts it between A5 and A4 and is the most useful metric page size for books.

There are several page sizes similar to A5 which are widely used in the publishing industry. Traditional paperbacks were printed in two sizes – **'A' format** (180 by 110 mm) and **'B' format** (197 by 125 mm). 'A' format is probably too small, certainly if you want photographs, although 'B' format might be worth considering for guide books intended to be carried in the pocket.

Before paper sizes went metric many books were printed as **Demy** (or **Demi**) **8vo** (pronounced 'dem-eye octavo') which is 8½" by 5½" (or 215 by 138 mm). This is just a little taller and a little narrower than A5, which is ideal for text-only books but not necessarily helpful if you intend to use landscape-format photographs 'right way up'. Another commonly used pre-metric page size is **Royal 8vo**, which is 234 by 156 mm. Assuming your book has a reasonable amount of text and pictures this can be an attractive page size (it is just a little smaller than the book you are holding).

Most printers can still work with Demi 8vo and Royal 8vo, although High Street copy shops may only offer A5, B5 and A4. All printers can of course cut the edges off the next-largest paper size but you will be paying for all the waste that ends up in the recycling bin.

When asking printers to quote you should be able to assess how easily or otherwise they will be able to work with the paper sizes you plan to use. Always listen to their suggestions – this book (and several others from Heart of Albion) has the non-standard page size of 245 x 175 mm because this fits in with both the capacity of the printer's digital press and the much larger standard sizes of paper sheets available from wholesalers. If I had designed this book for Royal 8vo (10mm by 19 mm smaller) I would simply have been paying for waste paper.

Page layout

Different page sizes are associated with different strengths and weaknesses. Everyone is familiar with A4 pages so let us start by looking at the pros and cons of designing publications to fit these fairly large pages.

The advantage of A4 format is that there is plenty of scope for illustrations. But the big downside is that text is tricky. When using the size of typeface usually associated with books then running lines of text across the full width of an A4 page in one column produces lines which are far too long for easy reading.

Increasing the point size and/or the leading (see page 142) helps slightly but means less words per page.

A4 pages can be divided into two columns, which greatly helps readability but makes for a boring page layout. Using three columns works well for magazines and newsletters, but looks all wrong for books.

Narrow columns work best when the right margin is ragged ('flush left'), rather than justified (lined up on both the left and right margins, like the text on this page), because DTP software usually copes badly with trying to justify short lines.

Another solution for A4 pages is to restrict the text to a width of about 125 mm (perhaps a little more if a larger type face is used) and leave a large margin down one side. This is ideal for publications with a large number of 'foot notes' as the notes can be put (usually in a smaller or slightly contrasting typeface) into the margins, rather than at the bottom of the page. This page layout is usually called 'side bar' style.

See opposite for examples of of 1, 2, 3 column and side bar pages.

Illustrations can 'spread' into the margin, of course. Indeed, small illustrations may fit into the margin, as may captions to the illustrations.

Margins and gutters

Page layout for books needs careful attention to margins. Do not try to overfill pages with text – there needs to be a certain amount of white space (margins, space around illustrations, space between lines, etc.) to make a book look attractive and inviting. Glossy 'coffee table' type books often include substantial amounts of white space.

This is an illustration of single column page layout, similar to the book you are reading. However with small font sizes and/or larger page sizes the number of words on each line becomes too much for easy reading.

There are a number of options to minimise this problem, such as increasing the font size, increasing the leading between lines and increasing the margins. However with A4 page sizes (297 x 210 mm) there is no sensible way of using single column page design with the sizes of fonts usually used for books. However single column layout can work well with smaller page sizes, such as A5 and Demi 8vo (215 x 138 mm). With generous margins and fairly large font sizes it also works for pages up to about 175 mm wide (e.g. the book you are reading).

This is an illustration of two column page layout. It makes the lines much shorter and therefore easier to read compared to using single column layout with the same page size and font size.

Unfortunately the disadvantage of two column page layout is that the pages look deadly dull. Unless you are writing an academic report that needs to conform to the usual academic conventions of being badly designed and decidedly boring in appearance then avoid the two column page layout.

For more design-conscious publications you can consider two columns of unequal width, but this may simply appear quirky.

This is an illustration of two column page layout. It makes the lines much shorter and therefore easier to read compared to using single column layout with the same page size and font size.

Unfortunately the disadvantage of two column page layout is that the pages look deadly dull. Unless you are writing

This is an illustration of three column layout. It is a useful format for A4 newsletters, although rather unsuitable either for books or for smaller page sizes (with the exception of A5 pages in landscape format, which are of course the same width as A4 paper in portrait format).

If you decide to use three column layout then you may prefer to use unjustified text (also known as 'right ragged') – as has been used for this paragraph. This is because DTP software finds it difficult to justify short lines of text without using lots of hyphens or leaving obtrusive unattractive spaces between multisyllablic words.

If you decide to use three column layout then you may prefer to use unjustified text (also known as 'right ragged'). This is because DTP software finds it difficult to justify short lines of text without using lots of hyphens or leaving obtrusive unattractive spaces between multisyllablic words.

This is an illustration of three column layout. It is a useful format for A4 newslet-

This is an example of 'side bar' layout, where the main text is no more than about 125 mm wide, although illustrations can fill nearly the full width of the page.

The rather large margin (usually a large right margin on left-facing pages and a large left margin on right-facing pages) can contain captions to illustrations, bibliographical details and/or footnotes, or small drop out boxes with additional information.

This page layout is the only stylish and readable way of designing books with A4-width pages as all other alternatives either produce unreadably long lines of text or simply look far too boring.

The 'sidebar' can be used for captions to illustrations, bibliographical references or other footnotes.

Examples of 1-, 2-, 3-column and side bar pages.

There needs to be space for page numbers and, usually, a 'running heading' (see page 140) at the top of the page.

The right-side of even-numbered pages and the left-side of odd-numbered pages will be incorporated into the binding. This means a few millimetres more margin should be allowed here. The printing trade refers to this as the 'gutter'. In PagePlus a four-step process is needed to set the gutter:

1. Select View / Go to Master Page.
2. Select File / Page Setup then tick the box for 'Two master pages'; also use this menu to change the size of page or create a custom size.
3. Select File / Layout Guides / Inside margin setting.
4. Select View / Leave Master Page.

The three outside edges of all pages will be trimmed after the book is bound (although probably only the outside edge for booklets). Allow 3 mm extra margin for such trimming. Margins are set in PagePlus by:

1. Select View / Go to Master Page.
2. Select File / Layout Guides and then adjusting as required
3. Select View / Leave Master Page.

Using the grid

To avoid pages looking messy, DTP software offers a 'grid' (visible only on screen and not printed out) to help line up illustrations, captions, etc. Many different grid layouts are possible but most people work with five or six column grids. Grids are set in PagePlus the same way as margins i.e.:

1. Select View / Go to Master Page.
2. Select File / Layout Guides and then adjusting as required
3. Select View / Leave Master Page.

All text and pictures should fit within the grid lines unless you are intentionally 'bleeding' images off the edge of the page (see next section).

Bleeding images

Professionally-produced publications include images which run off the edges of the pages – this is known in the trade as 'bleed'. However the image will have to overlap the edge of the page by at least 3 mm to allow for trimming.

While DTP software usually allows for such 'bled' images, the PDF format used for transferring files to printers (see page 155) may cause problems. This can be overcome by designing on a standard page size (say B5) while knowing that 3 mm will be cut off all the three edges of the page. Alternatively create a custom page size that is 6 mm higher and 3 mm wider than the one you intend to use.

If you are planning to bleed images I strongly recommend that you send suitable test files to your printer and get him to confirm that all is well with converting these into plates before you spend too much time typesetting a whole book.

In practice most local and family history publications keep all illustrations within the grid lines of the page, so bleed is not a problem.

Page numbers

There is no point in adding page numbers manually as all DTP software has facilities for doing this automatically. The problem is that the people who design DTP software make this basic function as darned difficult as possible. In PagePlus the sequence is:

1. Select View / Go to Master Page.
2. If there are no two pages showing then select File / Page Setup then tick the box for 'Two master pages'
3. Make sure the blue grid lines are set exactly how you want them (see above).
4. Select the Standard Frame Tool icon from the main tools toolbar.
5. Drag and drop a frame that goes the full width of the page grid on the left-hand page.
6. Go to Insert / Page number. This will create a page number at the left of the text box. If you are happy with a left-aligned page number then go to step 9 below
7. 'Highlight' this number with the mouse. Select the font (usually the same as for the main text) and font size (usually 9 pt) required for the page numbers.
8. Click on the 'Align centre' tool.
9. Repeat steps 4 to 7 for the right-hand page.
10. Click on the 'Align right' or the 'Align centre' tool.
11. Select View / Leave Master Page.

12. If you want Roman numbers (i, ii, iii, etc) for prelims then go to Format / Page Number Format and then click the appropriate option.

So now you will have page numbers on every page you create. Ah ha, I hear you say, what about the pages where numbers are not needed, such as the first page of a new chapter? Make sure the screen shows the page where the page number is not wanted. Select View / Master Page Objects and then untick for the required page, then click OK.

Running headers

Headers (and footers, if used) should be discreet. Conventionally the name of the book appears on the left-hand page and the title of the chapter (or an abbreviated version) on the right-hand page, although there may be good reasons to deviate from this convention (as with this book!).

Headers should not appear on the first page of a chapter and may need to be switched off on pages with full-page illustrations.

Most DTP software has an option for creating headers. With luck it also has an easy way of turning off headers on selected pages such as chapter headings. It may even allow different chapters of the book to have different headings. However the interfaces for such essential control of the header function are usually desperately complicated.

By far the easier option is to create a text box with the relevant text and then copy-and-paste this on all pages where it is wanted. The only trick is not to do this until the book is nearly completed because adding or removing a page will mean that left-facing pages become right-facing pages and vice versa, so all running headers would need to be deleted and replaced with the correct one.

Or you an pick and mix the best of both worlds. Create a text box on the left-hand *master* page with the title of the book (in the same way as inserting page numbers; see previous section). Then manually copy-and-paste text boxes (as described in the previous paragraph) with the appropriate chapter heading onto the right-hand pages.

For any pages where you do not want the chapter heading make sure the screen shows the page where the page number is not wanted. Then select View / Master Page Objects and then untick for the required page, then click OK. However this is where PagePlus reveals a stupid inability to cope with the real world as unticking Master Page Objects turns off page numbering as well, which is probably not wanted. However the page number can be put back as a 'manual' text box on the actual page (i.e. *not* the master page); be sure to use Insert / Page number so that this will automatically update if you add or remove pages.

Differences between typing and typesetting

Beware of three big distinctions between the conventions of typewriting and typesetting.

- Full stops are followed by *one* space in typesetting (whereas two spaces are normal for typewriting).
- Paragraphs are not indented *and* line spaced when typesetting (see page 143)
- Typesetters rarely if ever underline words. Use *italic* for emphasis and for the titles of books, etc. Underlining is *not* appropriate for typeset subheadings (see page 144).

Type faces

Computers come with a range of different typefaces (or 'fonts') and DTP software usually bundles in loads more options. To add confusion, extremely similar typefaces can be supplied under different names. But do not get bewildered by the apparent variety. Most type faces are decorative – suitable for headlines and covers but not for text.

Decorative typefaces just do not work for the main text! Type faces suitable for the main text of books (often called the 'body text') can be grouped into **serif** typefaces (such as Times Roman) and **sans serif** (such as Arial) typefaces. 'Serifs' are the little pointy bits at the end of letters that help the eye to read. Most sans serif typefaces are slightly less easy to read than serif typefaces. This book is typeset in a sans serif font traditionally called Optima but also available as Ottawa.

Many books use a different font for chapter headings. However never use more than two or three typefaces in the same publication. There is nothing as amateurish (and messy to read) as someone who think of fonts as a 'toy box' and tries to play with everything at once.

Point sizes

The size of type faces is traditionally measured in 'points'. One point (pt) is 1/72 of an inch (about 0.35 mm). But this does not mean that all 12 pt typefaces look the same height. The '12 points' (as an example) are measured from the top to bottom of a character such as 'T'. But different typefaces of the same type size can *appear* quite different. The relationship between the height of, say, an 'x' and ascenders of a 't' or the descenders of a 'y' vary greatly between different typefaces.

This is 12 pt Bright. **This is 12 pt Switzerland.**

The width of otherwise similar typefaces also varies:

This is an example in 12 pt Times Roman.

This is an example in 12 pt Bright.

This is an example in 12 pt Bodoni.

Using Bodoni rather than Bright will enable about ten percent more text on a page – which could be helpful, although be careful that the number of words per line is not excessive (see below).

Most books use 10 pt typefaces (this one does) although, had I used Switzerland for the body text (which has a large 'x' height) I could have tried 9 pts.

This is an example of 9 pt Switzerland.

This is an example of 10 pt Switzerland.

With local and family history books a substantial proportion of readers will be in the older age groups. This is especially true for village history booklets aimed at a wide readership. All of us suffer from eyesight deficiencies as we grow older – some more than others. I strongly recommend using 11 or 12 pt type faces for books that are likely to be bought mostly by older readers.

Line length

Two factors determine how easily (or otherwise) the eye follows a line of text on a page.

The main factor is how many words are on each line. Aim for an average of 56 characters per line and regard 80 as maximum (easily exceeded when using A4 pages or A5 pages in landscape format). To keep lines to a readable length there are several options:

- reduce the width of the text box;
- change to two- or three-column layout;
- increase the point size.

Secondly, if there are more than about 60 characters on a line then be sure to keep plenty of 'leading' between the lines – 10 pt type on 11 pt leading is typical for books but be willing to change to 10 pt on 12 pt to make it easier for the eye to follow each line.

Apart from the paragraph you are reading this book is set as 10 pt on 12 pt leading. However this paragraph illustrates how the same typeface appears when the leading is reduced to 11 pt. I find it less easy to read so opted to make the text just that little easier to follow by increasing the leading to 12pt, even though this added nearly 10 percent to the length of the book.

Paragraphs

There are two ways of breaking up paragraphs. One method, used in this book, is to have a space after each paragraph. The alternative method is to indent the first line of the paragraph. Note that spacing and indenting are *alternatives*. Forget that typists are taught to both line space and indent paragraphs. Typesetting is *not* typing and anyone who copies this convention when using DTP software simply betrays all too visibly their amateurism.

Also all-too-glaringly amateurish is using a double line return to space paragraphs. This gives the publication an unprofessional appearance and also wastes space.

If using space between paragraphs then this would normally be about half to two-thirds the depth of the leading. So 10 pt on 12 pt text would have about 6 to 8 pt of space between paragraphs (not 12 pt). Any more than 8 pt and it will look as if a line return has been used.

This and the following paragraphs are indented just to illustrate the different methods. Indenting enables more lines to be included on a page. Spacing between paragraphs helps readability and looks more 'friendly'. For most 'popular' local history publications I would favour spacing paragraphs. For longer and more 'scholarly' works then indenting is preferable.

In PagePlus indenting can only be set using the rulers at the top of the page (Go to View / Rulers if they are not visible). Highlight some of the paragraph(s) to be indented and then drag-and-drop the down-pointing grey triangle. (This is the same as setting paragraph indents in MS Word.)

With indented paragraphs, the usual indent is equivalent to the width of about three 'm' characters, although sometimes (with longer line length, for instance) an indent of up to 5 'm' characters works better. Very deep paragraph indents usually appear quirky. Remember, any typesetting that draws attention to itself is bad typesetting.

Note that the first paragraph after a heading or sub-heading is *not* indented. When typesetting you will need to click on the paragraph style for all such paragraphs and manually edit the indent.

Orphans and widows

'Orphans' and 'widows', in the world of printing, should be eliminated.

These terms refer to paragraphs being split in such a way that there is one line (a 'widow') or even one word (an 'orphan') on one page and the remainder of the paragraph on the following or preceding page. Most DTP software can be set to automatically eliminate orphans and widows. Otherwise careful attention is needed at a late stage in the proof-reading process.

Often creating (or removing) space around an illustration and/or caption will allow the widow or orphan to join up with the preceding or following lines. With all-text pages *subtly* adjust the letter spacing (but *never* adjust character width). With DTP it is probably easiest to shorten the length of the text box by one line. Make sure that the facing page does not look 'odd' as a result. Quite often the most effective 'tweak' needed to remove an orphan or widow is several pages back.

Displayed quotes

Short quotations (usually up to about two lines, or three in short columns) should be 'embedded' in the main text using quotation marks. Longer quotes should appear in their own paragraph, *without quotation marks*. Almost all book designers indent the left margin of displayed quotes. Traditional practice is to use a slightly smaller typeface for displayed quotations but this reduces legibility and is not recommended.

Often the right margin is also indented. Where the main text is justified I find that a combination of left indent with 'right ragged' (unjustified) – but no right indent – works quite well for quotations.

> If this paragraph was a substantial quotation (e.g. more than just a few lines) from a different book then it would appear indented like this. How far you indent on the left and right should be consistent with other indents. In this case both the left and right indents match the indentation used for bullet points.
>
> Alternatively you can use 'right ragged' (or 'unjustified') paragraph format for displayed quotations, as with this example. This is especially suited for shorter line lengths. With short line lengths it may not be necessary to indent the right margin, although this paragraph is indented as well as unjustified.

Above all, be completely consistent with the presentation of displayed quotations.

Hierarchical headings

Chapters have **headings**. As discussed on page 37, the text should be broken up, as necessary, with **sub-headings** and **sub-sub-headings**.

There should be a clear and distinct style for sub-headings and sub-sub-headings. Try out a few variations out – aim for a style that is distinctive but subtle. Always bear in mind that typesetting should make the text easy to read but not draw attention to itself.

The usual options are permutations of **bold**, *italic*, ALL CAPITALS and slightly larger point sizes. Another option, to be used with discretion, is to use sans serif sub-headings when the main body text is a serif font, or vice versa. In this book I have used the same type face for the chapter headings, sub-headings and sub-sub-headings, although I did consider using a more decorative font for the chapter headings.

Unless you want to look like a complete amateur, do not use underlining for sub-headings (or anywhere else for that matter!).

Captions

Conventionally captions for illustrations are typeset using the italic version of the body text, possibly one point size smaller (although usually retaining the same leading as the body text e.g. if the body text is 10 pt on 11 pt then the captions would be 9 pt italic on 11 pt). Often captions are unjustified and centred instead of left-aligned.

The hierarchy of headings used in this book is:

CHAPTER HEADINGS IN ALL CAPS 18 pt BOLD

Topic headings in 14 pt bold

Subheadings in 10 pt bold

sub-sub-headings in 10 pt italic

However look out for books which successfully break this convention (without drawing undue attention to the type setting!) and 'borrow' the more successful ideas. As with so many aspects of book design, find a solution that *consistently* works. Few readers enjoy playing 'hunt the caption'.

Book design

Even if you were not familiar with typesetting before reading this chapter I hope these brief remarks have shown that there are numerous possibilities for something as apparently straightforward as the pages of a book.

The trick with typesetting books is to decide on a particular style that will work. I often spend several hours designing and printing test pages (which should include typical use of illustrations, hierarchical headings, etc.). If there are few illustrations then this preparation may take longer than actually doing the nitty gritty of changing the raw text into a fully typeset publication. Making a significant change to an aspect of the design when part-way into the typesetting can be a major effort as this may require checking and redoing most of the previous work.

DTP software has facilities for setting 'paragraph styles'. Use them for hierarchical headings, captions, etc. This means that if you need to change an aspect of design fairly late in to the job there is no risk of missing some text 'tweaked' by hand. For instance, if in a late stage of typesetting this book I change my mind about the spacing of the 'bulleted' text I want all the bulleted text to change without manually changing (or even checking) each instance. If all the bulleted text has been created using the same paragraph style (used only for that purpose) then a few clicks on the paragraph style will change all the bulleted text 'instantly'; however check that page breaks and the like have not been affected.

Typesetting is a specialist skill. Professionals will know all about when – and, more importantly, when not – to adjust letter spacing, and be familiar with arcane terms such as 'kerning'.

Pages with illustrations

Illustrations bring a book to life. For books that need to have 'popular appeal' aim to have at least one illustration every four pages. Even better, make sure that every 'double page spread' includes a picture or two. This means that anyone flicking through the book will have plenty to grab their attention.

Work to a grid

However books with pictures can easily look messy. Either make the illustrations fit the full width of the text column(s) or fit the width to the invisible page grid (see page 138).

Sometimes, for instance when pictures are side by side, this will make the heights of illustrations different and clumsy-looking. Seriously consider cropping illustrations, if this does not affect the information, to enhance the appearance.

Illustrations should always have some white space between the border and the text. How much is up to you. About 2 mm is probably a minimum, 5 mm gives plenty of 'breathing space', but even bigger borders may be appropriate, for instance when the text itself has large margins. DTP software allows such 'text repel' features to be set.

Do not forget to leave space for the captions.

Know your four times table

Most short run printers use A4 paper. This means that A5 publications, especially stapled ('stitched') booklets and books 'sewn in ligatures' (see page 103), are made up of multiples of four sides. You cannot have, say, 30 pages. There can be 30 *numbered* pages but what are you going to do about the two 'spare' sides? The more pages there are in a publication gives more options for filling an odd page. But is a very real problem with booklets of up to about 40 pages. Just that extra bit of text, another illustration, or an index that ends up longer than expected and, instead of having say 36 pages, you have gone on to a 37th – putting up the cost and leaving you with the problem of what to do with the three 'spare' sides.

If you cannot easily remove something to get back to 36 pages, the usual solution is to adjust the prelim pages. Adding, or perhaps removing, a half title page (see page 125) with maybe a frontispiece illustration on the verso (i.e. page ii) takes up two pages. If you have used Roman numbering for the prelims then such 'shuffling' will not cause the main page sequence to be affected. PagePlus does not allow for mixing Roman and Arabic numbering in the same document. How it does allow for the main page numbering to start after the first page; the prelims can either remain unnumbered or the Roman numbering can be added manually.

An odd page at the end of a booklet does not look strange. Alternatively, typeset a simple advertisement for other publications you have produced (or have serious plans to produce).

Know your sixteen times table

As already discussed on page 106, offset litho books are usually printed on large presses which print 8 or 16 pages at the same time. If you are likely to be using offset litho then check with your printer before finalising the typesetting!

Proof reading

Once you have typeset the whole publication print off a copy; these are known as 'page proofs'. Even if you have already proof read the text at an earlier stage, read through again looking for any remaining errors in the text and also for inconsistencies with typesetting and layout. This is your last chance before committing all your mistokes to posterity...

Depending on the printer you are using (both ink jets and lasers can be misleading) the half-tones may look different to how they look on screen. *Do not panic!* If you are using digital printing then all that matters is how they look when reproduced by the printer's equipment. If you have not used the intended book printer previously then now is the time to send some sample pages to make sure that what you think you're going to get is really what you will get.

Indexing

Ideally all publications should be indexed. A simple index of places, people and the major topics will add only about one page for every 30 pages of main text (less if there are many illustrations). If even such a modest increase in pages will make the publication uneconomic (and this may be the case for simple booklets) then make sure that the contents page(s) contain full details of subheadings and sub-sub-headings.

An index can be prepared only after the book has been typeset and all the final changes made. Indexing requires much more than making an alphabetical list of all the 'key words', and much less than listing everything except 'the', 'an' and 'and'. Firstly, the indexer must be alert to the general theme of each paragraph and considerable imagination is needed to think in terms of words that the reader is likely to search under. This may requiring indexing against 'theme words' (i.e. words not necessarily in the text).

With books of interest to family history researchers (and that includes many *local* history publications) I strongly recommend indexing all named individuals, no matter how briefly they are mentioned.

The indexer must ensure that sub-entries are created when necessary, for instance, if the main entry would have more than about 6 different page references. Instead of:

churches 12, 14, 22, 25, 27, 31, 34–7, 42, 45, 47, 51, 54–5, 61

more helpful is:

churches 12, 25, 42; St Mary 12, 22, 25; St Nicholas 14, 27, 34, 47; St Thomas 31, 34–7, 45; St Wistan 51, 54–5, 61

If you have no experience of indexing then forget doing a bodged DIY job. How often in your research have you relied on a good index to locate important information? How much would you have missed if the indexing had been too hit and miss? Almost all local history publications will be of value to future researchers, and they are most likely to turn to the index when they first pick up your publication. No matter what other shortcuts you may have to take, do not compromise on the index.

Fortunately there are plenty of professional indexers and their costs are usually quite reasonable. Contact:

Society of Indexers
Globe Centre
Penistone Road
Sheffield
S6 3AE

telephone:	0114 292 2350
fax:	0114 292 2351
email:	admin@indexers.org.uk

Some specialist local history books may be indexes of historical records and sources in a collection or archive. R.F. Hunnisett's *Indexing for Editors* (British Records Association, 1972, reprinted 1997) is an essential guide for such projects and also a useful source for anyone who wants a better understanding of the special approach needed to prepare an index. *Indexing Books* by Nancy C. Mulvany (University of Chicago, 1994) is also helpful.

Typesetting the index

There are a few points to bear in mind when typesetting an index.

Almost always an index will be in two columns (on A5 pages) or three columns (on A4 pages). If you are pushed for space then the type size can be reduced by a point or two; sometimes reducing the leading (see page 142) by one point is preferable. Typesetting indexes is much easier if you opt for unjustified text and use the paragraph format command to make sure 'follow on' lines to automatically indent from the left margin.

There are two ways of laying out subentries, usually known as 'set out style' and 'run on style' (see opposite page). Note carefully the use of commas and semi-colons in the run on style. Usually each entry starts with a lower case letter, unless it is a proper name.

Note that the 'dash' between contractions (such as 34–7) is *not* a hyphen but the slightly longer 'en-dash' (see page 46).

Set out style: for indexes:

Lister Park 19
    brass bands 18, 22, 43
    Albion Band 22
    contests 18, 54
    Militia band 43
Lister, William 25

Run on style for indexes:

Lister Park 19; brass bands 18, 22, 43; Albion Band 22; contests 18, 54; Militia band 43
Lister, William 25

The final step is to check the index against the page proofs, and to double-check that there are no spelling errors in the index (mistakes are easily made, especially with proper names).

Writing back cover blurb

What is the first thing you do when you pick up a book in a bookshop? Unless it is highly illustrated, in which case you may just flick through, quite probably you will turn to the 'blurb' on the back cover. In about 150 words you need to achieve three objectives:

- grab the browser's attention
- summarise the contents
- 'tease' the reader into wanting to read more.

Keep everything crisp and to the point. Every word you use has to have maximum impact. Bear in mind that many browsers will not read the whole blurb! If they are not 'grabbed' by the first paragraph – maybe even the first sentence – the book will be back on the shop's shelf in a trice.

Writing 'blurb' is every bit as intense as writing poetry. Some would say that there is more satisfaction in writing a well-crafted blurb as there is in writing a whole descriptive chapter. You will end up making many revisions to fine-tune sentences, and sometimes completely redo whole paragraphs.

The opening sentence of the blurb for Heart of Albion's book *Musical Leicester* starts:

> There was an amazing diversity of music-making in Leicester during the eighteenth and nineteenth centuries, involving many nationally and internationally renowned performers.

So, go for a maximum impact first sentence, and keep the guns firing through the first paragraph. The next paragraph should outline the book's themes and the third (almost always the final paragraph) should stress who the book is aimed at.

The final sentence of the blurb for Heart of Albion's book *Musical Leicester* concludes:

> *Musical Leicester* will inform and entertain all those interested in music making, social history and local history.

One of the additional challenges of blurb writing is to avoid repetitions ('this book', 'the author', 'shows' and 'provides' are often problematic).

Keep all sentences short and direct, which means avoiding indirect constructions (see page 35) and passive sentences (see page 40).

If you have obtained endorsements (see page 129) then these need to feature prominently in the back cover blurb. Exceptionally, you may even want to include a short endorsement on the front cover if the endorsement is from an especially famous or respected person.

One trick that I now use regularly is to ask other people (especially those who have a good understanding of what makes a good 'blurb') to read the page proofs and make suggestions for the blurb. With luck one of these may be good enough to simply polish up but, in practice, I usually end up combining ideas from several different sources. (To avoid offending your helpers, always make clear from the beginning that you are seeking ideas and that their work may or may not be used in the final version.) The *Musical Leicester* blurb, for instance, was written by myself but some sections, including the final lines, drew heavily on a draft blurb made by the proof reader.

Least important are biographical details about the author. If the author is well-known in the field then the biography is largely superfluous and, if he or she is not well-known, extended biographical information appears as nothing more than self-aggrandisement and can be counterproductive. There is rarely any reason for the author's details to be longer than 25 words.

However, the blurb on the back cover of this book includes specific biographical information. Do you agree that this helps sell the book?

Cover design

So, since starting to read this chapter you have been trying out lots of ideas on your DTP software and, with any luck, are beginning to produce some professional-looking pages. Great! But there is one piece of design that is so crucial to the success of a book that I strongly suggest that a professional will do a far better job. Even (perhaps *especially)* if you think you have come up with a really great idea.

Contrary to an oft-repeated aphorism, people do judge a book by its cover. Indeed, a book may not even leave the shelves of a shop if the cover does not both 'grab' the browser's attention and give the impression of being professionally produced.

If you have been trained how to design a good cover (or dust jacket for a hard back edition) then you do not need me to help. If you do not know then there is far too much to learn for this book to be able to teach you.

Use a professional designer with previous experience of book cover designs. They will not charge the earth. You avoid the risk of something looking 'home grown' and, with two- and four-colour covers especially, will have a *much* easier time when it comes to getting suitable artwork to the printer.

The front cover text is usually restricted to the title, subtitle, author's name(s) and, exceptionally, the name(s) of illustrator(s). However, if you have succeeded in getting a foreword from someone influential (see page 128), then make sure this is clearly stated on the front cover. There is little point in having your book endorsed by such a person if the casual browser in a bookshop is likely to miss the fact.

Colour covers

How many colours?

The simplest covers are black photocopied line art on white or coloured card. With clever design some of these can be made to look quite attractive, but the design really has to be top-notch to avoid the risk of a cheap or amateurish-looking job. Digital printing allows half-tones as well as line art to be successfully printed.

The next step up is to use coloured ink on either white or coloured card. This will require offset litho, which allows for half-tones. In the right hands a number of clever design ideas can be explored. Using, say, dark red ink on white card allows white lettering on solid dark red, plus various tints of lighter reds and pinks.

Professional designers can create effective designs with so-called 'two colour' covers. Although it accurately describes the printing process (two different colour inks, one usually black) the name is a misnomer as the white of the card adds a third 'colour'. Furthermore, both the black and spot colour can be used as grey and 'tints' of the solid colour. Do not feel that, just because you have paid more to have an extra colour, you have to use it all over the cover! Some very effective cover designs are essentially black and white, with small areas of colour used to grab attention.

Cover of the Wolds Historical Organisation Newsletter 2002.
This simple half-tone cover for an A4 size annual newsletter was digitally printed in black on A4 light blue card and proved to be very eye-catching.

The ink used for single and two-colour printing can be just about any shade; these are known as 'spot colours'. The printing industry usually matches spot colours against 'Pantone' colour swatches. Metallic effects, such as gold and silver, can be done with spot colours although the strongest effects are produced by a separate process, usually known as 'foil embossing'. Predictably, this is rather expensive for short runs.

Full colour printing is also referred to as 'four colour' printing as the four 'process colours' (yellow, magenta, cyan and black) combine to reproduce the full range of colours. Providing artwork for full colour printing will be discussed later in this chapter.

Back cover

The back cover will contain about 150 words of carefully-worded 'blurb' (see above page 149) and a two-line summary of the author's expertise in the subject.

Although not essential, repeating the title, subtitle and author's name on the back cover is customary. Printing the price, ISBN and EAN-13 codes and a bar code on the back cover is helpful to bookshops. The bar code should always be in the bottom right corner

Bar codes

Professional book designers will create 'Bookland' barcodes for you. Otherwise there is shareware available; search for 'barcode shareware'.

I use an ancient Win 9x program called 'Wbar' which can be downloaded from www.hoap.co.uk/wbar195.zip.

WBar v.1.95 creates many different types of barcodes. For books make sure you use *Bookland*. To do this:

- Go to 'Special'
- Click 'Bookland barcode'
- Click anywhere
- Enter the ISBN *without spaces*
- Leave 'EAN' blank
- Click 'Pricing none/user'
- Click 'OK'

A bar code should now appear on screen.

Note that the number at the bottom is the EAN-13 number, not the ISBN – there are more leading characters and the final digit (the check digit) changes as a result. If you get a list starting 'UPC-A, UPC-E, 3 of 9' etc then click 'Cancel' and go to 'Special' then follow as above.

To copy this barcode for use in another application, such as DTP software

- Go to 'Action'
- Click 'Select'
- Place cursor to top left of barcode and drag-and-drop to bottom right of barcode (if you 'clip' the image just try again!)
- Go to 'Edit'
- Click 'Copy'

The barcode is now on the Windows clipboard and can be pasted into any image editing or DTP software.

Bar codes should *always* be printed in black on a white background that provides at least 5 mm of white border around the bar code. Above all, make sure that the lines of the bar code will print clearly – 40 mm width is minimum and 50 mm optimum.

If you are friendly with a local bookshop then I strongly suggest you ask them to scan some trial bar codes to make sure you are doing everything right. Create bar codes for other people's books that are probably in print and check that the correct details come up on the bookseller's screen.

Spine design

Unless your book will be stapled then the cover design will include the spine. Although much smaller than the front and back covers, the design of this is every bit as important as this small area of print may well be all that initially catches the eye of the bookshop browser.

Before you can design the spine you need to know how thick the book will be. This depends very much on the type of paper to be used and the type of binding – and there are significant variations between apparently similar types of paperback binding. The only person who can estimate the thickness of the spine accurately will be your printer – and only when you have finalised the number of pages and decided on a specific type of paper. Taking a book off your shelves and try to make your own estimate is totally misleading as different paper types greatly affect spine thickness.

Depending on the size of the spine you should try to include, in the following priority:

- The title of the book (abbreviated if it is rather long and the space is small)

- The name of the author (use initials rather than first names if necessary)
- The logo or name of the publisher (but never let this dominate).

Few local history titles are so thick that there is space for the sub-title (if indeed the book has one) on the spine.

The text on the spine should run *down from the top* not up from the bottom.

If you are going to ignore my advice about using a professional designer for the cover, then take a close look at the spines of books on your bookshelves and try to emulate those that catch your eye most effectively.

Sending cover artwork for the printer

The pages for a book will ideally be supplied as PDF files. PDF also works well for covers, although care is needed to make sure any 'bleed' around the edges (see page 138) is included in the files. In practice it may be easier to create the covers in Paint Shop Pro and send to the printer as TIFF format files.

If you are not familiar with preparing file formats such as PDF and TIFF for printers then I strongly recommend you use a professional designer for the cover. You may not even find out about problems until after the covers have been printed with the wrong font, or with part of the text missing. The colours you see on screen are *not* an accurate indication of how printing inks will reproduce the image. For example, yellows come out weaker. Professional graphics designers have gone down these learning curves before and if something still goes wrong it will be at their expense not yours. Of course designers cost money – but a lot less money than having to scrap several hundred books because a mistake on the cover makes them unsaleable.

Another option is to create a 'dummy' version of the cover yourself and then allow the printer to recreate the design in whatever software they use. However be warned that, no matter how enthusiastically they claim competence, many 'Mac operators' employed by printers have inadequate experience with the finer aspects of design and typesetting. Without supervision by someone with a design background they are likely to produce something that lacks the necessary finesse for a cover.

Sending your book to the printer

Traditionally artwork was sent to printers as 'camera ready copy' – in other words, physical pages that the printer would then photographically convert into printing plates.

Within the last few years all this has changed. Artwork is sent on a CD-ROM as PDF files. PDF is an acronym for 'Portable Document Format' and the standard was devised by Adobe. Software for reading PDF files is freely available. However writing and/or editing PDF files requires the necessary software.

PDF enables better quality printing and reduces cost. For example, the costs associated with making half-tones from photographs (often about £5 per image) have been eliminated.

The latest versions of PagePlus create PDF files, as do Pagemaker and InDesign. If you are not using any of these programs then you can create PDFs from *any* Windows software using either Adobe Acrobat (about £225 at the time of writing) or the various cheaper alternatives such as that available from FinePrint's PDF Factory (www.fineprint.com) which currently costs $50 (a trial version enables you to try before you buy).

With PDF Factory make sure:

- the paper size is exactly what you want (create a custom size if necessary)
- 'Enable international font support' is ticked
- 'Emulate printer' is *not* ticked
- Resolution is set to 1200 dpi
- 'Downsample bitmaps to 96 dpi' is *not* ticked
- The four margins are set to '0'

After you have clicked 'OK' and the pages have been processed then you must select 'Fonts' and embed all 'Fonts used in current document' before saving.

Then preview the PDF file and check for errors. Enlarge the viewing size to 200 percent or more to check that pictures have not come out 'blocky' (if so this probably means you did not *un*tick 'Downsample bitmaps to 96 dpi').

PDF is generally a reliable format, although hiccups can arise. These mostly fall into three types:

1. Even with international font support selected some fancy characters and accents may not come out correctly, even though MS Word and some DTP programs show them accurately. There is no way of over-riding such problems except by substituting a less quirky character. Different typefaces impose different limitations.

2. With some fonts any text in italic or bold may swap to Times Roman or Arial. This is because Windows has the capability to intelligently 'invent' italic and bold versions when they are not defined by the font file. However PDF plays by the rules and does not create italic and bold versions where they do not exist – but does not tell you it has hit a snag and substituted a different font!

ā ē ĕ ĭ ğ ġ ĥ ċ č ŋ ō ő ŏ ŕ ŗ ţ ŧ š ş ŭ ž

Examples of characters not supported by PDF.

If you think such a problem has arisen (and it will probably be with a fairly obscure 'fancy' font) then use My Computer and go into the Windows / Fonts folder. Some fonts will be listed thus:

fontname.ttf
fontname bold.ttf
fontname bold italic.ttf
fontname italic.ttf

The 'problem' font is more likely to be listed only as:

fontname.ttf

with no bold and italic versions. There are three solutions. The first is to forget using italic and bold. The second is to change to a fully-supported font. The third only works if the text is a heading – create the text in a graphics program and copy-and-paste it into the DTP software as an image (make sure the resolution is greater than 1200 dpi to avoid the text appearing 'soft' at the edges).

3. The third problem only arises if you have taken images right to the edge of the page. Some PDF-authoring software ignores any 'bleed' (see page 138). The solution is to create pages slightly bigger than final cropped size (see also page 138) and to make sure this larger page size is the one selected with writing the PDF file; this will probably mean creating a custom page size.

A printer can easily combine several PDF files into one book. With longer books I typically create one PDF file for each chapter and a separate PDF file for the prelims.

If you are using Pagemaker or Quark Xpress (and maybe InDesign) the printer should be able to take the DTP files without converting them to PDFs. However great care is needed to include all pictures and fonts correctly.

Placing an order with a printer

When you have decided on which printer you will use you will need to send the PDF files together with a formal order. This should be closely based on the quotation you have received. Indeed, if there are any differences between the quote and what your order states (such as more pages or more half-tones) then ask for a revised quote *before* sending the order.

The order needs to contain the following information:

- A unique order number.
- Date.
- Name, address and phone number of contact for queries, invoices, etc.
- Delivery address (if this is the same address state 'Deliver to above address'); alternatively state that the books will be collected.
- The size of the publication (A4, A5, Demi 8vo, etc.).
- The number of pages. Total up prelims, main text and any blank pages at the end. The number will *always* be an even number and always a multiple of four for stapled booklets.
- Type of binding (preferably use trade terms such as 'case bound', 'perfect bound' and 'stitched' – see page 103).
- Type of paper to be used for the body of the book e.g. '100 gsm white bond'. If the printer has supplied samples then these will be identified by trade names – use the trade name if you know it. If there is any possible ambiguity then include part of the sample with the order.
- Specification for end papers, if any.
- Type of card to be used for the cover – again cite trade names or return part of the printer's sample.
- Number of colours to be used for cover. Clearly identify 'spot' colours by Pantone reference (the printer may be able to loan swatches).
- Whether or not cover will be laminated.
- How many copies you want.
- How many spare covers you want (see page 110); you may well want about 50 flat covers for promotional purposes.
- State 'Proofs must be submitted before binding' (Do not forget this – it is probably the most important phrase in the whole order; see below).
- The signature of an 'authorised person'.

If in doubt, state your requirements, or ask for specific details to be confirmed. Verbal agreements count for nothing if there are problems to be resolved when the proofs appear. Finally, double-check that all details are correct – this is a legally-binding document. Any mistakes or 'extras' will almost certainly lead to extra costs – and expect to pay more than if this work had been part of the original quotation. Finally, do not forget to sign the order.

If the printer comes back with any queries then respond *in writing*. A fax is often best. If you use email then keep printed and dated copies; insist on an acknowledgement.

If using offset litho preferably state in writing that you want the printer to retain the plates (in case a reprint is needed). Most printers will only agree to store plates for a maximum of one year. In this case storing them yourself may be preferable (although bear in mind that scratched or creased plates are useless). With digital printing the files are usually kept on computer disc 'indefinitely' (check with your printer what this really means!) although colour covers are usually produced by offset litho, so the above remarks still apply.

Approving printer's proofs

Most printers will do a good job. But the last thing you want is for boxes full of books to arrive with some glaring fault – especially if it is on the cover. This is why approving proofs before binding is *essential*. Few printers will agree to redoing the whole printing job, even they have made a big mistake.

With digital printing the proof copy is simply a 'first off' and will look exactly how the subsequent copies will appear. Check *every* detail of digital proofs – did you really want the price on the back cover to be in Courier typeface? Was the running heading really meant to be in a different typeface? Have all strange accents come out correctly? Are there any words in italics or bold where the typeface has changed?

Half-tones rarely reproduce as well as original photographs. Do not expect the printed half-tones to look as good as the originals but simply check that they show all the necessary detail and that there is a good range of greys from very light grey to near black. If necessary go back to the original file of the image and tweak differently. Try to allow for the difference between how images appear on screen and how they have printed out.

If there are problems you can redo the relevant pages and resend revised PDFs. If only a few pages are affected then modified pages can be created as individual PDF files; such small PDF files are usually small enough to be emailed.

With offset litho the printer has probably already printed all the copies and is simply waiting for approval before binding. At the very least any changes with offset litho will require new plates (fairly expensive) or a reprint (very expensive).

If you really do not like something, and it is not a fault with your artwork, then tread carefully. Few printers will respond positively to demands such as 'You must reprint this page', even if the fault is blatantly theirs. The cost of reprinting will erode most of the printer's profits. The cost of reprinting a cover will often, because of the cost of the card, represent about a third of the cost of the whole job.

If the problem relates in any way to an ambiguity in your written order then the printer is unlikely to meet the costs of any reprinting. Except for blatant mistakes caused solely by the printer then, in my experience, the best you can usually hope to achieve is to split the costs of the rework with the printer. Some printers will try to persuade you to you live with the fault in exchange for a discount on their final invoice.

Check printer's proofs carefully before signing and faxing (or posting) the acceptance form. If you live close to the printer's and visit the works to approve the proofs, do not be rushed into approving them. I strongly recommend that you bring the proofs home, unless you are the sort of person who can remain cool and completely focused under all circumstances.

Remember, once you have 'signed off' the proofs you have no come back on the printer should any faults remain.

Final thoughts

Designing and typesetting books is probably the trickiest of all the skills to develop to a professional standard – there are simply so many aspects, each requiring a subtle understanding of the pros and cons. Sadly the widespread availability of DTP software has resulted in rather too many poor or even bad book designs. This chapter offers advice on some of the most important aspects, but cannot provide an in-depth guide to the finer points. The ability to mimic *accurately* book designs you like will help develop sufficient awareness of the more arcane aspects of typesetting.

If you consider that design, typesetting and liaising with printers is a part of the writing and publishing process that they would prefer to subcontract then Heart of Albion will be pleased to quote.

Further reading

The Non-designer's Design Book, Robin Williams, Peachpit Press Inc, rev edn 2003

The Thames and Hudson Manual of Typography, Ruari McLean, Thames and Hudson, 1992 [still by far the best introduction to typography]

The Complete Manual of Typography: A Guide to Setting Perfect Type Jim Felici, Adobe 2002

Chapter Seven

DESIGNING WEB SITES AND CD-ROMS

Web sites, CD-ROMs and ebooks are different forms of electronic publication. They are all fairly new ways of presenting information. Nevertheless Web sites and CD-ROMs have been enthusiastically adopted by many local and family historians. The advantages are obvious:

- They are much cheaper than printing books.
- Web sites can be accessed by anyone with a computer.
- Far more information can be included (especially colour photographs) than in affordable books.
- Video clips, sound and animations can be readily included.
- 'Hypertext' links allow easy cross-referencing of ideas.
- Web search engines make finding information easier and more reliable than using an index.
- Web pages and CD-ROMs can be created as easily as designing and typesetting books.

However many of these strengths are also potentially weaknesses. The amount of information that can be included means that considerable care and planning is needed to help the user find the necessary details. Also the prevailing 'DIY' ethos of Web site creation often leads to poorly designed sites.

What sort of content is suited to Web sites and CD-ROMs?

One answer is 'anything'. You could produce electronic versions of previously-published books, booklets or articles. Or you could publish raw data such as transcriptions of census returns or parish registers. In between there is the option for sharing work in progress with other people, perhaps to solicit feedback.

The range of local and family history information already published electronically is vast. Individuals have produced CD-ROMs of most of the old antiquarian county volumes, census transcriptions, parish registers, and such like. Leicester University has made many nineteenth century trade directories available over the Web (www.historicaldirectories.org).

Taking Leicestershire as an example, so far there have been CD-ROMs of:

- Phillimore marriage registers
- Transcriptions of the 1086 Domesday Survey, Lay Subsidies. Hearth Taxes, Court Rolls, Fines, etc. up to the 1666 Hearth Tax for over half the villages in the county.
- Extracts form the Archives of the Corporation of Leicester 1103–1603; originally published between 1899 and 1905 as three books.
- Scans of all the volumes of John Nichols' *History and Antiquity of the County of Leicester*, originally published between 1795 and 1811.
- Photographs of all the sepulchral effigies in Leicestershire and Rutland together with transcriptions of all the inscriptions and brief biographies of those commemorated and the sculptors.
- Details of all the holy wells, standing stones, medieval crosses and other 'little-known' aspects of the county's history.
- Nearly 300 examples of medieval carvings on or in Leicestershire's churches.
- Historical details for all the city centre streets, with about 1,800 images. This CD-ROM includes nearly 800 biographies of eminent citizens and incorporates the text and illustrations from five previously-published booklets.
- A history of Great Glen, based on a previously published booklet but with many more photographs and an additional 'chapter' on more recent history.

These show the range of topics – from transcriptions of old documents to photographic surveys of specialist topics. None of these could be published in paper format at an affordable price without severely reducing the number of pictures. For example a book based on the medieval carvings CD-ROM contains only half the photos and has none of the benefits of hypertext indices to specific topics.

The number of Web sites relating to the local history of Leicestershire and all other places is ever-evolving. Sadly some of the best sites 'die' (although if you know the previous Web address you may be able to find it on www.archive.org). As an interesting example of village-based local history on the Web visit www.wymeswold.org/localhis.htm which links to over 60 different articles about the history of the Leicestershire village of Wymeswold, mostly previously published in booklets and magazines that are now out of print. This Web site also has transcriptions of the village's census returns from 1841 to 1901 and the parish registers from 1560. All of this information can be found by Web search engines.

Web sites are an obvious way of publishing family history, and very many such sites have been created. The designs usually reflect the whims of their creators much more than the rules for good design but, because there is usually only limited amounts of information on any one site, this rarely causes too many problems.

'Look and feel' and 'information architecture'

This chapter is devoted to creating professional-looking CD-ROMs and Web sites that will be easy for other people to use. The emphasis is on drawing attention to potential problems so many of the sections are in the nature of 'do's and don't's' rather than detailed practical advice.

Some of the advice will be about the design of the on-screen appearance – often referred to as the 'look and feel'. Other advice is perhaps even more important. This is about structuring the content to make it easy for users to find what they are looking for, and for them to move around the hyperlinks without a mental sense of getting lost. This is referred to as 'information architecture'.

But before we get too lost in jargon, let's start by thinking how information is best presented on screen.

Writing for screen reading

On-screen reading is different to books. With Web sites and CD-ROMs most people 'skim' through text and only stop to read fairly short sections that grab their attention.

When they stop skimming and start to read in more detail they will read more slowly than if the information was on paper. What might take 4 seconds to read when printed out will take 5 or 6 seconds to read on-screen (and even longer if an inappropriate font face or size has been used).

Text must be brief and easy to read. Information must be presented in small bites – 'less is better' is an important maxim when writing for on-screen reading. This means adapting the way you write. Pay attention to nine 'rules':

1. Present ideas simply. Think of a Web page as akin to a TV advert – you need to focus on getting your message across. Never bury key information or arguments within rambling digressions.
2. Write in an informal style. Communicate *with* readers, not *at* them. Write as if you were chatting to friends. However use

metaphors sparingly – they slow down comprehension and may be misinterpreted.

3. Provide plenty of sub-headings and other clues as to what the text is about. Sub-headings both break up the text and help the skip reader identify topics of interest.
4. The opening sentence of a paragraph should give a good indication about the rest of the paragraph. Always keep to the 'one idea = one paragraph' principle.
5. Use much shorter paragraphs – normally no more than 90 words, and ideally about 70 words – than are typical for books.
6. Keep sentences to a maximum of 30 words.
7. Use bullet points and numbered lists wherever appropriate.
8. Use bold to draw attention to key words. Avoid italics as these are difficult to read on screen. Never use underline for emphasis – underline should *always* denote a hyperlink. (Hyperlinks also add emphasis; used sensibly these too help to 'structure' information; see page 179.)
9. Provide summaries before and/or after each section.

These are also rules which work well for books. Indeed, these last few paragraphs, although written for a printed book, are a self-referential example of effective writing for on-screen reading.

Comparative data should always be put in a table. Use illustrations and diagrams as much as possible. (See later in this chapter for more details of using tables and illustrations). However do not add standard 'clip art' just to make the page look 'busy' – this is the opposite of good design.

Break up into pages

One school of thought says that Web pages should be kept very short and never more than three scrolls of the screen deep. However this all depends on what information you are presenting. If you are producing a Web version of a 5,000 word article then such short pages could result in a great many 'next page' links which is tedious for the reader and also causes problems for anyone who wants to print out the article.

My preference is to keep pages as short as reasonably possible but where information genuinely belongs together – as with the 5,000 word article – then create one long page. However ensure that subheadings appear frequently – ideally about one for every scroll of the screen. Be prepared to add subheadings and break up paragraphs when converting text originally published in print for on-screen reading. You may also need to add hyperlinks – for example to footnotes, a glossary, bibliographical details or other articles.

Do not overload the home page

The first page of a site should give a clear indication of what the site is about rather than some vague atmospheric image or cryptic statement. As with every other aspect of life, first impressions count. Complicated, badly-designed or wilfully unconventional home pages do not create good first impressions. Spelling and grammatical mistakes also set poor expectations about the reliability of the information.

'Whacky' home pages or failure to provide clear links will simply mean that most visitors will not bother to try to navigate the site. They will either not realise that there is information relevant to their interests, or consider too much time and effort will be needed to find it, or assume that such a badly-designed site could not possibly have reliable information.

Most of the home page should be devoted to links to the rest of the site. Make sure all aspects of the content of the Web site or CD-ROM are listed from the home page (perhaps by using 'nested' lists/sub-menus). Each of these links must be self-explanatory – no one will thank you for obscure puns or arcane 'cleverness'. Make sure the navigation design and nomenclature on the home page is consistent with the rest of the site.

Make sure that all the important links can be found without scrolling down and the whole of the home page occupies no more than two complete screens (i.e. no more than 1600 pixels high at 1024 screen resolution). A prominent link to 'search this site' and/or a comprehensive and hierarchically-organised 'site map' is essential for more complex Web sites or CD-ROMs. About 30 percent of Web users prefer to find information using 'search this site' rather than drilling down through unfamiliar navigation links.

A few images may be helpful but keep them small; you can always include bigger versions elsewhere in the site. Home pages with animations are usually bad news and shout 'amateur'. Animations grab attention and are therefore useful for, say, banner adverts. However once someone has entered a Web site or CD-ROM you no longer need to grab their attention in this rather offensive way. No one wants to be distracted by continually-moving images in their peripheral vision while reading text. At the very worst include an animation on the home page that stops after a few seconds. (However, away from the home page animated graphics may help to illustrate a topic better than a static graphic and, used intelligently, *may* be helpful.)

The 'three clicks' rule

Plan in reasonable detail how different sections of the site will link to each other. All important parts of the site should be no more than three hyperlinks away from the opening screen. Only the most obscure 'background information' should be four links away.

This means careful planning of 'index' pages. The real advantage of Web sites is that the same detailed page can be accessed in different ways.

For example, with the CD-ROM of sepulchral effigies in Leicestershire and Rutland the underlying structure of the information is based around individual churches. Each church may contain one or more effigies so each of these is given its own page. Predictably one index lists the churches parish by parish. However another index lists the names of the people commemorated – the links are direct to the page about their effigy. Furthermore some of the effigies are by notable sculptors so there is an index of sculptors' names with links to their work (there are also links to the sculptors' biographies from the pages with details of the effigies created by them). All these different indices mean that the same information can be accessed in different ways, depending whether the reader is primarily interested in the deceased, or the sculptor, or the parish and its church.

The same 'three click' principle is used for the Heart of Albion Web site (www.hoap.co.uk). Information about individual books is one or two clicks 'deep'. The next click will either take you 'deeper' – to reviews of the book or details about the author – or remain at the same 'level' and link to details of other books.

Offer a tour

Every page should also offer a link to the next related page. If your work is about a whole county and there is one page per village, then create links to 'Next village' and 'Previous village' at the end of the page. Likewise if you are dealing with only one place then the links could be to 'Next street' and 'Previous street'. More biographical content could be linked to 'Next person'.

Unless there are good reasons otherwise (for example if the tour is in chronological order) then 'next' and 'previous' should be based on alphabetical listing. Such alphabetical tours may not be the most logical way of finding information on specific topics but what they do offer is the opportunity for someone to 'browse' through, as they may well want to the first few times they use the Web site or CD-ROM.

These ways of 'browsing' electronic publications are the equivalent of flicking through a book – it allows the user to get an overall assessment of the scope of the information and the way it is presented. They may not seem necessary to you, simply because you created the content and have a good idea of what it is all about. In contrast, the ability to 'flick through' and get a feel for sites and CD-ROMs is an essential facility for electronic publications, although one frequently ignored by the creators. The more content there is, the greater the need for such tours (and the more work needed to create them!).

Having to click on the 'Back' button to go back to an index is most emphatically *not* the same as clicking on 'Next village' or 'Next person' as it offers *too many* choices rather than a clear (if somewhat arbitrary) option. Repeated use of the 'Back' button is psychologically similar to trying to find your way out of a maze where every way you turn seems to end up in a cul-de-sac. We are much happier when we have the illusion of moving onwards.

In some cases you may want to organise one or more specific 'tours' yourself. A CD-ROM by Max Matthews called *A Stroll through Dublin* (Eneclann 2004) includes, among much else, a tour of all the locations featured in James Joyce's novel *Ulysses.* My CD-ROM of Leicestershire and Rutland medieval carvings allows 'tours' according to what is depicted – such as dragons, or foliate faces, etc – and by period, such as Anglo-Saxon or Romanesque carvings.

The Web site design 'gospel'

Making Web sites easy to navigate is a skill that needs to be learnt. The best-known book on the subject appeared in 2000 but the ideas have stood up to the test of time. It is *Designing Web Usability: The Practice of Simplicity* by Jakob Nielsen (New Riders Publishing; http://www.useit.com).

On-line family history

If your main interest is a family history Web site then track down a copy of Cyndi Howells' *Planting Your Family Tree Online: How To Create Your Own Family History Web Site* (Rutledge Hill Press 2004). It is an American book but the information requires little if any adaptation for UK readers.

File formats

HTML

HTML (Hyper Text Mark-up Language) is the language for writing Web pages. HTML is essentially about turning on and off commands like you do when you ask for **bold,** *italic* or a new paragraph in a word processor. The difference is that in HTML you type in the codes for such commands as well as typing in the content of the pages; see pages 172 to 197 for a more detailed discussion of HTML authoring.

HTML pages can include links to other pages (known as 'hyperlinks'), images (still or moving), sound, and 'code' or 'scripts' for doing clever effects written in other languages such as Java or JavaScript (see below). HTML pages can also automatically send information back to the server computer which then generates 'shopping carts' and such like – this is how e-commerce sites such as Amazon operate.

Most local and family history Web sites simply do not need the complexities of JavaScript code or 'shopping carts'. Text, hyperlinks, images and even sound can all be included in Web pages with use simple use of HTML.

This book does not offer detailed advice on learning HTML, simply because that information is readily available on the Web (see page 173). Because I have to assume that readers have little or no prior knowledge of creating Web sites and CD-ROMs then predictably I will offer the easiest solutions. In contrast, if you want to develop your expertise with the more arcane aspects of HTML and/or learn JavaScript then by all means seek out suitable tutorials. However complexity for its own sake is rarely, if ever, a good basis for designing Web sites and the like. In this book I will be keeping things simple.

Why CD-ROMs should be written in HTML

Exactly the same HTML that is used for on-line Web sites can be used 'off-line' to write CD-ROMs. Indeed, for the purposes of this chapter I will regard CD-ROMs as being off-line Web sites. I am fully aware that there is a range of specialist programs for writing CD-ROMs (such as JASC's Opus Pro or Macromedia's Director) but they are expensive and require considerable time and effort to learn how to use. Furthermore the ability to run such CD-ROMs is dependant on the ability of the program to cope with future changes to computer operating systems. At the present time it would be very foolish to assume that programs which run on Windows 9X or Windows XP will run on operating systems current in ten or more years time, even if the content of the CD-ROM is transferred to a different media. As local historians are likely to want their information to be available to researchers in the indefinite future, creating CD-ROMs in proprietary software (such as Opus Pro or Director) is exceedingly risky.

However future-proofing is much less of a problem if CD-ROMs are written in the same language as that used for Web pages i.e. HTML. While HTML will continue to evolve there will always be extremely powerful reasons for maintaining backward compatibility.

Most of this chapter will concentrate on HTML format. However there are other options for making information available on the Web.

Ebooks

Ebooks are set to become an important aspect of mainstream publishing. However at the time of writing the proprietary standards are still evolving. Frustratingly, the standard of conversion of printed texts to ebook formats is mostly quite appalling – even the major publishing houses have a long way to go to demonstrate the advantages of ebooks. Passing on advice about 'best practice' is clearly not possible when no one has yet developed such approaches. So, somewhat regrettably, I am simply going to ignore this way of publishing until a future edition.

PDF

PDF files can be a very compact way of making publications available via the Web. All Web browsers now read PDF files, and the major search engines search the content.

If you have already designed and typeset a paper publication and have PDF *authoring* software (see page 156) then the PDF version is just a few mouse clicks away. However for the Web version be sure to

- select 150 dpi resolution
- downsize all images to 96 dpi

Failure to do this will create an unacceptably large PDF file with no benefits to the person viewing.

Creating PDF files from paper documents may seem like an 'instant' solution to Web site authoring. However there are two problems:

Firstly, PDF files created from documents designed to fit on a portrait-format A5 or A4 page are more difficult to read on the letter-box shape of computer screens. So, if you are creating PDF documents specifically for Web use (although I would want to query why you are not doing this in HTML!), then use a landscape-format page.

Secondly, the way information should be structured for on-screen viewing is often quite different from how similar information is prepared for print. Later sections of this chapter will provide plenty of clues as to the differences.

MS Office file formats

As with PDF files, MS Word (.DOC), MS Excel (.EXL) and MS Powerpoint (.PPT) files all can be read by current versions of Internet browser software. Likewise the contents are indexed by the major search engines.

Word DOC files are inherently rather large – an 'empty' DOC format file with no content is already 19 Kbytes – and can be huge if images are included. Excel XLS rarely contain images so are usually between 15 and 50 Kbytes – big but not too big. In contrast Powerpoint PPT files often contain images and so can quickly end up quite large. However text-only PPT files are fairly compact. Larger Powerpoint files can be reduced in size by converting to Flash (SWF) format; the most affordable software for doing this is Swish Presenter (see www.swishzone.com as prices not confirmed when this book went to press), although Articulate Presenter (see www.articulateglobal.com) is another option if you can afford $599.

Large file size is not usually a problem when reading files offline but is a serious issue for both the person downloading them and for the person paying for the 'bandwidth' of the server (see page 193 for more discussions about bandwidth).

Flash

Macromedia Shockwave Flash, or just 'Flash' to its many friends, was invented as a way of creating simple animations in a way that was compatible with the small file sizes needed for the Web. However it soon outgrew this original concept and is now capable of creating complete Web sites or CD-ROMs. There are some disadvantages to this, not least the much greater amounts of time needed to create the pages and difficulties of making changes. Note also that any text content in Flash files is *not* indexed by search engines.

Typically Flash files are called up from HTML pages. This is fairly easy to do and, starting on page 198, there is a whole section of this chapter devoted to creating Flash animations.

Flash files can quickly become very large. This is rarely an issue with CD-ROMs but certain tricks are needed with Web sites to avoid making the user too aware of the download times (see page 199).

Java and JavaScript

Another way of doing clever 'tricks' on Web sites is to incorporate short programs written in Java or JavaScript. The similarity of the names is deceptive as there are substantial differences between these programming languages. In practice most such programs are written in JavaScript.

Unless you have prior experience in computer programming then I do not recommend trying to write such programs. However this does not mean you cannot use them! Java and JavaScript developers often make their code available to others. Web sites such as www.tucows.com provide huge lists of such code. By copy-and-pasting the JavaScript into the right part of an HTML page, and then tweaking some of the fine details according to the instructions provided, you should get the effects being offered.

There are very few such effects which are essential to local or family history Web sites so, with only a few passing exceptions, I will ignore such complexities.

XML

The next big thing in file formats is XML, which stands for eXtensible Mark-up Language. XML is taking over as the 'internal' file format for word processing software, spreadsheets, and databases (although proprietary formats such as Word DOC will still be supported). XML is already incorporated into the latest MS Office applications and will become integral to future Microsoft operating systems.

XML is very different to HTML, Word DOC and most other file formats which simply control how words and numbers appear on the screen – e.g. font size, colours, italics, bullets, size of margins, and so on. In complete contrast the primary function of XML defines the 'function' or 'structure' of the text; defining the appearance of the words on screen is very much a secondary (although still important) aspect.

Two examples should help show how XML works. Firstly, think of a book. The information can be split down into several categories:

- title
- subtitle
- author
- chapter number and title

- subheadings
- text
- captions
- etc, etc

In XML the text belonging to each of these categories of 'data' would be labelled according to the category. There would then be a 'document type definition' which says what font etc should be used for each of these categories. HTML codes, or relevant parts of a Word DOC, or DTP file can all be thought of as akin to such 'document type definitions'.

A more specific example would be bibliographical references where the categories include:

- author's surname
- author's first name
- author's initials
- names of other authors, if any
- title of the publication
- subtitle
- details of periodical if applicable
- details of editor etc if part of an edited work
- publisher
- year of publication
- previous publication details

Again each of these categories will be labelled in the XML file. The aim would be for the bibliographical data in *all* XML documents to have a similar structure, so that 'document type definitions' could be easily created, making it possible to exchange XML data with other people and still easily format it the way you prefer.

This concept will be familiar to genealogists who use the GEDCOM data format; it remains to be seen if GEDCOM will adapt to integrate with XML or simply be superseded by it.

In many ways XML can be thought of as a 'high level' database format. However the document type definitions associated with XML have more in common with HTML, DTP or word processing software. XML is a whole new way of thinking about data and how it is presented on screen. XML is being combined with HTML in an evolving new standard called XHTML; however HTML will continue to exist alongside XHTML.

So far XML is mostly a powerful concept with only a few rather specialist applications. But within the next few years XML – mostly through XML-compatible programmes such as XHTML – will become a powerful and ubiquitous aspect of storing and processing data. To what extent computer users rather than programmers will really be aware of the changes is yet to be seen. We must wait and see how it affects publishing.

Getting started with HTML

Despite all these alternative options, the rest of this chapter will be based mostly around HTML, the language currently used as the 'backbone' of Web publishing, and which is entirely suited for writing CD-ROMs.

HTML may sound intimidating but the basics can be picked up quite quickly even by people who are not in the least 'techie'; thankfully the more complex bits are mostly not needed for local and family history Web sites and CD-ROMs.

HTML authoring software

Once you have learnt the basic commands then writing HTML is so simple that you can simply type in all the codes and content for a Web page using a basic word processor such as Notepad or SimpleText (Wordpad and Word are almost too complicated for this!). However some codes (such as those for hyperlinks and images) are tedious to type out repeatedly so dedicated HTML authoring software will help speed things up considerably.

Most HTML authoring software tries to make it too easy for the beginner but, in so doing, creates problems. To create effective Web pages you need to know the basics of HTML and not leave the software to muddle along trying to cope with what you think you want. So HTML authoring software that works in roughly the same way as word processing or DTP software but does not allow you to edit the code is counter-productive. Such WYSIWYG (What You See is What You Get) software may be fine for word processing and essential for DTP but is not the answer for HTML authoring where you need to metaphorically get under the bonnet and fine tune all the mechanics.

Microsoft's FrontPage is WYSIWYG. It also has a reputation for creating HTML code which is vastly more complex than anyone would ever hand code. This means the HTML files are vastly bigger than they need be. And to add insult to injury if you 'tweak' a file created by FrontPage in any other software then FrontPage will no longer edit it. All-in-all FrontPage is not what is needed to help you master HTML.

The professionals use Macromedia's Dreamweaver or, more rarely, its competitor Adobe's GoLive. Both currently both cost around £350. As you might expect for this price they are the heavyweights of HTML authoring programs. However all the powerful extra features they offer are not needed for straightforward Web sites and

CD-ROMs, and simply add vast amounts of complexity which is not relevant – and most certainly not helpful – when trying to learn the more basic aspects.

At the time of writing the easiest HTML authoring software for beginners is Netobjects' Fusion (available for about £120). This software's main strength – a wizard-based approach – is also its weakness, as the wizards tend to lead the user down rather pre-defined paths. Fusion is WYSIWIG but also allows the HTML code to be edited, although again what might have been a benefit – helpful comments on the code – are overdone, while the code is excessively compressed making it difficult to sort out what does what (and triply difficult for a novice to HTML coding).

Frankly the best way to get to know the basics of HTML is not to use WYSIWYG Web authoring packages at all but to use a really basic HTML editor and sit down with a text book on how to write HTML. In practice, you can economise on the text book, as there are hundreds of 'how to write HTML' sites on the Web, and the best of these are excellent. Simply search for 'HTML tutorial' and you will be overwhelmed with choices. If you cannot get on with the first one you try then simply pick another. My favourites include NCSA – A Beginner's Guide to HTML (www.ncsa.uiuc.edu/General/Internet/WWW/HTMLPrimer.html and numerous mirror sites) and Joe's PageTutor (www.pagetutor.com/pagetutor/makapage/index.html) although I've certainly not tried them all. HTML is not complicated and you will soon be creating basic pages.

For many years I have been creating Web sites and CD-ROMs using a simple HTML authoring shareware program called Arachnophilia (www.arachnoid.com/arachnophilia). Version 5 runs on both PCs and Macs but version 4 (for PC only) is much easier to install and has worked well for me.

Arachnophilia offers enough help with setting up hyperlinks, importing graphics, creating tables and such like without 'getting in the way'. One of Arachnophilia's most endearing features is the ability to set up 'Keyboard Macros' which means that frequently used words or commands (even long complex ones) can be typed in with a two-key combination. Another useful feature is the ease with which 'find and replace' can look at multiple files – even all the files in a complete Web site or CD-ROM.

Arachnophilia does not have in-built Cascading Style Sheet (CSS) tools; see next section. Nor does it have wizards for different Web page designs. Although this lack of wizards is perhaps a strength rather than a weakness. Why? Because beginners should get experienced help with designing the 'look and feel' and 'information architecture'; this is the scope of the next section.

In recent months I have moved from Arachnophilia to a program called HTMLPad 2002 Pro (www.bluementals.net). This offers similar functionality with the additional of CSS support, some frequently used items of code, and extensive help files. It costs about £20. The beginner might find the 'bare bones' simplicity of Arachnophilia least distracting but, once you have got your head around the basics, the extra features of HTMLPad make this the better of the two.

Cascading Style Sheets (CSS)

Making HTML pages easy to change and update is crucial. Dreamweaver's page template tools are powerful, but a beginner cannot be expected to understand how to use them effectively.

Cascading Style Sheets (CSS) are a part of HTML that are designed to make tweaking the appearance of the site much easier. However CSS is one of the more arcane and tricky aspects of HTML – not an aspect a beginner will find easy to understand and use. Once you have some basic understanding of HTML then enter 'CSS tutorial' into a Web search engine and work your way through the many options.

Note that in this book I will be using only 'External Style Sheets' so you can ignore embedded style sheets and advice on how to put CSS commands into <head> tags. This means that each HTML page has the following line in the <head> section:

```
<link rel="stylesheet" type="text/css" href="mainstyle.css" />
```

and that there is a file called mainstyle.css in the same folder as the HTML pages (the filename can be changed in the <link> to any filename ending with .CSS).

The contents of CSS files have an awkward syntax where every semi-colon – or its absence – is crucial, and finding exactly the right term for what you want to achieve is sometimes tricky. If you have not worked with CSS before then try to find a mentor to help your through any initial difficulties. The rest of HTML is a doddle compared to the awkwardness of CSS.

Simple Web sites can be created without CSS but to future-proof your work, especially if it grows to more than a few pages, then the use of CSS external style sheets will be of great benefit in the long run.

Getting started with a Web site

I have helped a number of people to get started with HTML. Even though none of them were especially familiar with computers they soon picked up all the necessary basic skills. However I made sure that they had a basic Web page design that was appropriate, had a good understanding of making it easy for the user to read the information and navigate the site, and had planned out the structure of the information as thoroughly as possible. These are exactly the topics I will concentrate on in the next few sections.

Before you go any further with this chapter you will need to read an HTML tutorial such as the NCSA Beginner's Guide to HTML or Joe's PageTutor mentioned above. You will also need to know roughly how Cascading Style Sheets (CSS) work in conjunction with HTML.

Get help with site structure and page design

While learning HTML is not tricky, clearly someone new to creating Web sites cannot be expected to know all the finer points of making pages look good, easy to navigate, and – most crucially of all – to plan ahead for the structure of the site.

Failure to get these key aspects right in the first place can mean lots of time-consuming changes later, with plenty of scope for getting things slightly wrong. Far better to have got nearer to being right in the first place!

If you have little experience of designing Web pages then clearly there are going to be difficulties making your first attempt look good and work well. There are three options:

1. Get someone competent to design the pages; brief them by keeping a list of Web sites that you think work (either overall or in part). The easiest way for 'non-techie' people to update sites created by Web site designers is Macromedia Contribute (www.macromedia.com/contribute) which currently costs about £99 and has an interface like a word processor and has some very clever tricks hidden behind the scenes to make everything work very smoothly.

2. Get to grips with the basics of HTML and adapt existing page designs. Look at the code for Web sites that you like (or at least like part of). Clicking on 'View / Source' opens up MS Notepad with the HTML visible. So long as it does not have commands like <frameset> or vast amounts of <script> then you should be able to work out roughly what each part of the code is doing.

   While 'borrowing' a complete page design will infringe copyright, copying specific details is unlikely to cause a problem. With a bit of experimentation you should be able to adapt different parts of different sites to get more or less what you want. If you get stuck on some aspect then find a friend who can mentor you through the sticky bits. In practice sending HTML files by email is easier than face-to-face contact, so the mentor does not have to live locally.

3. Use Netobjects' Fusion templates, although be prepared to 'tweak' these by borrowing ideas from other Web sites.

The best way to learn about page design is to play with other peoples' pages and see what bit of code does what. Clearly I cannot copy code from other peoples' Web sites to use in this book. Handily Heart of Albion's own Web site (www.hoap.co.uk) was written by me and includes examples of all the topics to be discussed in this chapter. You are welcome to copy files to see how they work, and to 'play' with them to change the appearance and content.

However note that if you want to see any modified pages off-line you will also need a file called 'mainstyle.css'. This file cannot be accessed using your Web browser. To overcome this I have created a file called www.hoap.co.uk/css.htm which contains the contents of mainstyle.css. Simply copy the text between the rows of asterisks and paste into Notepad and save as 'mainstyle.css' in the same folder where you are saving offline versions of Heart of Albion Web pages. Do not modify any of the content of this file until you have some understanding of how CSS files work.

Keep it consistent

All the pages should look as if they belong to the same site. Bear in mind that most of your visitors will come via search engines which simply drop the visitor into the content pages, not the home page. So every page should also state clearly whose site it is and what it the overall scope is. The obvious option is to include a logo or slogan at the top or bottom of every page. Above all keep the pages looking consistent.

Where to put navigation links?

All but the most simple Web site needs a list of links to other key pages in the site. This information should be presented in a consistent way throughout the site. Often nicknamed the 'menu' it is also often referred to as the 'navigation column' because it often appears down the side of the Web page. Even if it appears across the top or bottom of the screen it is still usually referred to as the 'navigation column'.

Putting the navigation links across the screen makes the space available for the content of the page more 'letter box' shaped. Because long lines of text cannot be easily read this may mean that much of the screen remains unused. Whereas putting the navigation column down one side of the screen reduces the letter box effect and helps keep line lengths readable. For this reason I always create Web pages with navigation columns down the side.

Whether the navigation column should be on the left side or the right side is more a matter of personal preference. If the viewer is likely to make extensive use of a detailed list of navigation links then the left-hand side is more intuitive.

Because navigation columns can scroll off the screen longer pages should have a simple text-only version of the navigation links at the bottom of the page.

<frame> tag

The <frame> tag can be used to keep the navigation column on screen at all times. Unfortunately it is all but useless for Web sites because most people find a Web page via search engines which link to pages *without* including the associated navigation frame. This means the visitor has no idea how to find other parts of the site.

In contrast, the <frame> tag is very useful on CD-ROMs where this problem does not arise.

Future proofing navigation columns

There are three ways of providing navigation columns on every page without using frames. One is to delve into the intricacies of 'CSS driven drop down menus'. However Internet Explorer 6 is not fully compliant with relevant parts of CSS, making this even more complicated. If you feel like taking on a challenge then type 'CSS driven drop down menus' into a search engine and get stuck in, but don't expect a smooth ride!

Those who are using Dreamweaver and GoLive can create page templates. The navigation column code belongs in the template and so any changes need only be made once. However few readers of this book will be using such expensive HTML authoring software and learning to use these templates is a skill in its own right.

The third way is to simply put the navigation code on every page, almost certainly using the <table> tag. Assuming you have mastered the <table> tag (and this is so useful you will need it frequently) then there is nothing tricky about doing this. That is, until you need to change anything. Even the most simple change could mean manually editing every page (and not missing any out by mistake).

However planning in advance can minimise this problem. If every page has *exactly* the same code for the navigation column (e.g. no spurious spaces or line returns) then software such as Arachnophilia can be used to open up all the pages in a site then use find-and-replace to put in the new code.

For example, this is the current navigation column for www.hoap.co.uk pages:

```
<ul>
<li><a href="index.htm"><span id="navigation">home</span></a>
<li><a href="explore.htm"><span id="navigation">Explore
    Books</span></a>
<li><a href="alternative.htm"><span id="navigation">Alternative
    Albion</span></a>
<li><a href="general.htm"><span id="navigation">general
    titles</span></a>
<li><a href="localhis.htm"><span id="navigation">local history
    titles</span></a>
<li><a href="authors.htm"><span id="navigation">authors</span></a>
<li><a href="howtobuy.htm"><span id="navigation">HOW TO
    BUY</span></a>
<li><a href="advice.htm"><span id="navigation">advice for
    authors</span></a>
<li><a href="mailto:albion@indigogroup.co.uk"><span
    id="navigation">email</span></a>
<li><a href="copyright.htm"><span id="navigation">copyright</span></a>
</ul>
```

When I launched the Alternative Albion imprint mid-2004 I was able to find

```
<li><a href="explore.htm"><span id="navigation">Explore
Books</span></a>
<li><a href="general.htm"><span id="navigation">general
titles</span></a>
```

and replace with

```
<li><a href="explore.htm"><span id="navigation">Explore
Books</span></a>
<li><a href="alternative.htm"><span id="navigation">Alternative
Albion</span></a>
<li><a href="general.htm"><span id="navigation">general
titles</span></a>
```

Job done! How was I so sure that none of the pages had spurious spaces or anything else that would trip up the 'find' process? Simply because I created a file called 'blank.htm' at an early stage in developing this Web site. This contains all the code and text that appears on every page. Every page on the site was created by making a copy of blank.htm, then adding the content without changing any of the code.

This way of creating web sites from a template or 'blank.htm' may be low-tech but it has worked well for me – and I have been creating Web sites regularly for eight years now.

Links must be obvious and easy to follow

Some people prefer to have images – 'buttons' – rather than plain text for navigation links. These buttons have either short text or icons. There is an inherent conflict here. On the one hand navigation links must be instantly self-explanatory. On the other the text on buttons must be kept very short to be readable. Worse still, icons are rarely instantly obvious to anyone except their designers. So, while buttons may look more 'cool', if you want to include reasonably detailed descriptions of the links in the minimum of space then stick with text links. If the rest of the site looks well-designed and, more importantly, functions well then the absence of buttons will not make the site any less 'cool'.

All navigation links must always indicate clearly what they link to. Never leave the viewer guessing for more than a split-second – either a link is obvious or it is bad design. There is already far too much of the latter on Web sites so do not add to the problem. What the designer thinks is 'clever' is all too often just a damn nuisance to visitors. If you really are clever then you will want to make your site work unobtrusively, not do quirky things that will identify you as a twerp, or worse.

Sometimes – although certainly not always – buttons which change when the cursor moves over them (so-called 'mouseovers') can be helpful; see page 197 for details of how to do this.

A variation on this is navigation menus which expand into submenus when the mouse moves over different options. These are frustrating because it means you need to open up the submenus before you can see what the options are. This frustration is usually aggravated because the graphics associated with the menus have text in font sizes that are too small to be easily read. Furthermore the coding for them requires a reasonably good grasp of JavaScript or a very good grasp of CSS. Forget such fancy effects and simply list all the options under subheadings. This may take more space but it is much easier to use by someone who does not know what lurks underneath each of the buttons (i.e. everyone who visits your site). If there are several quite long submenus then it may be simpler and easier to create these on a page of their own, with a suitably self-explanatory link to the sub-menu page.

Site maps

An *additional* way of guiding the visitor around Web sites is to list *every* page, usually in some sort of hierarchical sequence(s), with hyperlinks to each page. These are known as 'site maps'. Such pages rarely look pretty – function rather than appearance is the critical issue. The downside of site map pages is that modifications to the site may require this page to be kept up to date (although this is not a problem for CD-ROMs which, once sold, are not changed).

One advantage of site maps is that they help search engines to find and index every page of a site. If you ever need to manually submit a Web site to a search engine then point them to a comprehensive site map page rather than to the home page (unless the home page happens to have direct links to every other page in the site, which is unusual).

Provide landmarks

In the real world we remember our way around our regular haunts by taking note of specific buildings, road junctions and the like. When trying to find our way to somewhere new we follow directions based on relevant pubs, roundabouts and other landmarks. On-line navigation similarly benefits from equivalent landmarks, especially if your site is quite complex.

For example different topics, or different 'levels' of the site, could be indicated by changing the background colour. Or create a series of simple graphic motifs which appear in the top-left or top-right of the page, with the appropriate motif for each set of pages.

Landmarking external links

A common and very helpful use of landmarks is to distinguish between 'internal' hyperlinks (i.e. to other pages of the same site) and 'external' hyperlinks (to other peoples' Web sites). Such hints are essential on CD-ROMs where the user may not be online while browsing the pages.

One way of 'landmarking' external links is to include the URL (i.e. Web address) in the main text. For example an external link to the Heart of Albion Web site could appear as:

> More information on the <u>Heart of Albion Web site (www.hoap.co.uk).</u>

Whereas an internal link would simply be underlined:

> More information about <u>dragons</u>.

I always add the <target="blank"> tag when linking to external sites e.g.:

> <a href="http://www.hoap.co.uk/" **target="blank**">Heart of Albion Web site</a>

This opens up a new browser window, leaving the user able to easily get back to your site. The slight downside is that the new window may mask the old one, but experienced users of Web browsers become familiar with this minor hiccup. See also the next section about the 'title' parameter.

If you use target="blank" to create new windows *within* your own site (and this can be helpful when linking to big pictures from thumbnails) then include the following code on the 'pop up' page:

> <a onclick=self.close()>Close This Window</a>

Links in text should add suitable emphasis and be easy to follow

Use hyperlinks to add *appropriate* emphasis to sentences. Compare:

> This is a <u>good site</u> about HTML design.

with:

> This is a good site about <u>HTML design.</u>

The 'title' parameter

One way of helping the user find out more about a link is to use the 'title' parameter. This means that extra text appears on screen when the cursor hovers over a link, very similar to the 'alt' parameter for images.

For example:

> <a href="http://www.hoap.co.uk/" target="blank" **title="external link**">
> Heart of Albion Web site</a>
>
> displays the words 'external link' when the cursor hovers over the link.

A more informative example, for an internal link, might be:

> <a href="dragons.htm" **title="A tour of dragons in Leicestershire churches**" >dragons</a>

Remember than links can be to sections within a longer page by using:

> <a href="filelinkedto.htm#link">words linked from</a>

and then adding <a name="link"> (there is no need for a closing </a>) in the appropriate part of filelinkedto.htm . This is used extensively in www.hoap.co.uk to link to specific book titles.

Note that the name is case sensitive – so <a href="filelinkedto.htm#link"> will *not* find <a name="Link"> because of the capital 'L'.

If you link to a section further down the *same* page then the usage is:

<a href="#link">words linked from</a>

The 'title' parameter used in the previous example of an <a href> tag can also be included in the <h1>, h2>, etc and <div> tags. This means that any block of text (not just hyperlinks) can create a pop up when the cursor hovers over it.

Specifying fonts

Always specify fonts that are designed for screen reading, such as Verdana (sans serif) or Georgia (serif).

An example of Arial:

> In contrast to printed pages, where serif fonts such as Times Roman are easier to read than sans serif, with on-screen reading sans serif fonts are much easier to read. Indeed Times Roman is seriously bad news for on-screen reading.

An example of Verdana:

> In contrast to printed pages, where serif fonts such as Times Roman are easier to read than sans serif, with on-screen reading sans serif fonts are much easier to read. Indeed Times Roman is seriously bad news for on-screen reading.

An example of Georgia:

> In contrast to printed pages, where serif fonts such as Times Roman are easier to read than sans serif, with on-screen reading sans serif fonts are much easier to read. Indeed Times Roman is seriously bad news for on-screen reading.

An example of Times Roman:

> In contrast to printed pages, where serif fonts such as Times Roman are easier to read than sans serif, with on-screen reading sans serif fonts are much easier to read. Indeed Times Roman is seriously bad news for on-screen reading.

However you have no way of knowing which fonts are installed on the users' computers, so you must also include standard PC and Mac fonts (Arial and Helvetica respectively for sans serif). With CSS this is covered by the font-family declaration:

```
p, ul, ol, li, h1, h2, h3, table, tr, td
{
font-family: "verdana", "arial", "helvetica", "sans serif"
}
```

Font and background colours

Font and page background colours should be specified by the CSS style sheet. If you are using CSS style sheets then *never* use the 'old fashioned' HTML <font> tag.

Just because thousands of colours can be specified for Web pages does not mean that you need to use all available options! Good site design makes use of a limited palette of colours, with perhaps lighter and darker tints of the same colour. Think in terms of a *maximum* of three colours (plus black and white) for each page.

Use colour variations to help provide 'landmarks' and give structure to a site. *Never* use coloured text in an arbitrary way just to 'liven things up'. What might look 'lively' to you will look cluttered, confusing and amateurish to everyone else.

Note that in CSS the spelling 'color' is necessary. So CSS declarations include:

```
body {background-color: #FFA32A}

table {background-color: #FFA32A}

img {border-color: #FFA32A}

p, ul, ol, li, table, tr, td {color: black}
```

Colours are specified either in words (from a restricted 'glossary' – use a Web search engine to find the full list) or in hexadecimal code preceded by the '#' symbol. Paint Shop Pro is especially useful here as the Colour Dropper tool shows the HTML hexadecimal code (e.g. #FFA32A) for colours – simply copy-and-paste the #FFA32A or whatever from Paint Shop Pro into your HTML or CSS authoring software.

Paint Shop Pro's Colour Dropper tool also allows you to create a palette of related colours by changing the hue, saturation or luminance *one at a time*. For example you could create pastel shades of blue, green and yellow:

pastel blue: Hue 150, Saturation 255, Lightness 200

pastel green: Hue 100, Saturation 255, Lightness 200

pastel yellow: Hue 40, Saturation 255, Lightness 200

Because the saturation and lightness are constant these are clearly 'related' shades, in a way that creating three shades from the colour wheel would not give such a pleasing effect.

Always select font and background colours to provide adequate contrast. Black and white provide the highest contrast of course, but this can be excessive. Be wary of using light coloured text on dark backgrounds. This is rarely easy to read. If you must do this then try making all the text bold as this helps the legibility of such 'reversed out' effects (e.g. the navigation column of the Heart of Albion Web site [www.hoap.co.uk] currently uses bold white text on a saturated red background).

Remember that seven percent of the male population has defective red-green discrimination, and a few others are blue-green colour blind. So red text on a green background would not only look awful but be all but invisible to about seven percent of male visitors.

Font sizes

HTML allows designers to specify font sizes in points. This is seriously bad news for the users of Web sites and CD-ROMs as they are prevented from making changes according on their screen resolution or to overcome less than perfect eyesight.

HTML also allows designers to specify relative font sizes. This is excellent news for Web site and CD-ROM users as this enables them to make changes depending on their screen resolution and to overcome less than perfect eyesight.

Do you want to design a Web site that is seriously bad news for users or excellent news for them? Legions of people with 20:20 eyesight and no foresight for people working on higher resolution screens than themselves chose the seriously bad news option. I assume you will want to take the excellent news option. So the gospel of effective Web design says you need to add the following statement to the CSS style sheet:

```
p, ul, ol, li, h1, h2, h3, table, tr, td
{
font-family: "verdana", "arial", "switzerland"
font-size: small
}
```

Make sure your browser is set to View / Text Size / Medium. If the on-screen text is not right for you then select from the other font-size options: 'xx-small', 'x-small', 'medium', 'large', 'x-large' and 'xx-large'.

With other styles which are hierarchically related to this parent group of elements you can use the relative terms 'smaller' and 'larger'. So one of the Heart of Albion elements is:

```
#welcome
{
text-align: left;
color: black;
font-size: larger;
font-weight: bold
}
```

You may think there is no difference between this and the declaration:

font-size: large (N.B. 'large' not 'larger').

However, because the styles are related hierarchically, if I change the parent size from 'x-small' to, say, 'small', then the 'welcome' style will automatically change in proportion to the parent style if I specify it by the relative term 'larger'; whereas if I use the absolute term 'large' it will remain the same size if the parent size changes.

Font leading

CSS style sheets allow the font leading (space between lines) to be controlled. However unless there are exceptional reasons leave these undefined – Web browsers make a good job of defaulting to easily readable line spacing.

Controlling text lines

To make on-screen text easy to read there should be no more than about ten words on each line. However, unlike typesetting where the page designer directly controls how many characters make up a line, with Web pages the HTML code does not determine where the line breaks fall. This is determined by the user's browser and depends on:

- the screen resolution they are using (e.g. 800, 1024 or 1280)
- how they have selected View / Text Size in their browser (e.g. Largest; Large; Medium; Small; Smallest).

Beginners to Web site design find it very hard to accept that what looks good on their screen may look quite different on other people's screens. Even when they have accepted that things change dramatically, they then want to take control by forcing in line breaks with the <br> command. This is time-consuming and totally counter-productive because if the user goes to View/ Text Size and opts for larger font sizes then the <br> tags will create unwanted short lines.

There is a much simpler solution which really does solve the problem. Create a <table> (if you haven't already to create a navigation column) then use the 'width' attribute of the <td> tag. With Heart of Albion pages the main text appears in a table defined thus:

<td width="660px" valign="top" bgcolor="#efeadf">

Clearly you must define the width in pixels (numbers followed by 'px') rather than a percentage width as that would simply change with different screen resolutions and defeat the main purpose. The 'valign' ensures that the table appears at the top and I have also defined the background colour of the table here (although the colour could have been set in the CSS style sheet instead had I not wanted some table cells to have a different background colour).

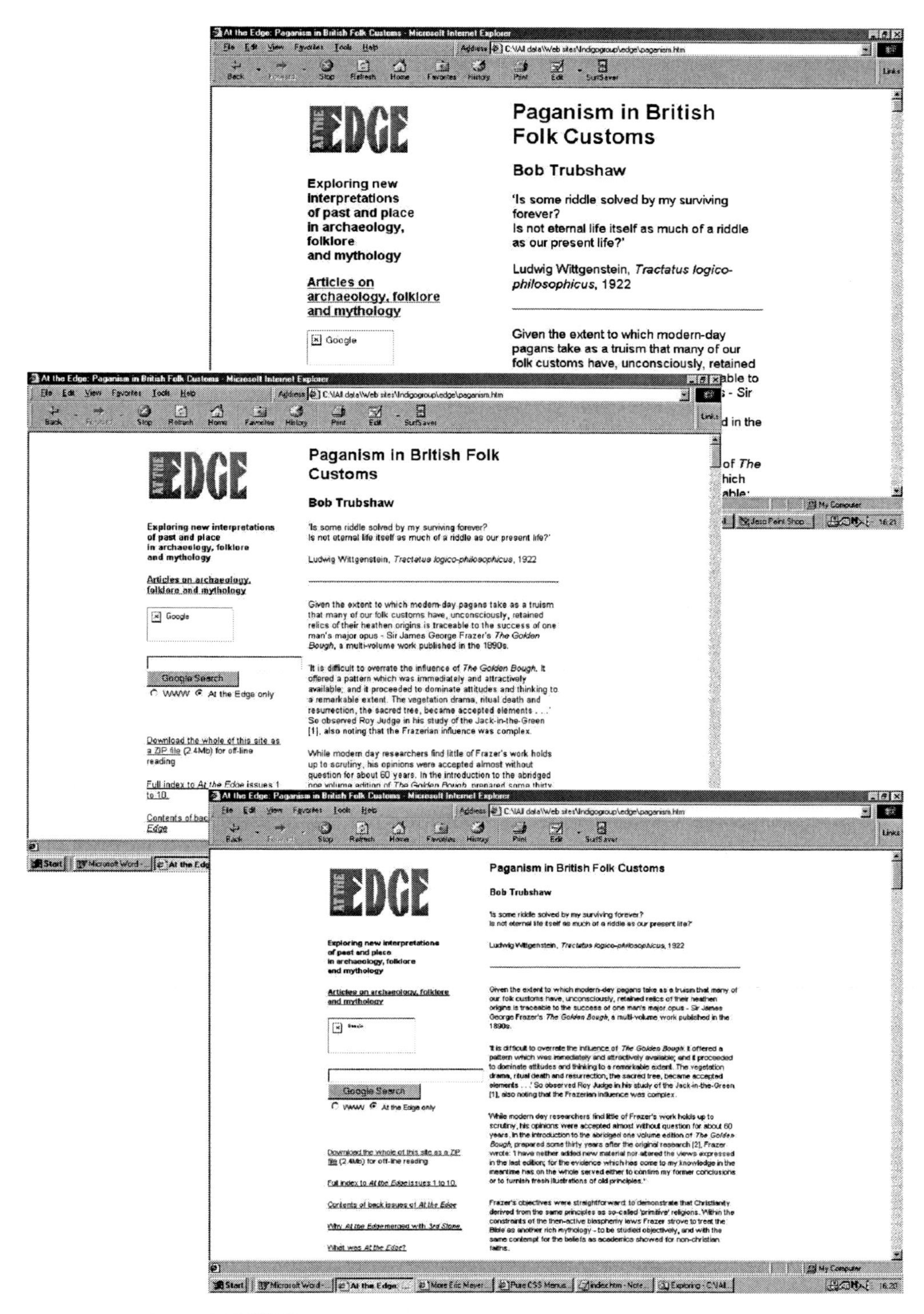

The same Web page with the Text Size set to 'Largest', 'Medium' and 'Smallest'.

I accept that this leaves plenty of blank screen on the right of screen set to 1280 pixels or more. But this is much better than giving users of such screens lines of text that are far too long to read.

Look at the code for any page of www.hoap.co.uk to see the <table> tag being used to create a red navigation column down the left of the screen and controlling the width of the main part of the page to 660 pixels. However, the <table> code is a little more complicated because it is also creating the black lines either side of the red column and creating narrow blank areas either side of the text to keep the words away from the black lines.

Unfortunately most introductory guides to creating Web pages miss out practical advice on controlling the length of text lines. This is very unfortunate because a wide variety of screen resolutions are now in use and keeping text lines to about ten words is a crucial to making a Web page easy to read. Even if you ignore most of the other advice in this chapter, please take on board the need to make your site work well with the different text sizes available in the browser and on different screen resolutions.

Nitty gritty aspects of HTML

There are some details of working with HTML that seem to get left out of tutorials. So here are some helpful thoughts.

.HTM or .HTML ?

Should the files be called 'filename.htm' or 'filename.html'? Both work equally well. The answer is to be consistent – either always call your files '.htm' or always '.html'. Mixing them up is a sure way to getting broken links. If your HTML authoring software creates .html file extensions by default (some do) then go with the flow rather than have to remember to delete the 'l'.

What should the home page be called?

Most servers are configured to default to:

index

default

main

home

with HTM, HTML, PHP or CGI extensions.

This means the Web address www.hoap.co.uk will automatically open www.hoap.co.uk/index.htm. If I had called the home page 'main.html', 'default.htm' or 'home.html' then typing in www.hoap.co.uk to an Internet browser would still open the home page.

Most people opt for index.htm or index.html as the name of the home page.

The only thing to watch out for is *not* to use more than one of the four file names (index, default, main and home) or to create both .htm and .html versions of any one of these file names (e.g. both index.htm and index.html) in the root directory of the Web site or CD-ROM as this will leave the server confused as to which is supposed to be the default.

Unless you are using relevant back-end software then you will not be using PHP or CGI file extensions.

Case-sensitive filenames

Working with Windows and Macs means that filenames are not case-sensitive. This means that <a href="filelinkedto.htm"> will find FILELINKEDTO.HTM, FileLinkedTo.htm and any other permutations. Likewise for files ending JPG or GIF or SWF, etc.

However your Web site is likely to be hosted on a server running Linux. And Linux is case-sensitive. In the land of Linux a file called Dragon.jpg is a different beast to dragon.jpg or dragon.JPG. Many people have carefully-tested their Web sites offline only to find masses of broken links when they go online. When they finally find out why, they then need to go through changing the case of many or all the filenames. All very tedious and liable to leave uncorrected errors.

There is one simple rule that avoids this nightmare. *Always* use only lowercase letters for filenames that will be used on the Web.

Spaces and non-alphanumeric characters in filenames

Linux also does not like spaces in filenames. And some of the symbols which Windows and Macs allow in filenames are not supported by Linux – although the hyphen and underscore characters are.

If you are tempted to call a file 'file name with spaces.htm' then you can either use 'filenamewithnospaces.htm' or 'file_name_with_underscores.htm'.

HTML tags – upper or lower case

The 'tags' used in HTML – such as <h1>, <img>, <a href>, <table> and the many others are *not* case sensitive. They work just as well if you type <H1>, <IMG>, <A REF> or <TABLE>, or a mismatch of cases. However it is easier to type only in lower case, it is slightly easier to read HTML code when it is consistently in lower case, and professional Web site designers (and the HTML authoring software they use) only use lower case HTML tags.

So all lower case HTML tags look cool whereas upper-case looks like you wrote the HTML code when Noah was a lad (and some of us were writing HTML before the Internet was flooded with Web sites…).

Semantic mark up

CSS allows the style of the text to be defined in a way that also relates to the 'function' of the content. This is known technically as 'semantic mark up'. It makes for easier updating of the CSS and should help to future proof your HTML as XML and XHTML begin to become more important.

Use <h1>, <h2>, <h3> wherever possible for headings and subheadings. Define the size and style of font using CSS.

Use <strong> and <em> *not* <b> and <i>. In the CSS style sheet define that you want <strong> to appear as bold and <em> to appear as italic.

Use <cite> when giving bibliographical sources and <abbr> when using a phrase that needs glossing. Both these tags can be used with the 'title' parameter that appears as a tool tip with many browsers when the cursor hovers over (this has already been discussed on page 180).

For example:

> <cite title="A.B. Smith 'A History of Anytown' (Bigcity UP 2003)">(Smith 2003)</cite>

Will appear simply as (Smith 2003) on screen but when the cursor hovers over the words 'A.B. Smith 'A History of Anytown' (Bigcity UP 2003)' will appear. Unfortunately with the 'title' parameter it is not possible to put the title of the book into italics.

Be sure to specify a font face and style for <cite> and <abbr> in the CSS style sheet.

Defining styles using <id> in CSS

Beginners to CSS are often confused by <p>, <div> and <span> especially when these are used to define styles with the 'id' parameter. If you want, say, authors' names to appear a particular way and have defined a style called '#author' in the CSS style sheet, should you call this style up with <p id="author"> or <div id="author"> or <span id="author">?

Bear in mind that each of these styles ends with the corresponding </p>, </div> and </span> tag. So if you want the style to automatically end at the next </p> break then it would be easiest to use <p id="author">; this still allows you to include <br> tags if necessary.

However more often you want the style to continue across <p> tags, as with the use of <span id="reviews"> in the Heart of Albion Web site. Because the <span> tag has no other function that to 'span' a section of text (unlike either <p> or <div> tags, which have other functions) then this is the simplest to use when you only want to define the text style and such like.

Span can be used inside the <a href> tag thus:

```
<a href="index.htm"><span id="navigation">home</span></a>
```

The <div> tag is something of a halfway house between <p> and <span> in that <div> styles run across <p> and </p> (but are less accommodating with <table>). Note that the <div> tag also allows the 'title' parameter which creates pop ups when the cursor hovers over the text (see page 180).

Horizontal rules

As with printed pages, a simple horizontal line can be effective at unobtrusively helping to structure pages. HTML provides the <hr> tag for this purpose. The design can be specified each time it is used e.g.:

```
<hr noshade align="center" width="70%" size ="2">
```

Much more usefully <hr> can be defined in the CSS style sheet. The Heart of Albion Web site defines horizontal rules thus:

```
hr
{
color: #F43400;
align: center;
width: 80%
}
```

**Avoid

 and <p><p>**

Internet browsers are capable of fixing 'bad' HTML. But different browsers – and different versions of the same browser! – fix bad HTML in different ways.

According to the rules of HTML
 (line return) and <p> (paragraph beak – equivalent to two line returns) should only be used 'solo'. So
<p> or

 or <p><p> are bad HTML (and 'ordinary' spaces and 'ordinary' line breaks only visible in the authoring software are ignored by HTML so

 is just as bad as

.

Such 'bad' HTML is interpreted differently by different browsers. Some will do the right thing and only use the first such tag; others will interpret the multiple tags as multiple line breaks.

This means when you see your site on different browsers you could be in for a nasty surprise. The only way to avoid such issues is to religiously check that you have not used multiple <br> and/or <p> tags without any 'content' in between.

But what happens when I really want a big space? Then use:

```
<p> <p>
```

This puts a 'non-breaking space' on the line in between; such spaces are not ignored by HTML so you will always get a double line return.

Importing from Word into HTML

If you have a substantial amount of text in Word and want to import it into HTML then this can be done quite simply.

1. Open the Word document
2. 'Save as' to create a duplicate copy
3. Use 'Find and replace' (or Ctrl+H) to replace **^p** with **^p
^p** (just type in these characters into the find and replace fields – the ^ character is shift+6).
4. Then use 'Find and replace' to find **^p
^p^p
^p** and replace with **^p<p>^p**.
5. Then 'Select all' (or Ctrl+A), copy (Ctrl+C) and paste into your HTML authoring software.

Depending on how disciplined you were about using single and double line returns in the Word document will depend on whether this has created any
<p> type duplications. Go through carefully checking that either <br> or <p> appear in the required places. Despite the need for accurate checking this is still much quicker than putting all the <p> and <br> breaks in by hand.

Bullet points and lists

HTML provides two basic types of 'bullet points' – so-called 'ordered lists' (which are numbered) with the tag <ol> and the so-called 'unordered lists' (which have bullets) with the <ul> tag. Both require the corresponding </ol> or </ul> tag at the end.

Such lists can be nested inside each other. The Web browser will automatically provide different styles of bullet points for up to about five levels of such nested lists. So an <ol> or <ul> can have one or more <ol> or <ul> lists nested inside.

Furthermore you can change <ol> to list with upper- or lower-case Roman numbers, or upper- or lower-case letters instead of the default Arabic numerals. These are selected by the tag <ol type="I"> (i.e. upper-case 'i' not lower-case 'L'), <ol type="i">, <ol type="a"> and <ol type="A"> respectively. If you want to insist on a list being numbered in Arabic numbers rather than just assuming that it will appear this way by default then use <ol type="1">.

So:

```
<ol type="i">
        <li>first list item
        <li>second list item
</ol>
```

will produce a list prefixed with the numbers i and ii.

The style of bullet used with the <ul> can also be specified. The options are <ul type="disc">, <ul type="circle"> or <ul type="square">.

E.g.:

```
<ul type="disc">
        <li>first list item
        <li>second list item
</ul>
```

Accents and other funny characters

As with word processing and DTP software it can be tricky incorporating accented characters and other 'funnies' that are not shown on the standard keyboard. However a vast number of such special characters are supported by HTML.

They appear as either an abbreviation (e.g.) or as a number (e.g.) – with the '&' and ';' characters 'topping and tailing' the abbreviation or number. Both   and   create a non-breaking space.

Not all special characters have an abbreviation, although all have a number. The number can be either decimal or (if you want to be decidedly obtuse) hexadecimal formats. However there are 'bugs' with some of the browsers, which interpret some of the abbreviations and the hexadecimal numbers incorrectly. Fortunately, at the time of writing, all the browsers interpret the decimal number codes correctly. In practice the more commonly used abbreviations – such as é (for 'é') or © (for '©') – are interpreted acceptably.

Note also that 'insert symbols' tools in FrontPage and Dreamweaver are also flawed – some characters produced this way may not show correctly with Mozilla or Opera browsers.

The answer to these problems is to put in the decimal code by hand. To find out which codes you need search the Web for "ISO characters chart" (including the double quotes). At the time of writing a useful link was at http://home.earthlink.net/~atomic_rom/iso.htm

Useful special characters include:

£ sign	£
©	©
Opening single quote	‘
Closing single quote	’
Opening double quote	“
Closing double quote	”

- If you need to show '<' (less than) or '>' (greater than) in HTML then you can only do this with < and > respectively as the characters '<' and '>' are always interpreted as HTML code.

If you are using Arachnophilia then the Keyboard Macros tool is very useful for setting up short cuts to frequently used special characters.

Hyphens, en-dashes, em-dashes and minus signs

We have already discussed hyphens, en-dashes and em-dashes in relation to books (see page 46). To reiterate: Hyphens are not dashes. An en-dash is shorter than an em-dash.

Re-read this sentence — at least 2–3 times — to see how hyphens, en-dashes and em-dashes are used. Note the hyphen in 're-read', the em-dashes to indicate a break in thought, and the en-dash to separate two numbers.

The HTML code for an en-dash is – and for an em-dash —

If you want a minus sign for mathematics then strictly you should use the code − rather than a hyphen as this lines up more neatly with the '+' sign.

Elipsis

The three dots that mark a break in a quotation ('… ') are tricky in HTML because a line break may be forced between three full stops. However if use the special character … instead of three dots then all will be well.

Enable people to email you

Every Web site should include the ability for people to email comments and suggestions to you. HTML includes the simple command:

<a href="mailto:you@yourdomain.com">you@yourdomain.com</a>

Although this works well enough, never use 'mailto:' anywhere on your Web site. Why? You will start received hundreds of 'spam' emails every day.

The way to get around this is to use the <form> tag. This requires a script provided by your Web site host, usually in a folder called 'cgi_bin' or something similar – check with your Web site host. To generate the HTML code correctly either search for an on-line tutorial to the <form> tag or adapt someone else's code (e.g. www.indigogroup.co.uk/foamycustard/fc001.htm).

Linking to non-HTML documents

Some file formats that are not in HTML format can be read by the more recent versions of Web browsers. These include PDF, Rich Text Format (RTF), Word DOC, Excel XLS and Powerpoint PPT.

The code is no different to that linking to an HTML document e.g.:

```
<a href="localhistory.doc">local history MS Word DOC</a>
```

The potential problem is that these file formats can be quite large. This is not usually a problem when reading the files offline but is a serious issue for both the person downloading them and for the person – presumably you – paying for the 'bandwidth' of the server (see next section for more discussions about bandwidth).

Large page sizes and bandwidth limits

Large file sizes have two implications. The obvious one is that they take longer for the reader to download. While you may be using broadband, many people are still using 56k modems. And even broadband is only as fast as the server supplying the pages and any bottlenecks on the Internet. Research reveals that pages under 32 Kbytes have a bail-out rate of seven to ten percent, whereas for those over 40 Kbytes the rate increases to between 25 and 30 percent.

The less obvious implication is that Web sites are hosted by companies who normally expect the total amount of files 'served up' each month to be less than 1 Gbyte (unless you are paying extra for a higher-bandwidth hosting arrangement) and will either impose rather excessive extra costs for exceeding the limit or simply take the site offline once the monthly quota has been reached, which is frankly a disaster.

Although 1 Gbyte each month may seem a lot when your site is made up of files which are individually under, say, 50 Kbytes remember that calling up one page will also call up all the associated graphics. So the total amount of files from a heavily illustrated page could be over 100 Kbytes. Even if the viewer has clicked their 'back' button and gone elsewhere before all this has completely downloaded (a very probable scenario!), the server will have clocked up that it has provided these pages.

This can become a real issue if you have long text-rich pages which contain lots of words commonly searched for on the Web. At one time I was hosting a page for someone interested in dialect. He had produced a long list of dialect terms for everyday words which came to about 40 Kbytes of HTML. Overall it was only of interest to people with fairly specialist interests in dialect. The problem was that this long list of 'everyday' words was frequently found by search engines, presumably by people who had little or no interest in dialect. The page was getting several hits an hour, so the bandwidth was around 200 Mbytes per month – one-fifth of the total available for the whole hosting package. If there had been five such pages then the whole of the available bandwidth would have been used up. Had the list been produced as a Word DOC then it would have been at least 60 Kbytes for the same amount of text, or 300 Mbytes per month for the same number of 'hits'.

The answer is to make sure that any one page together with all its associated images comes to no more than 50 Kbytes in total, and ideally no more than 30 Kbytes. If necessary split up long and/or heavily illustrated pages. This makes for both speedier downloading for the viewer and optimum use of your bandwidth.

Indeed once you have more than about 100 Kbytes of different images linked to the same page your visitors may find that some of the images are replaced by the little red cross that denotes a broken link. This is not because the link is broken but simply because the files were taking so long to download that the browser 'timed out' and assumed, incorrectly, there was a broken link. You may not be aware of such problems, especially if you are using broadband, so the best way of avoiding such serious hiccups is to make sure that a page together with all its images never totals more than about 100 Kbytes. If necessary break the page down and/or make the images into 'thumbnails' which link to larger versions.

Use the <img> tag effectively

Plonking an image on an HTML page can be done with <img src="filename.jpg">.

But I hope readers of this book will want to do more than just plonk their images. The proper way of putting an image on a page is:

```
<img src="filename.jpg" height="200" width="150" hspace="5"
vspace="5" alt="description">
```

The <height> and <width> attributes 'warn' the browser how big the picture will be. This is important for online Web sites and helpful for CD-ROMs.

<hspace> and <vspace> define how many pixels are to left between the image and any text (or other images).

The text associated with the <alt> parameter appears when the cursor hovers over the image or if the link to image is shown as broken. It is also used by software which helps the visually handicapped to access Web sites and provides search engines with something to index. All-in-all the <alt> parameter is very useful.

Only use <hspace> and <vspace> is you need to define a space around the image – there is no point in using hspace="0" for instance. However the <height>, <width> and <alt> parameters should *always* be used for Web sites and CD-ROMs.

If you are using Arachnophilia then the 'NewImg' tool automatically works out the <height> and <width> and provides an <alt> tag ready to be completed.

Thumbnails linked to larger images

If a large image is necessary – as is often the case with maps – then you need to create a link from a 'thumbnail'. The relevant HTML code will look like this:

```
<a href="page_with_bigger_image.htm"><img
src="thumbnail_image.jpg" width="150" height="210" border="0"
alt="description of image"></a>
```

The border="0" parameter prevents a coloured line from appearing around images which are hyperlinks.

If you do remove the border from images which are hyperlinked then be sure to use the <alt> parameter. The words provided for the <alt> parameter will appear on screen when the cursor hovers over the image. As a minimum it should say 'Click for a larger version of this image' although a more informative text would be preferable.

Writing HTML for CD-ROMs

In general using HTML to write CD-ROMs is exactly the same as using HTML for Web sites. There are just a few differences to watch out for.

<frame> tag

Whereas the <frame> tag creates serious problems when used online (see page 176), with CD-ROMs there are no drawbacks so this is an excellent way to keep navigation menus on screen at all times.

file sizes

Neither are there are limitations to file sizes. This means substantial sound and animation files can be incorporated and JPGs do not need to be heavily compressed.

large pictures

However with pages with lots of images I would recommend keeping the sizes down to about 300 pixels maximum width or height and linking these to a separate page with a larger versions of one image, together with a suitably detailed caption (even if this caption repeats information on the page with lots of smaller pictures).

generating content from a database using templates

The 'classic' Web site or CD-ROM is made up from lots of different pages all individually written. These are known as 'static' Web sites. In contrast e-commerce sites (such as Amazon) and news portals (such as www.bbc.co.uk) generate all their pages 'dynamically' by using templates which call up the required content from a database. Such dynamically-generated HTML is known as DHTML.

If you have an exceptionally large online Web site then it would be appropriate to write the code to dynamically generate pages. If you are experienced with Dreamweaver then this software supports DHTML. However Dreamweaver makes this tricky task even more difficult because of the unfriendly interface. Much easier to use for DHTML but still very powerful is EasyGen 2 (www.easygen.com) which currently costs £80. However setting up DMHTL Web sites is well beyond the scope of this book.

With CD-ROMs dynamically generated pages are difficult because DHTML means installing a suitable 'back end' program to create the pages. However there is an interesting half-way house that could be helpful for writing CD-ROMs. Ultimately the CD-ROM is purely a static site – but the pages are not individually crafted but generated from a database using templates. This approach would be especially interesting if the information you want to include in the CD-ROM is already in one or more databases.

If you know anyone with a good knowledge of JavaScript then they should be able to devise a template that creates static Web pages from a database. The only program I have come across (but not used) which does this task is WebMerge (www.fourthworld.com/products/webmerge/).

Generating static pages from a database is fairly future-proof because this readily allows for greater use of XML and XHTML. However I have to be honest and admit that this is not an approach to creating CD-ROMs that I have used yet – my experience is only with 'handcrafted' HTML pages.

searching CD-ROMs

One disadvantage of CD-ROMs is that they cannot be searched in the way people are accustomed to use Web search engines. However there is a JavaScript program which is easy to use to create searchable CD-ROMs. It is called 'SiteSearch Indexer' and can be downloaded from a number of sites – just run a Web search on the exact name of the program. The current version (3.0) costs $50 but can be used for free in trial mode (the trial mode is limited to indexing a maximum of 25 pages).

SiteSearch indexes HTML, PDF, Word DOC and Rich Text Format (RTF) documents and the search facility runs on PCs and Macs. It is easy to set up with only a basic knowledge of HTML; there are plenty of tutorials with the software and more online. The final search function is very straightforward for users.

auto run

Anyone with limited knowledge of computers knows how to 'kick start' a CD-ROM which does not automatically run when it is put in the drive. As you are competent enough with computers to write HTML for CD-ROMs you probably fall into this category. If you use a Mac you have no choice. However the vast majority of PC users do not have this basic knowledge. CD-ROMs must auto run otherwise you will get endless complaints that 'it doesn't work'.

Creating CD-ROMs which auto run is easy. You need two files in the root directory of the CD-ROM. These can be downloaded from www.hoap.co.uk/autorun.htm

One is called autorunexe.exe and the other autorun.inf. *Do not change these file names!* As downloaded they will automatically run a file called index.htm. Make sure there is an HTML file called index.htm (N.B. *not* index.htm**l**) in the root directory alongside the two autorun files. When you burn these onto a CD-ROM then it should automatically run index.htm with both Windows 9x and Windows XP operating systems.

If you really cannot live with the index.htm file name then open the autoexec.ini file in a simple text editor such as Notepad and change the file name (twice). Do not change anything else.

keeping things simple for Mac users

Mac users will need to find the index.htm file to be able to run the CD-ROM. If the root directory contains lots of other files they will be confused about which one to click on. Make life easier for them by including only three files in the root directory – index.htm and the two auto run files.

The rest of the content should be tucked away inside one or more folders (directories).

Getting clever with images

Basic advice about preparing images for publication on Web sites and CD-ROMs was included in Chapter 3. This section is about more sophisticated use of images in electronic publications and assumes you already have a basic understanding of file formats, optimising the compression of images, and the other topics discussed in Chapter 3.

Making things change

Animated GIFs

The GIF file format can be used to sequence a series of images and is commonly used to created simple animations. Most of the annoying banner adverts that use rapid movements to draw attention to themselves are animated GIFs. Animated GIFs are also encountered on too many amateurs' home pages where they annoyingly blink away for no good reason. Indeed the phrase 'animated GIF' is frequently linked to the word 'annoying'.

Little icons flickering in your peripheral vision while you are trying to read text is seriously annoying. 'Gratuitous' use of animated GIFs to make a page look 'busy' is always bad design. However when simple animation is essential to illustrate an idea then animated GIFs are probably one of the easiest options.

Animated GIFs are created using software specific for the purpose. Paint Shop Pro comes with a standalone program called 'Animation Shop' which is easy enough to learn to use.

Mouse overs

However does the animation really need to change all the time? Wouldn't it better if if 'came to life' only when the viewer brought their cursor over the image? If necessary the caption to the image could prompt the user to move their mouse, or in some instances it could come as a 'nice surprise' – for example, if the 'next' link changes into a new image before it is clicked.

If you think a mouse over will be helpful then this are accomplished with the following HTML:

```
<A HREF="linkedpage.htm"
onMouseOver="document.pic1.src='image2.jpg'"
onMouseOut="document.pic1.src='image1.jpg'">

<IMG SRC="image1.jpg" BORDER=0 NAME="pic1"></a>
```

Change 'image1.jpg' and 'image2.jpg' to the actual filenames of your images, and change 'linkedpage.htm' to the name of the hyperlinked file. If you use this code more than once on the same page then change 'document.pic1.src' to 'document.pic2.src' etc.

Again use such effects only if they are necessary, never simply to distract the user or make you seem 'clever'. Remember – clever Web site and CD-ROM design never draws attention to itself, it just works smoothly and unobtrusively. Putting your ideas across smoothly and effectively takes real skill; achieving this is much more 'clever' than scattering a toy box of effects on the screen.

Getting Flash

If you need to provide more complex animation than can be provided with animated GIFs or mouse overs then you need to enter the world of Flash.

Formally known as Macromedia Shockwave Flash, this file format (.SWF) was invented in the late 1990s to provide a way of including animations based on text and vector graphics. Quite small files could include a lot of animation and the format took off fast among trendy Web designers.

'Hot spots' in the images could be defined as hyperlinks and there was sufficient coding available that simple computer games could be designed to run in Flash. A huge number of such Flash animations were created.

Flash also allows the use of pixel-based graphics (e.g. digital photographs) and sound. Recent versions of the file format also support video clips. However photographs, sound and video rapidly make the Flash file rather large. Large files mean long downloads and the all-too familiar 'Please wait' messages annoying Web users the world over.

Large Flash file sizes – unless exceptionally large – are not a problem with CD-ROMs. This means that Flash is a useful way of creating 'slide shows' that automatically change to the next photograph, for example to act as a sample of the contents.

You could create an entire CD-ROM using Flash, but this would make it more difficult to update. The better option is to use HTML for text-rich areas and use Flash for the more 'interactive' aspects. However if you like the idea of a CD-ROM that does not run inside Internet browser software then Macromedia Flash and Swish Studio both can create Flash files which run independently of any other programs. If you take this route be sure to create plenty of navigation controls, especially an equivalent to the 'back' button on every page. You will not be able to include 'external' links to other peoples' Web sites however.

At the time of writing an old version of Macromedia Flash is available for £130, although the current version is £450. Apart from the intimidating price, Macromedia Flash is also tricky to learn to use. However do not let any of this put you off creating Flash-format files. A remarkably easy to use but powerful program called SwishStudio also creates Flash-format files and is available online for $50; it also has a big brother called SwishStudio Max for $100 which is even more powerful. SwishStudio is remarkably good value and so easy to use you risk becoming addicted to creating Flash animations.

Go to www.swishzone.com for more details. If you want to see a Web site which makes good use of Swish then go to www.pansoftstudios.co.uk/ecws.htm

The trick with Flash files is to avoid making the viewer wait for the full file to download before they start to see something interesting. Provide a simple image or small vector animation to start things off, preferably with a reasonable amount of text to keep the viewer reading while the rest of the file is downloading.

Never start a Web site with a lengthy Flash intro. Let's put that another way – only start a Web site with a lengthy Flash intro if you want between 80 to 90 percent of your visitors to click their 'back' buttons out of boredom or frustration.

Family trees on Web sites and CD-ROMs

A tricky problem is shared by all family history Web sites and CD-ROMs: how to present family trees.

Scanning in a hand-written or printed version of the family tree simply generates a vast GIF file (JPG format files would be even larger unless compressed to the extent that the text is no longer readable). This is not usually an option.

If your family history data is stored in GEDCOM format then various GEDCOM-to-HTML conversion programs are available online, although these seem to have limited abilities for creating family trees.

Painstaking use of the <table> tag can create family trees using only HTML, but providing the vertical lines to denote offspring makes this decidedly hard work. The slightest change later on can mean earlier work has to be redone. Frankly most people would regard this as vastly too frustrating and time-consuming.

Flash allows text and lines to be readily created and accurately located. The nature of the file format allows zoom functions (for example, to create 'overviews' of the tree, albeit with the text too small to be read) and for scrolling in all four directions. Just to add an element of real sophistication, you can include hyperlinks from one part of the tree to either another part of the Flash animation or to 'supporting' HTML pages. Clearly this requires considerable effort and the bigger the family tree the longer it will take. But the resulting tree is easy to view on screen and not too tricky to update.

However there is an easier way to make a detailed family tree available on-line. Create a new document in your DTP or word processor software. Change the page size to A3 (or even bigger with 'custom page size' – for example A2 is 420 by 594 mm). Type out the family tree (with Word use the Insert / Text Box tool to help lay out text easily) and use the 'draw' tools in the software for the necessary lines. Then create a PDF file (remembering to select the same page size as used for the document). This PDF file will be reasonably compact (about 350Kbytes for an A2 document) and can easily be incorporated into a Web site (see page 192).

Testing, testing, testing

Once you have a Web site design that works reasonably well and a good idea of how different sections and pages will link together, do not get carried away and start putting in all the content. Now is the time to do some serious testing.

Just because at the time of writing most people use Internet Explorer does not mean you can ignore other browsers. Microsoft seems unlikely to develop IE very fast in the next few years, allowing rival browsers a chance to offer improvements (and IE leaves plenty of scope for improvement). Get your hands on recent versions of Mozilla and Opera browsers either from magazine cover discs or by downloading.

Change your Screen Resolution to 800, 1024 and 1280. In Windows this is done by going to Start / Settings / Control Panel / Display / Settings then sliding the slider to the pre-set options and clicking 'OK' then 'OK' again.

At each resolution try different options for View / Text Size in Internet Explorer.

Also look at your site with the three different browsers.

Burn a copy of your site on CD-ROM and take it along to anyone you know who uses a Mac and test it out there.

Is the line length staying under about ten words per line? Are any images or sections of text moving about too much? What other problems can you see?

Keep detailed notes of any problems. When you have completed such testing then plan the most effective way of overcoming them (and effective does not mean the least time consuming!). Then test again!

Testing navigation

Because you know your own Web site all too well you may well be 'blind' to the problems quirky navigation causes visitors. Step back from what you have created and put yourself in the mental situation of someone who has never visited the site before. Which parts of the site would you not easily find?

Even better, watch someone else try to use your site navigation (it does not matter if all the content has been added yet, so long as there are not too many 'broken links'). Better still, ask several people to test out the site navigation.

Resist every temptation to chip in with helpful advice (unless they are totally stuck – and that reveals serious problems with your navigation design). Never argue with feedback. Simply accept that *all* the problems that arise are caused by your site design, and never put the blame on the user. After all, in the real wired world you cannot choose who visits your site, still less help them if they get stuck.

Keep adequate notes of any problems, major or minor, and afterwards decide what is the most effective way to minimise or eliminate the problems. Yes, I said the most effective, not the quickest or the one that has least impact on the design.

Much as you may get carried away adding content to a new site, bear in mind that if you leave such testing to late in the development of the Web site or CD-ROM you may have to make extensive and time-consuming changes.

Only when you have tested the design and navigation with several users, and made any necessary changes, then tested again with other users should you think about putting together all the content.

Check spelling and proof read

Spelling and grammatical mistakes quickly reduce the credibility of the content. Make sure all content is spell-checked *before* it is pasted into the HTML pages. This does not stop changes and errors creeping in later, but should minimise the risk of unnoticed mistakes being perpetuated.

Once most of the content of the site of CD-ROM is in place and only a few last tweaks are needed then ask someone who is a good proof reader if they will go through the whole thing. You may need to provide them with a 'site map' to enable to check whether they have found all the pages.

The problem with proof reading Web sites and CD-ROMs is how to notify mistakes without doing masses of print outs. Ask the proof reader to copy and paste two things into an email or Word DOC:

1. The filename of the HTML page (if you are not using <frame> the this will appear in the browser's Address window; if you are using <frame> then you will have to ask the proof reader to identify the file in other ways – it may even be worth creating a version without <frame> just to assist the proof reading).

2. Copy the sentence or paragraph *with the problem uncorrected.* They should then indicate the correction as briefly as possible.

This second step will enable you to copy and paste the problem into the Find function of your HTML editor, making it easy to find the offending sentence.

Otherwise you may find proof readers who less-than-helpfully say 'the word "the" is spelt wrong' leaving you to find out where 'the' that is not a 'the' is in the text.

Apart from all the usual issues of spelling, grammar and consistency of abbreviations, dates and capitalisation that would apply to print publications (see pages 50 to 52) with electronic publications there are a few specific issues to watch out for. Be consistent with referring to either the 'Web', or 'web', or 'World Wide Wide' or 'WWW' Likewise decide whether you are going to refer to the 'Internet', 'InterNet' or even the 'internet'? Will you mention 'emails', 'e-mails' or 'E-mails'?

While the jury is still out, some sort of consensus is emerging. The 'Internet' (capitalised) is used to refer collectively to the World Wide Web, emails and the Usenet. The 'Web' (capitalised) is used to refer to the World Wide Web (i.e. pages based on HTML and viewed using a Web browser). In contrast 'email' is not capitalised, nor is it hyphenated.

Check <title> tags

Most Web sites and CD-ROMs have at least a few pages where the <title> tag is wrong. It is one of the easiest things to miss when checking. So open up every HTML page. Scan each page.

Is it quickly obvious what the topic(s) are? If not perhaps some more subheadings are needed.

Does the <title> tag accurately summarise the topic(s)? If not change the <title>.

Always create useful page titles, never quirky ones. Remember that visitors may enter your site other than through your home page. Search engines and portals may list a page from your site only by its title. Page titles are used in browser history lists, so make them meaningful and unique to one page.

Check broken links

If there are any broken links then the proof reader may pick up at least some. However they are unlikely to find them all. Checking every link is essential, especially for CD-ROMs where there is no way of retrospectively modifying the files.

Checking links by hand is very tedious and inevitably a few will be missed. However Dreamweaver has an excellent tool for automatically checking links, although predictably the user interface is far from helpful. If you can't afford a copy of Dreamweaver, try to make friends with someone who has. Send them a copy of your Web site on CD-ROM, or the CD-ROM you plan to publish, and ask them to give you a print out of the report of broken links.

No 'under construction'

Messages and icons which say 'under construction' say a lot about the authors of the Web sites where they are encountered. What is says is not repeatable in mixed company. If you want people to think you are one of this bunch of utter twerps then by all means include 'under construction' messages on your Web site (I hope you aren't so totally daft as to even think about including them on a CD-ROM...).

No visitor wants know about what you intended to do but have now probably forgotten all about. Simply create a complete-looking site, even if you know that more is planned for the future. As and when you are able to update and extend the site simply do so (and perhaps add a page which provides details of the updates if these are not immediately obvious from the navigation menu).

Testing is the key to good Web sites and CD-ROMs

The Web is awash with quirky and badly designed sites. Rather too many CD-ROMs are produced without the necessary attention to how the users will navigate the contents. Almost always the problems would have been spotted if the designers had done some testing with representative users.

Never think of testing as some sort of 'optional extra' – it is key to producing professional Web sites. It is even more essential for CD-ROMs where there is no chance of updating the content after copies have been sold.

Packaging and manufacturing CD-ROMS

Jewel case, DVD case or white card box?

So you think CD-ROMs always come in brittle, clear polystyrene cases measuring 140 x 124 mm and only DVDs come in tougher, black polypropylene cases measuring 190 x 135 mm? Think again. So-called 'DVD cases' are better for packaging CD-ROMs than the brittle so-called 'jewel cases' associated with CD-ROMs. This for three reasons:

1. The DVD cases do not easily break in transit or when being handled.

2. They look more like a book and so are more suited to being sold alongside books

3. Most importantly, they offer a bigger area for graphics and text.

While you can get a feel for a book by flicking through or even reading a few pages, you have no such options with CD-ROMs. You can only judge a CD-ROM by its cover. The more space you have on the cover the better!

However do make sure that both the front and back clearly show that it is a CD-ROM otherwise people will understandably wonder if it is a DVD.

Another option, although adding to the cost, is to package the CD-ROM in a clear jewel case but to package this in a much larger white cardboard box, then wrap the box with a colour sleeve. This is of course the way used by manufacturers of software programs and computer games. I have used this technique once when I wanted to sell a CD-ROM together with a printed guide book. Learn from my mistake and choose a box which can be wrapped with an A3 sheet of paper (allowing for a small overlap) – this means the width and the height of the box should total no more than 200 mm as the maximum length of a sleeve printed on A3 paper is 420 mm.

Produce the colour sleeves on an A3 inkjet printer or by digital photocopying on an A3 colour printer. Budget about £1 per sleeve at current ink jet and colour copying costs; on top of this there is the cost of a suitable box and the CD-ROM. These extra costs mean that the 'white box' option is not the cheapest option, but it does provide the maximum impact in shops. Remember to include a strong design on both sides of the sleeve (as well as the front and back) in case it is displayed on shelves sideways on.

Designing the cover

The cover of a CD-ROM – whether it fits a jewel case or a DVD case – needs to work hard. It needs to grab attention in a shop. It must give a clear impression that the contents are well-produced – an amateurish-looking cover will seriously damage sales. There must be a clear indication of what the CD-ROM contains. There must be 'technical stuff' about which types of computer it runs on and how to start it (see below). Yet all this must be done without the cover looking excessively cluttered. Definitely a job for a professional designer – but even then you must brief them with suitable snippets of text and a selection of eye-catching photographs.

One option is to include screen grabs on the back cover, although these will usually be reproduced too small to do more than give the most tentative impression of the look and feel of the content.

Back cover text needs to be short and snappy. Heart of Albion's *Interactive Gargoyles and Grotesque Carvings of Leicestershire and Rutland* CD-ROM sells itself thus:

> On this CD-ROM are photographs of 280 carvings of gargoyles, green men, tongue pokers, dragons and much, much more.
>
> Includes introductory essays, indexes and bibliography

The *Sepulchral Effigies of Leicestershire and Rutland* CD-ROM is equally concise:

> This CD-ROM contains detailed information about all the sepulchral effigies in the counties of Leicestershire and Rutland.
>
> A total of 177 effigies in 85 different churches and private chapels are described and illustrated with 518 photographs.

Despite the auto run facility, always provide written instructions of how to run the CD-ROM manually. Assuming you are not creating an insert for inside the DVD case then this must be on the back cover; do not put such instructions on the CD-ROM label itself as this will be inside the drive when needed. Here is an example of suitable wording:

> On most Windows PCs this CD-ROM will auto-run. If this does not happen then select 'Start' then 'Run' then D://index.htm and press 'Enter'.
>
> On Macs select the CD-ROM drive and double-click 'index.htm'

Spine design

Make sure the spine design looks effective – DVD cases will be slipped in alongside books in bookshops.

Artwork format

Designs for sleeves are best produced as 600 dpi TIFF files, although I suspect most manufacturers can also work with PDF files.

Making cases pilfer-proof

Jewel cases and DVD cases are not pilfer-proof. If your supplier cannot package them with proper tamper-proof sticky tape then simply tear neat strips of clear adhesive tape and apply these to the opening edge of the case.

Designing the CD-ROM label

In contrast to the case itself, the 'label' on the CD-ROM itself can be straightforward. Include the title of the CD-ROM, the ISBN, a copyright declaration, and an address for the publisher. Add the publisher's logo and maybe a couple of small images from the content. Prepare as a 300 dpi TIFF file and double-check that it prints accurately into the available area of a CD-ROM (the clear area in the middle is surprisingly intrusive!).

The label could be simply black only, but the additional costs for colour are usually small.

Manufacturing CD-ROMs

With a decent inkjet printer and a supply of the suitable-shaped sticky-backed labels for CD-ROMs, together with blank CD-ROMs and empty DVD cases (available from all the leading office supply companies) you can easily 'home brew' your CD-ROMs.

There are three problems:

1. The results always look 'home brewed' – seriously bad news if you intend selling in shops.

2. It takes ages to produce more than a few copies.

3. It costs almost as much as buying in CD-ROMs professionally produced.

By all means use this route for 'prototypes'. Indeed the last thing you want to do is pay for a batch of CD-ROMs to be made and then find there are errors.

However once all the bugs have been ironed out then send off the artwork to a company specialising in producing CD-ROMs (they will probably also be producing audio CDs too). They have the equipment to print direct onto the CD-ROM rather than using the amateurish sticky labels. They will also use more cost-effective ways of printing the cover inserts. And, above all, it is all done for you!

For a batch of 50 CD-ROMs in DVD cases with colour 'labels' and colour cover inserts currently expect to pay about £3 plus VAT and carriage; CD-ROMs in jewel cases are slightly cheaper. The company I have found easiest to work with is:

dbMasters
9 Waterside Close
Faversham Reach
Upper Brents
Faversham
Kent
ME13 7AU

telephone: 01795 597755
fax: 01795 597766
email: info@dbmasters.co.uk

Send them one CD-ROM which is an exact master of what you want replicated. Send a second CD-ROM with the artwork for the label and cover (as 300 or 600 dpi TIFF files).

Promoting CD-ROMS

Promoting CD-ROMs is mostly like promoting books (see Chapter 8). A key part of the promotion will be sending out review copies. Make sure the accompanying press release gives a good indication of the contents – do not expect all reviewers to have the time or inclination to explore the CD-ROM in any depth.

You may well get about the same amount of publicity in local papers, specialist magazines and Web sites as you would for a paper-based publication. However sales are likely to be much less spectacular. There is a rule of thumb with says you will sell one-tenth the number of CD-ROMs that you would a book of similar scope and price. So if a guide book to some aspect of your county's history might sell 500 copies, be happy if you sell more than 50 copies of the CD-ROM.

Clearly CD-ROMs which appeal to large numbers of tourists are going to better than those about obscure topics – but that is equally true of books.

If you have taken out an ISBN number for the CD-ROM (see page 122) then you will need to send off six copies to the Legal Deposit Office and A.T. Smail, just the same as for a book (see page 229). Remember to send Advance Information sheets to Neilsen BookData and BDS (see page 217), ideally three months before publication date.

Be sure to create a simple Web site promoting your CD-ROM, with clear information about how to obtain it and how to email for further information. If the CD-ROM is written in HTML or Flash then you may be able to include part of it as a 'sample'. However be sure not to leave broken links – replace pages not available online with a page simply stating 'This information not available in this sample version'.

Contact all local bookshops and other retail outlets in the same way as if you were promoting a book (see page 243). However some bookshop managers will flatly refuse to consider stocking something which is not printed on paper. If the CD-ROM is likely to appeal to a wide range of visitors, and is attractively presented, then you may get useful sales in tourist information centres and museums.

Licensing CD-ROMs

A novel opportunity may arise for selling CD-ROMs: licensing copies for use in relevant public and academic libraries, especially ones that operate computer networks. Telephone to find out who you need to speak to. Be prepared to send a copy of the CD-ROM on approval.

How much you charge for licensing the use of CD-ROM is typically based on how many individual computers there are on the network (or, more pedantically, how many computers will be authorised to access your CD-ROM). A good basis for negotiation is to work out what your net profit is on each copy of the CD-ROM you sell (i.e. retail price less trade discount less the cost of manufacturing the CD-ROM and its case). For example, if you are selling the CD-ROM for, say £12, and your trade discount is 33% you would invoice £8 per copy. If manufacture costs are £3 then the net profit is £5. If the library has 50 computers then offer to licence the CD-ROM for 50 x £5 (i.e. £250); be prepared to negotiate if there are vast numbers of users.

Usually licenses are for an agreed period of time – say 3 or 5 years. With local history material such time limits may not be so useful. Instead you may usefully plan to produce an updated version in 3 to 5 years and licence the upgrade (probably for about half the original license fee).

Clearly such licenses can have a major impact on the income from specialist CD-ROMs. Usually such licence fees are split such that the publisher keeps half the total and the other half is split between the author(s) and illustrators(s); see page 210 for more discussions on planning for allocating royalties.

Most computer network managers will copy the contents of the CD-ROM onto their hard-drive servers and then use software which limits the numbers of users according to the terms of the license.

Promoting Web sites

In contrast to books and CD-ROMs the promotion of Web sites is quite different. The best way to promote a new or significantly revised Web site is to email anyone and everyone who you think might be interested. State the URL (Web site address) clearly – and double-check that you've not made a typing mistake! Include a 'tempter' – some snippet of information that you think will interest the recipients and make them want to visit the Web site – rather than just a bland 'Please visit my Web site'. Do not include so much information that no one bothers to read to the end or, if they do, feel they have read so much they do not need to visit the Web site for more information.

To ensure you have a good list of people to email I suggest you keep a file or database of such contacts. Make sure to include anyone who runs a related Web site which contains lots of relevant links.

If it is a new Web site then submit to the main search engines; at the time of writing these are Google, MSN and Alta Vista. There are links from their main pages for submitting URLs. Unless your home page has plenty of links to most of the pages to the rest of the site then create a comprehensive site map page (see page 179) and submit the filename of this page instead.

All the main search engines are fairly efficient about finding new sites and checking established sites for changes – most seem to work to a two to four week cycle of checks.

Other people may link to your Web site from their Web sites – make sure there is a clear way of contacting you by email (see page 192). Quite understandably they may expect a reciprocal link so you may want to include a special page which includes such links (and probably other useful links as well).

In addition to promoting by email you can create a press release (see page 223) and send to relevant specialist paper-based publications.

Web sites usually receive few visitors for the first few weeks or months but if there is a topic of interest to other people then you will receive a steady flow of 'hits' via search engines. If other sites, especially heavily-visited ones, create a link to your site then you can expect plenty of on-line visitors.

Legal aspects of Web sites and CD-ROMS

In addition to the legal matters outlined in Chapter 2, there are some issues which are specific to Web sites and CD-ROMs, or at least more likely to arise with electronic publications than books and magazines.

Enforcing copyright and moral rights etc

Rather than have masses of 'small print' relating to copyright, moral rights, etc on every page of a Web site or CD-ROM it is better to have a link marked 'copyright' in the navigation menu of every page. This link can call up a page which includes all the necessary declarations relating to copyright, moral rights and terms of licensing CD-ROMs. Note that moral rights need to be asserted using the same simple statement that would appear in the prelim pages of printed publications.

Heart of Albion CD-ROMs include the following words:

> © All text, photographs and drawings on this CD-ROM copyright R.N. Trubshaw 2004.
>
> The moral rights of the author have been asserted.
>
> All rights reserved. This software and the information contained therein may not be reproduced in whole or in part in any manner whatsoever without prior written permission, except for those pages containing the following statement:
>
> 'No unauthorised copying or reproduction except if all following conditions apply:
> a: Copy is complete (including this copyright statement).
> b: No changes are made.
> c: No charge is made.'
>
> By accessing the information on this CD-ROM the user agrees to the following conditions:
>
> 1. The right to use a single copy on a single computer. [Users should apply to Heart of Albion Press for terms of use on networked computers.]
>
> 2. A single back-up copy may be made solely for back-up purposes. The back-up copy must be complete (including all copyright information).
>
> 3. No additional copies of the information, in part or in whole, can be made in any media without written permission from Heart of Albion Press.
>
> 4. Transfer of the software requires prior written notification to Heart of Albion Press.
>
> 5. **Under no circumstances can the software be transferred, assigned, leased, sold or otherwise disposed of on a temporary basis.**
>
> 6. Heart of Albion Press guarantees the media on which the software is supplied to be free of defects in material and workmanship, under normal use, for ninety days from date of supply. In the event of defects Heart of Albion Press will replace any defective products which are returned and shown to be defective.

7. All other warranties, express or implied, are excluded. Heart of Albion Press shall not be liable for any direct, indirect, consequential or incidental damages arising from the use or inability to use the software.

Agreeing your rights

While books and Web sites are typically the work of an individual or a small number of people, with CD-ROMs the sheer amount of work, together with the wide variety of skills needed, means that they are typically the work of a group of people. Furthermore, CD-ROMs (unlike Web sites) are usually sold, which means there is – potentially at least – a profit to be shared among those who have rights in the content.

And that could be a great many people. Everyone who writes a section of text will own the copyright in their contribution. Everyone who makes a photograph or video clip available will own the copyright in their image or clip. Anyone who composes music or sound effects will likewise own the relevant copyright. The people who perform the music will have rights too. The person(s) who design the appearance of the pages will own the relevant copyright. Anyone who writes the HTML or Javascript coding, or prepares Flash animations will be the owners of the copyright for this part of the content. Add to this the person who designs the cover and so on and so on – the list of copyright owners soon grows rapidly.

If the CD-ROM is being sold then all these people have a right to be paid for their contributions. However the person or persons who had the overall ideas for what to do will *not* own any copyright unless they created the work as well – there is no copyright in ideas only in their 'execution'. Coming up with good ideas but not doing the work to bring them into existence means you have no legal claim on any profits!

While everyone may understand what is what initially, the very nature of group projects is that everything gets increasingly blurred over time. People make various assumptions, or misunderstand verbal agreements. At some time it is inevitable that people fall out. At this stage a key contributor could legitimately withhold the rights to publish their contribution.

To avoid such problems arising, at an early stage all contributors should sign a written agreement which assigns their copyright and publication rights. If necessary they should be paid a one-off fee for assigning the relevant rights, or some percentage of the sales price agreed as a royalty. Ideally these rights should be assigned to a formally-constituted committee (an existing local history group may be ideal), but in the absence of such a committee then one key person *may* be an acceptable alternative.

Note that moral rights cannot be assigned, although they can if necessary be waived. Waiving moral rights would only be necessary if the nature of the CD-ROM made it difficult to credit individual contributions – although a straightforward 'acknowledgements' section would suffice.

At the same time any member of the group who is mostly contributing 'ideas' rather than any substantial amounts of writing, images or HTML coding, etc should also assert their moral rights and, if appropriate, agree a fee or royalties.

For further details on protecting your rights obtain a copy of *Buying and Clearing Rights* by Richard McCracken and Madeleine Gilbart (Blueprint 1995); sections of this book deal specifically with CD-ROMs and other multimedia publications produced by teams of contributors.

Clearing rights

Never use any text or images on a Web site for which you do have the relevant rights. Just because you paid to use a picture in a book or even a CD-ROM most certainly does not mean that you have the rights to put it on a Web site.

Picture libraries and the like usually charge several hundred pounds for including a photograph on a Web site. And this fee will be time-limited, usually to less than three years. If you use photographs without permission expect to be charged a retrospective fee of *twice* the standard fee. So including half-a-dozen pictures scanned in from a museum catalogue could easily cost you over £2,000 in fees if the copyright owner is alerted. It is *not* sufficient to take them down from the Web and expect the fees to be waived – you have already been using the images and the copyright owner can quite legitimately claim their fees from you.

Bear in mind, as discussed on page 60, that publishing photographs you have taken yourself inside museums, stately homes, churches and the like still require permission and there is no obligation for this to be granted (museums and the like would much prefer to license one of their own photographs).

Libel

Unlike books, Web pages are more likely to incur problems with libel because people on the Internet are accustomed to communicating in an informal manner. This means that there is considerable risk of remarks that may be considered libellous. While hopefully someone creating a Web site will consider carefully the tenor of any remarks they put on a Web page, if you also create the opportunity for 'feedback' to be displayed on the Web site – something akin to a 'blog for example – then *as publisher* of the remarks you will be liable for other peoples' opinions.

Historical sources can be very candid about individuals. Such 'revelations' can make interesting reading, but care needs to be taken to avoid statements that 'bring into disrepute' or could be considered a breach of confidence. Every effort should be made to check that the more 'sensational' stories are, indeed, true. Individuals who are still alive should be contacted before publication and ask to sign a 'waiver'. If serious allegations are made (and 'serious' should be interpreted from the perspective of the subject) then a libel lawyer must be consulted, even if there is good evidence to support the remarks.

You may think that some humorous remark about a distant cousin is worth including on your family history site. However that cousin may have quite different ideas about the remark and, if he has the ability to pay for legal action, you may find yourself on the receiving end of a legal bill that could easily exceed £100,000, with the 'damages' to find on top.

The crux of libel is that a remark must be judged to be both untrue and call into question someone's reputation. Furthermore the person being libelled must still be alive (although very serious instances of libel can still be prosecuted after death as criminal libel). Libel action is also more difficult (but not impossible) if over a year has elapsed since first publication.

In practice libel actions can usually only be brought by someone living in the same country as the person who makes the libellous remark and/or who publishes the remark.

The potential for huge financial loss makes libel a real issue for Web site creators and owners. However it is a somewhat specialised topic within the overall scope of this book. If you want an easily-understood overview of British libel laws, see Chapter 7 of *Publishing Law* by Hugh Jones and Christopher Benson (Routledge, 2nd edn 2002).

Archiving CD-ROMS and Web sites

Books are likely to be readable in many years time. Even if the binding breaks, the pages can be rebound. The same is not true of electronic publications. There are two issues that need to be considered if your research is to be available in the long-term future.

The first issue is the software used to read the data, which in turn is reliant on specific operating systems and hardware – none of which will be current in a decade or two. This is one reason why I have recommended working with HTML rather than more proprietary formats – HTML is likely to remain compatible with future developments such as XHTML. Other file formats which are likely to remain readable in the future include Word DOC, RTF and PDF, together with JPG and TIFF for images.

The second issue is the 'physical media' on which the data is stored – hard drive, CD-ROM, etc. None of these are likely to be especially long-lived. Hard drives are dependent on computer motherboards which share the same interfaces; the pace of technological change means that this year's technology will be incompatible with technology a decade or so in the future. CD-ROMs are notoriously prone to failure and original claims for 25 year durability have not been matched by practical experience – durability of 1 to 5 years seems to be more typical, even for the better quality 'gold standard' brands (cheap CD-Rs may fail within a few months). Failure of CD-ROMs may be limited to specific files but is quite often total – without any warning none of the data can be accessed.

What to do? Data kept on your computer's hard drives can 'migrate' to a new computer without too much effort. Even if the computer you own in 20 years time will not talk to the one you own now, each of the computers you have owned in between will talk to each other, so the data has been passed on without any problems.

Bear in mind that external hard drives that communicate with the main computer using USB 2 or Firewire interfaces are fast and enable 'off site' back up. Such a drive together with a 120 Gbyte drive will currently cost between £120 to £150. Few researchers can quickly fill a 120 Gbyte drive so this allows for plenty of backing up of data. (Being totally paranoid about losing data, DTP files and digital photographs accumulated over the last 20 years I have two such external back up drives, one of which is always off site at any given time; the cost of the drives is low compared to the irreplaceable contents.)

If you want to take 'snap shots' of ever-changing Web sites then this can be done by creating complete copies before any changes. Unless the Web site is huge this should not take up too much of your back up drive. Other people burn a copy of their Web site to a CD-ROM every month or so. This is fine for backing up but does not solve the problem of archiving the data for long-term access – assume that the CD-ROMs will be have become unreadable within a few years.

If you publish CD-ROMs make sure you keep a master copy on your back up hard drive – never rely on your CD-ROM copies still being readable when you come back to them in a few years.

So far record offices and similar archives have simply not worked through the implications for long-term archiving of electronic data. However there is one way you can help. If you deposit a copy of your CD-ROM with the local record office include a covering letter which authorises the record office (or whoever) to copy the CD-ROMs as needed to preserve the content. At least this way they can renew the physical media without infringing copyright laws.

Final thoughts

Preparing Web sites and CD-ROMs requires a moderately good understanding of HTML. This is not too difficult to achieve, although a suitable 'mentor' is helpful in the early stages. The advice on HTML coding in this chapter is mostly restricted to aspects that seem to be rarely discussed in tutorials, or which have seem especially useful.

However the most critical aspect of electronic publications is not the 'code', still less all the clever tricks that are possible. To a certain extent the most critical aspect is not even the 'content' – but rather how this information is structured and how the site or CD-ROM enables users to access the material. So what I have termed 'information architecture' – and associated ideas such as the 'three-click rule' – are the most critical aspects, together with a suitable 'look and feel' for the site which provides appropriate menus and 'landmarks' to help navigate with confidence.

There is a huge gulf between the person who develops the site – and is therefore very familiar with the content and how to find it – and all the users who (even if they later develop greater familiarity) come to the site of CD-ROM with no idea of what it contains and how to find the information. While the developer must continually think from the perspective of the 'ignorant' user there is only one way to check if the site works for users – and that is to repeatedly test the design and menus. Anyone who simply keeps adding content without user testing has missed the main message of this chapter and risks adding to the vast number of badly-designed Web sites and CD-ROMs already created.

Chapter Eight

PROMOTION AND PUBLICITY

This book is getting slightly out of chronological sequence. By the time an order has been sent to the printer several key aspects of the promotion and publicity should be taking shape.

I will bet serious money that your publication is not going to grow legs and a mouth to promote itself. You are the publisher and will need to put considerable effort into making people aware that it is available. If you think sufficient publicity will be achieved just by sitting in a comfortable chair and thinking positive thoughts you are going to be storing lots of boxes of books or CD-ROMs for a long time.

This chapter will help you take advantage of all relevant opportunities for promotion, and to plan for all these activities.

When to start planning the launch

Ideally at least three months before the planned launch date you will send details of the book to relevant book trade bibliographies (see below).

About a month before the launch date you need to send out promotional copies and, for local history books, visit shops to make sure they have copies *before* any publicity appears in local papers.

Sometimes it is helpful to have a launch party, although this is by no means essential. If you do have a launch party this will need to be planned a couple of months in advance, with a list of who is to be invited prepared at least a month in advance.

At the time of the launch you will need to liaise closely with local papers and specialist periodicals; a list of names and addresses is essential. An interview on local radio is quite probable. You may need to write promotional articles summarising key aspects of the book – these are best drafted before you become too busy with other promotional activities.

When to launch

When should a book be launched? The simplest answer may be 'As soon as the books come back from the printers'. However the simplest answer is not always the best. Avoid late July to early September as any publicity you may get will be missed by people away on holiday. Avoid January as everyone is 'tight' after Christmas and the New Year sales – books are very often considered 'non-essential' when trying to keep expenses under control.

Guide books should appear about Easter time. Books on specialist subjects and those costing over £10 are best launched in September or October, to take full advantage of the Christmas market (although bear in mind that all publishers regard this as the optimum time for book launches, so there will be plenty of competition for publicity).

Village history books can be launched any time from February to July or September to November. Indeed, there are some advantages to launching in the first half of the year, as this avoids competition with all the other books being published in the autumn. If promotion will involve door-to-door leafleting or selling (see page 251) then it makes sense to wait until the weather is tolerably warm.

The printer will have quoted a delivery time, usually four to six weeks. The printer may print within a week but remember that you will need to approve proofs between printing and binding. If there are any minor problems with cover artwork, half-tones and the like, this can cause a week or two's delay. Unless you plan to collect then allow time for delivery too.

Whatever delivery time the printer quotes *always* allow *at least* another two weeks in case problems arise (indeed time consuming hiccups are almost certain if you have not used a particular printer before). Then you need to allow another four weeks between delivery and the official launch date. This will allow review copies to be seen and reviewed by local papers in time for publicity to coincide with the launch. Adding all this together means a book to be published on the 1st September needs to be sent to the printers in the early part of June.

Who to contact

At about the time the book goes off to the printers you need to have addresses (and preferably names of key individuals) for the following:

- All bookshops in the area where your book is of interest
- Tourist information offices
- Museums and other heritage centres
- Local papers and county magazines
- Local radio stations

- Any specialist local history magazines, family history magazines, county society periodicals, etc.

Yellow Pages should identify most bookshops and tourist information offices. Your local library will have up-to-date annual directories (such as *Willing's Press Guide*) listing national publications. Few national publications are interested in specialist titles, least of all ones of regional or parochial interest.

With local papers and local radio stations phone up and find out who is likely to be interested in writing about local history, or which radio station producer or presenter (if any) is involved with programmes that interview local authors. *Never* send a book to a newspaper or radio station without addressing it to a specific person by name and including a personalised letter.

Specialist magazines can usually be tracked down on the Internet, but you may well be subscribing to them anyway.

If you are not self-publishing then the author and any other key people involved in the preparation of the publication should be approached for suggestions for who to send review copies to, although make it clear that you will regard these only as 'suggestions' not mandates.

All names and addresses need to be entered into a database or, at the very least, typed up on a word processor in a way that will quickly and easily print out as labels.

Library suppliers

You should send an advance information leaflet (see page 220) to the major library suppliers (such as James Askew; T. C. Farries, Holt Jackson, JMLS, Lindsay and Howes Booksellers, Morley Book Co [part of the Cypher Group], Woodfield and Stanley). A Web search should yield contact information for all these but there is a trade directory called *List of Library Suppliers* that will have reasonably up-to-date information about these companies.

Bibliographical databases

As soon as possible (ideally three months before launch dates, but small presses rarely work to the 'leisurely' time-scales of major publishers) you need to send all the relevant bibliographical information to Nielsen BookData (previously Whitakers) and Bibliographic Data Services Ltd (usually referred to as BDS).

Contact information is:

Nielsen BookData Ltd
3rd Floor
Midas House
62 Goldsworth Road
Woking
GU21 6LQ

telephone: 0870 777 8710
fax: 0870 777 8711
email: infor@nielsenbookdata.co.uk
Web: www.bookdata.co.uk

Bibliographic Data Services Ltd
Annandale House
The Crichton
Bankend Road
Dumfries
DG1 4TA

telephone: 01387 702251
fax: 01387 702259
email: info@bibdsl.co.uk

These two organisations supply the book trade with up-to-date information. If you have ever gone into a bookshop and said 'I think there is a book called *History of Sometown* but I don't know who the publisher is' then, if this book has been listed by BookData or BDS, they will be able to order a copy. If it is not listed then most bookshops will not be able to track it down.

BookData will automatically also include details of new books in *The Bookseller,* which is the UK's leading trade journal. Libraries regularly order their loan copies as a result of seeing details in this periodical. At the time of writing, BookData supply the information used by on-line book stores such as Amazon.co.uk. In due course you will also be approached by the publishers of yearbooks listing British publishers; such listings are unlikely to generate much business directly but will help people to contact you.

The information sent to BDS also makes its way on to the British Library Cataloguing in Publication (CIP) database. If you send Advance Information (see page 220) *at least three months before publication date* this entitles you to put the following words on the imprint page (see page 126):

British Library Cataloguing-in-Publication Data
A catalogue record for this book is available from the British Library

Because it takes time for information about new books to circulate (although most bookshops now use on-line computer access to get around this) get information to BookData and BDS at least a month (ideally three months) before you plan to launch the book. However they do need to know quite a few specific details, so the information cannot be sent before the final page proofs have been produced.

BookData have a standard form for submitting bibliographical information, known as the 'CIP Book Information'. They will send the forms, together with guidance information, on request. A copy of the information sent to BookData is appropriate for sending to BDS.

Completing the CIP form

There are one or two conventions on the CIP form that are worth noting. There are tick boxes for 'cloth' (hard back) and 'paperback' binding but stapled booklets need to be shown as 'Other'.

Under 'number of pages' count only printed pages and not blank (or advertising) pages at the back. If prelims are numbered in Roman then show these separately.

So the bibliographical information for this book is 262 + xviii.

For 'number and type of illustrations' show line art separately from half-tones. If there are colour illustrations (other than the cover) then list these first.

The 'Brief description of subject matter' needs careful consideration. The words that you enter here can be searched by bookshops, so try to include as many 'key words' relevant to the subject as possible.

Submitting cover images to BookData

At about the same time you send off the CIP Advance Information form you can also email the front cover image to them. This will appear in the trade database and, even more usefully, on the Amazon.co.uk Web site.

However the image needs to be prepared *exactly* as BookData and Amazon require it.

1. The image should show **only the front cover** – i.e. no spine
2. The image must be resized to exactly **648 pixels high** (I always click on Paint Shop Pro's 'Sharpen' tool after resizing; this usually adds 'crispness' but if you do not think it helps then click on 'Undo'! However small text is unlikely to be legible at this size.)
3. The image must be submitted in **JPG format**. There is no need to compress to any great extent – a compression value of 10 is the most that should be used.
4. The **filename must be the ISBN** (with no spaces) [So the cover image for this book was submitted with the filename 1872883591.jpg]

Double-check that you have complied with all these four requirements (and sent the CIP Advance Information to BookData so they have a title etc to match the image to) then email to images@nielsenbookdata.co.uk

After a couple of weeks search Amazon.co.uk for your book and, with luck, the book's details and cover image will appear. If there seems to be an unnecessary delay then phone BookData on 0870 777 8710 to discuss.

Advance Information leaflets

The book trade circulates Advance Information (AI) leaflets to library suppliers and other major trade outlets about three months before publication. Such potential purchasers are of limited use to local history publishers, although still consider sending them an AI.

Local history publishers can make much more effective use of promotional leaflets than simply sending them out as AIs. There are almost certainly a number of local societies whose members may be interested in your book. You may already attend some of these meetings fairly regularly; sometimes you will need to make a special effort to attend. Contact the organiser in advance and ask if you can hand out publicity leaflets; you will rarely be refused. Try hard to generate interest in the book *before* it appears (you can then revisit the same organisations soon after the book has been printed and sell copies direct). The AI leaflet is a useful way of 'softening up' people and going to two or more meetings also ensures that you will catch more people than just turning up once after publication with a box of books.

Some specialist magazines will also include promotional leaflets with the mail out of the next issue. They will understandably expect a contribution for the effort of 'stuffing' and/or extra postage costs but this is usually modest in proportion to the publicity benefits.

Advance sales

Some people will want to give you money at the meetings and ask you to post the book when it appears. Make sure they fill out their address and write on it clearly that they have paid, and – above all – do not lose the details!

Other opportunities for using leaflets successfully

Leaflets are also an excellent way of promoting books at specialist conferences *after* publication date.

For instance, Heart of Albion's *Cinema in Leicester* was successfully promoted at annual history of cinema conferences using quite simple leaflets run off on the office laser printer.

At the other extreme, with *Stonehenge: Celebration and subversion,* which is a history of the midsummer festival, 6,000 full colour A5 leaflets were professionally printed. The author and helpers handed these out to as many as possible of the 20,000-plus crowd at the solstice celebrations

Designing a promotional leaflet

There is one essential rule for promotional leaflets that must never be broken: they must look good. A poor-looking leaflet will make people assume that the book is also poorly-produced and you will lose potential sales.

For the book trade promotional leaflets should incorporate all information that appears on the CIP form plus the blurb from the back cover. Do not forget to state the planned publication date and how to obtain copies!

For leaflets to be handed out, include essential bibliographical information (size, number of pages, number of illustrations, publication date) and the blurb. Add a tear-off order form at the bottom showing clearly how much the book will cost (perhaps with an additional charge for post and packing), who to make cheques out to, and where to send them.

Usually some sort of discount is offered to people who order before publication date. Typically this is 10 to 15 percent of cover price, or maybe the postage and packing costs are waived.

Unless you intend handing out more than about 300 of these leaflets then laser printing, photocopying or digital printing is probably the best option; High Street copy shops may offer to use offset litho for 300 upwards. Investigate the cost of using tinted paper – the extra cost is probably worth while as this will give extra impact.

Advertising

Paid advertising in magazines is rarely worthwhile for local history publications. At the time of writing this book *Local History Magazine* offers a free 'noticeboard' advertisement service for its subscribers. This is probably well worth the price of a year's subscription.

Shared mailings

Major publishers often circulate flat covers (perhaps overprinted with additional sales information on the back) or promotional leaflets to libraries and bookshops. To reduce costs these normally go out as shared mailings.

Currently only one organisation offers shared mailings to libraries. This is:

Bookfile
Orbital Park
Ashford
Kent
TN24 0GA

telephone: 01233 214400
fax: 01233 214440

At the time of writing there are about 270 recipients at libraries responsible for purchasing. The cost of leaflets and the shared mailing is therefore reasonable.

Solo mailings to libraries work out more expensive and are offered by both Bookfile and:

Hamilton House Mailings Ltd
Earlstrees Court
Earlestree Road
Corby
Northamptonshire
NN17 4HH

telephone: 01536 399000
fax: 01536 399012

Bookfile and Hamilton House both offer shared mailings to bookshops. However my experience is that shared mailings to UK bookshops – and there are over 1,500 of them (excluding the major chains, such as Waterstones, W H Smith and Borders, who only purchase at head office not at branch level) do not generate the volume of sales necessary to even begin to cover the substantial costs, least of all when promoting relatively specialist titles.

Lectures and stalls

Giving talks is an excellent way of promoting and selling your book. If you are already an experienced speaker then this should hold no terrors. If not, go to your library and borrow some books on presentation skills. As with riding a bicycle, driving a car and a great many other 'life skills', it seems difficult to start with but after a moderate amount of practice it 'just comes naturally'.

Although public speaking can be nerve-wracking the first few times it soon becomes an enjoyable way of sharing your ideas and getting feedback.

When setting up speaking engagements make sure the organiser knows you are bringing along books to sell. If there is any doubt about whether tables will be available pop a folding table into the car – the sort used for pasting wallpaper is cheap and easy to carry. If you think it will look rather scruffy (especially if it is a wallpaper table that has seen real DIY use) then take a tablecloth to cover it with.

Make sure you take plenty of change, plus a notepad and pen to keep track of sales.

Sometimes there are opportunities to set up a book stall at specialist conferences and local history fairs. This can be very successful, especially if you have back issues of magazines and the like.

With village history publications you may have the opportunity to sell at local car boot fairs, or at charity events. If you have suitable display material this can be used to make up a small exhibition. Do not be tempted to take original photographs, documents or artefacts – there are too many opportunities for damage or even theft. A table with books in front or alongside the exhibition will usually result in sufficient sales to cover the costs of preparing the exhibition material.

Planning for the launch

After the book has gone to the printers there are several key checks and preparations to be made. These are:

- preparing a press release
- checking the list of recipients for review copies
- checking the list of shops etc that will need to be visited to sell copies
- planning where to store the books until they are sold

If you plan to have a launch party then details will need to be finalised and invitations sent out.

Press releases

Local papers have an insatiable thirst for news, features and 'excitement', such as:

- Genuine news stories
- Interesting features (invariably about people rather than just places or things)
- Odd statistics
- Provocative quotes
- Interesting photographs (with attention-grabbing captions)
- Exclusive 'scoops'

The rules of writing press releases

Professional editors expect a press release that conforms to professional practice. They expect to *quickly* find out 'who, what and why'. Bear in mind the media are sent hundreds of press releases each week. Editors will never bother to read beyond the first paragraph of 'waffle' – any wording that seems to them unprofessional will be sufficient excuse to add your press release to the large collection already in the waste paper bin rather than have to carry on reading.

- The headline should grab attention (although no one will use your headline – no paper will risk 'sharing' a headline with another paper).
- Start with the most important information. Make sure the first paragraph states 'who', 'what', 'where' and 'when'. Write about the most interesting aspects of the subject, not the book itself.

- Explain 'how' and 'why' in the next paragraph or two. Offer opinions, ideas, odd statistics or unique claims ('This is the first book on eighteenth century horse racing in Wiltshire'). Offer benefits to the reader. Again, put the most important ideas first.

- State why the author is an authority on the subject (write in the third person if you are self-publishing).

- Emphasise any interesting or quirky aspects of the author's life, especially their local connections. Note that local papers usually publish stories about the *authors* rather than about the content of their books.

- The least-important information should be in the last paragraph (such as where to obtain copies – see below). Often the last paragraph will state who will be interested.

- Write from the reader's point of view, not yours

- Avoid anything which reads like a sales pitch. Be impartial.

- Eliminate all jargon. Do not waffle. Be precise and concise.

- Include a quote from an 'authority' (perhaps from the foreword), or a short quote from the book.

If the author has 'good credentials' then it may be worth putting together a *brief* biography. But an A4 page full of self-aggrandisement is quite likely to backfire – professional editors are both busy and prone to being cynical.

If you are happy for people to order direct from you, then ensure that your press release states:

- how much post and packaging will cost (if you are not charging for postage then make this clear too!)

- who to make cheques out to

- where to send orders.

At the end of the press release you *must* give a contact name and *daytime* phone number for both the publisher and (where different) the author. Such contact information will not be published if the press release is laid out correctly – see next page – but is *essential* if you want your press release to result in an article. The media wants everything *now*, not in an hour's time. Journalists typically leave everything until deadlines are hours away; even if this is not the case in an hour's time the journalist's priorities will have changed and the interest in writing a story based on your press release will have passed. Daytime telephone numbers where the journalists can reliably get hold of the publisher and author (not merely leave a message!) are therefore essential.

Journalists and editors will not be happy if they have to speak to an answering machine in the hope that someone will phone them back – everything they do has to be done now and tomorrow will always be too late.

How to lay out a press release

Press releases are always printed on A4 paper, on one side only, with double spaced lines.

Rarely is it necessary to extend to a second A4 page – long press releases are more likely to be binned unread than shorter ones. If you need to start on a second page then go back and reread every sentence on the first page and ask 'What am I saying here?', 'Is it really essential information?' 'Am I waffling?'.

If a second page is essential (it may be if ordering information is included, for instance) then do *not* print this on the reverse of the first page – both pages should be blank on the back.

To give the impression your press release has been professionally written, at the top of the first page state either 'For immediate release' or (exceptionally) 'Embargoed until [launch date]'.

At the end of the main text, but before contact information, centre the following (including the dashes):

– ends –

This makes it completely clear what information is intended for publication and what information – such as the author's phone number – is for the journalist's information only.

Who to send press releases to

The press release should be mailed or faxed about a month before launch date to monthly and weekly periodicals and about a week before launch date to daily papers. (You may want to accompany the press release with an invitation to the launch; see page 229.)

Review copies will be accompanied by a copy of the press release and, where appropriate, a personalised covering letter.

All local papers, monthly county magazines and local radio stations should receive a copy of the press release even if you do not send them a review copy – but in this case make it clear that review copies are available on request.

If you have come up with a *really* 'sexy' story for the press release then also send to national weekend papers (the chances of them 'biting' are low but, if they do, the publicity is superb). Do *not* send them a review copy 'just in case' as this is counter-productive (how will you know they are a little bit interested if they do not need to contact you for a copy?).

If you really have come up with something of a coup that will interest the book trade outside your geographical area then also send a copy of the press release to the leading trade weeklies:

Publishing News
7 John Street
London
WC1N 2ES

telephone:	0870 870 2345
fax:	0870 870 0385
email:	rodneyburbeck@publishingnews.co.uk

The Bookseller
Endeavor House
5th Floor
189 Shaftesbury Avenue
London
WC2H 8TJ

telephone:	020 7420 6125
email:	webeditor@bookseller.co.uk

Promoting on the Web

Even if you do not plan to have a complex Web site, at the very least create a simple page containing the 'blurb' of the book and details of how to obtain it.

Consider including a sample chapter or section (this will greatly enhance the chances of someone finding your page by searching for key words), and include a *small* image scanned from the cover.

Bear in mind that the Web is very international so be prepared to add some sort of explanatory comments about where places are located. Anyone in Leicestershire might be expected to know roughly where Melton Mowbray is, but on the Web many people may not even have heard of Leicestershire...

Also explain any terms which are 'local' or specialist. For instance, except in Britain few know that 'Norman architecture' refers to 11th to 13th century buildings.

Do not assume that everyone will start beating a path to your door. There are over a million new Web pages created each day, so your site is less than a spit in an ocean. What you need to do is make as many people as sensibly possible aware of your on-line publicity. Without being overly commercial, try to find a pretext for mentioning the site in postings to relevant email lists or Usenet groups. Above all try to get other sites to link to your site (although, quite understandably, they may expect a link back to their site). At the time of writing the *Local History Magazine* Web site <www.local-history.co.uk> contains some of the best links to on-line UK local history.

For family history there is a vast number of on-line sites, some of these are known as 'portals' i.e. they primarily list other relevant sites. The leading genealogical portal for the UK is GENUKI (www.genuki.org.uk). Follow their links to mailing lists and identify ones that are relevant to your publication; post an 'informative' message rather than an out-and-out sales pitch. Also send details for inclusion in GENUKI's weekly email newsletter called *UK Family History News*. Try to get relevant specialist family history sites to link to your site (again, quite reasonably they may expect a link back to their site).

Search engines such as Google tend to be quite good at automatically finding new sites, although to be on the safe side manually submit to Google and the MSN search engine. However there is little or no point in submitting to large numbers of specialist search engines and absolutely no point in wasting money on paying other organisations who claim to submit to large numbers of search engines – these are best thought of as a con.

See Chapter 7 for more information on creating and promoting Web sites.

Storage

Where will you store the books when they arrive back from the printers? Bear in mind that books are heavy! A typical paperback weighs between 250 and 700 grams. This means 300 copies will weigh somewhere between 100 and 200 kgs.

Assuming you will receive no more than about 500 books of less than 250 pages, then storage in a house is realistic. But, once you start to accumulate stocks of several titles, or decide to go mad and get 1,000 or more copies printed at once, then bear in mind that the floors of domestic houses are not built to take the weight. More than about 1,000 books in the middle of a back bedroom may lead to loud creaking noises followed by a sudden descent into the room below. Your insurance company will *not* cover the costs, as they will (rightly) say you were negligent in putting them there in the first place.

If you have a ground floor with solid concrete floors then this is more suited to reasonable quantities of books. However, for many people the only place capable of taking the weight will be the garage. Paperback and hardback books fare quite well, providing the boxes are kept off the floor using blocks of wood and there is no risk of rain blowing in under the doors. If the roof is suspect then cover the boxes with polythene sheets to avoid problems from drips. In general, err on the side of caution as, once books get damaged, they are scrap.

Stapled booklets *must* be kept warm and constantly dry, otherwise the staples will rust. Garages are not suitable. Even unheated back bedrooms may cause problems.

The printer will usually pack the books or booklets in boxes that weigh about 10 to 12 kg. These can be stacked 4 or 5 high without too much risk that those at the bottom will get damaged. Keep all your stock in these boxes until needed. Sunlight will fade covers and may turn the edges of books yellow. Garages and such like are often dusty.

If you plan to sell by mail order then you will also need somewhere to store packaging. While this is much lighter it is rather bulky and also needs to be kept perfectly dry.

Mailing review copies

Copies of books sent out for review should be accompanied by a 'review slip'. Like the press release this should state full details of the size of the book, number of pages, number of illustrations (half-tone and line art), type of binding, ISBN number, name of the imprint and, most importantly, the price.

Including this information on the review slip means that if the book is sent out to a reviewer then the editor is able to keep these details handy in case the reviewer does not include them all.

Many publishers reprint the back cover blurb too. If there is a foreword by someone 'famous', make this clear also.

If you are happy for people to order direct from you, then ensure that your review slip also states:

- how much post and packaging will cost (if you are not charging for postage then make this clear too!)
- who to make cheques out to
- where to send orders.

The packaging used to send out review copies *must* be stiff enough to protect the corners of the books. *Never* send books or booklets wrapped in 'Jiffy' bags or similar unstiffened products as they will arrive with the corners damaged.

Booklets can be sent in board-backed envelopes. Books should be sent wrapped in rigid corrugated card, folded to extend beyond the corners of the books. The leading supplier of such packaging is:

Ready Case Ltd
PO Box 862
Brookwood
Woking
Surrey
GU24 0WX

telephone: 0870 873 5535
fax: 0870 873 5536

Ready Case have a wide range of standard sizes. Before you telephone their sales department make sure you have the size of your book handy. You want a pack that is between 5 and 10 mm longer and wider than the cover of your publication. At the time of writing their minimum order is a reasonable 100 off; while you may not need this many for review copies alone this is a sensible minimum for all but the most specialist title.

Legal deposit copies

Now is the time to fulfil one of the few legal obligations of a publisher – to send *one* copy to the British Library and *five* copies to A.T. Smail. These will end up in the Bodleian Library (Oxford), Cambridge University Library, Trinity College Dublin Library, and the national libraries of Scotland and Wales.

Both organisations will send receipts. Keep these safe as, in the very unlikely event of someone breaching your copyright, they will provide proof of the date of publication.

While there is a legal obligation to send one copy to the British Library within one month of publication legally you can wait until A.T. Smail approach you. However they will pick up on any ISBN or ISSN information (see page 122) and catch up with you in due course, so there is little point in waiting to be asked.

This requirement applies to anything which can carry an ISBN or ISSN, so includes all booklets, books, periodicals and CD-ROMs.

The current addresses are:

Legal Deposit Office
The British Library
Boston Spa
Wetherby
LS23 7BY

A T Smail
100 Euston Street
London
NW1 2HQ

The launch

A book launch is not essential. If well-publicised, they are sometimes useful. But few launches fully achieve what the publisher sets out to achieve, and many achieve very little – while still costing money!

The aim is to bring together local bookshop owners, local media representatives, and everyone involved in the research and publication of the book. The reality is that the bookshop owners and media rarely turn up.

The key question is 'How much can you afford to spend on the launch?' Only the most modest of launches costs under £100 and a more realistic budget is £300 upwards.

If you are on good terms with a local bookshop, and the owner (or manager) has expressed real interest in stocking your book, then he or she may be interested in hosting the book launch. Typically this will take place early on a weekday evening, soon after the shop has shut for normal trading. The owner will probably have experience of arranging similar events and be able to offer considerable practical advice.

Whether or not the shop is willing to meet all the costs of the launch needs to be discussed; splitting costs is probably realistic. Clearly, the shop expects to sell copies of the book at the launch and in the next few days and weeks.. Customarily publishers offer a bigger discount than usual (perhaps 50 percent) on copies sold at a launch, to help the shop meet the costs incurred hosting the launch. However if the shop asks for a significant contribution to the cost of refreshments then there is no need to offer anything more than your usual discount.

Where a local history publication is the result of a 'group effort', or where residents of a community have contributed to the contents, then a book launch is an excellent way of saying 'thank you' to all involved. If a bookshop venue is unlikely or too expensive, then a local pub will be able to provide a simple buffet. There may be advantages in organising a book launch at lunch time or early afternoon instead of early evening. My preference is to avoid a start time of later than 7.30 pm, as this is less attractive to journalists and those who are attending as part of their day job.

Another option that may be appropriate is a village hall. Avoid using private premises (houses, barns, garages) unless the owner has suitable public liability insurance; you will also be unable to sell drinks without applying for a licence (which are only granted monthly so pay attention to timing!). Note that there is no need for a license if there is no charge for admission or for the drinks themselves.

Set a date that is at least four weeks after that when the printer said they would be delivered. (This also means that review copies can be sent out at an appropriate time.) Printers tend not to be the most punctual of creatures and genuine problems may arise. The last thing you want is having to postpone a launch because there would be no copies of the book.

Send invitations to all the local papers, local radio stations and local bookshops. With 'village history' publications invite the C-of-E and non-conformist clergy. For books dealing with towns and cities then invite representatives from the local history societies, museums, record office, libraries, and maybe also from industry and commerce (especially where long-established organisations feature in the publication). Aim to invite anyone who has 'influence' and is remotely involved in the subject of the book. Indeed the Great and the Good and people known to be 'movers and shakers' should get an invitation even if they have no direct connections with the book – with luck they will help spread the word to their contacts.

Many of those invited will send their apologies or simply not respond. You will be doing well if half of those invited actually turn up. Nevertheless you have made them aware of the book. Invitations should be sent out at least 10 to 14 days before the event. There is little point in invitations to the local papers and radio stations much further in advance – they tend not to plan their lives that far ahead.

All invitations should be to individually-named people (*not* just 'The Editor' or 'Managing Director'). If there is any doubt phone up to check you have the correct name and spelling.

If the launch is at a bookshop then they will want to display posters. These could be simply flat covers but it may be better to make a colour photocopy of the front cover blown up to A3 size. (Alternatively if you have access to an A3 inkjet printer then print out the cover to fit an A3 sheet of paper.) If there are some eye-catching illustrations in the book then enlarge a few of these to A3 as well. With luck the bookshop will include these A3 images in their window for a few days before and after the launch.

For a village book launch you may want to display posters. Only use locations, such as shop windows and parish notice boards, where posters are regularly displayed. 'Fly posting' is illegal and many local authorities enforce the law vigorously so you may find yourself before the bench being addressed as Mr Bill Sticker.

The poster should contain only essential information in big print. Be sure to include a contact telephone number.

Following up launch invitations

With local press and radio (and possibly a few other key people) phone up the named individual the morning of the day *before* the launch party to get confirmation that they, or a deputy, will be attending.

The reality is probably that the person genuinely never saw the invitation, or completely forgot about seeing it, or asked someone else to 'look into it', or simply had no intention of turning up. Your phone call will focus their thoughts and still allow enough time for a reporter and photographer to be scheduled to attend.

If your guest list includes contributors to the book who are elderly or frail then contact them in advance to discuss if they need to be picked up, any special seating arrangements, and such like.

The launch will probably not require large quantities of champagne to be freely flowing (though, if the budget allows, I would not discourage this!). In practice still white wine, red wine and soft drinks for the drivers and diet conscious are all that is required. 'Nibbles' are not essential. Indeed bookshops may sensibly discourage any snacks (such as crisps) which leave people with greasy fingers – fingers that will probably then be browsing books, leaving indelible marks on covers and pages.

Where the author and/or leading illustrator is female, a bouquet of flowers from the publisher is a tradition worth sustaining.

Be willing to hand out review copies (with a copy of the press release) at the launch – but be sure to keep track of who has had what, so you do not end up mailing out duplicates.

Before proceedings get underway appoint helpers to take care of specific tasks. The author(s) and publisher will – hopefully! – find themselves too busy talking to a rapid succession of different people to be able to effectively help with nitty-gritty aspects. One or more people need to act as wine waiters. Someone else should keep track of review copies. If the launch is not at a bookshop then appoint at least two people who are not otherwise actively involved to take the money (make sure they have plenty of change). If there are limitations on car parking you will need to appoint one or more car parking attendants, especially if spaces need to be reserved for celebrities or people with mobility limitations. You may also need to prearrange who is going to help with clearing up.

Most essential of all, make sure that someone competent takes photographs on a digital camera – the author and publisher cannot take photographs of themselves 'in action'. Plan in advance for whoever is organising publicity to have copies of the photographs by early the next day (see next section for why).

You may want to include a display of related activities. This is especially true for local history societies. Indeed enlarged copies of photographs from the book can make excellent talking points. But make sure someone from the society is delegated to be politely listening in and taking notes, otherwise valuable snippets of local information may be lost.

Launches mean speeches. There is only one rule to such speeches – shut up and sit down as quickly as possible. This is doubly true if a 'celebrity' has been asked to 'say a few words' and you are simply acting as master of ceremonies. However do remember to sincerely thank everyone who has helped with the preparation of the publication and the launch itself.

The author(s) can expect to be asked to sign copies of the book at a launch. However, apart from complimentary copies to people who have helped, it is not 'the done thing' to offer to sign books – wait to be asked! Where authorship is by more than two people make sure the relevant people sign a box full of books *in advance*.

Radio interviews

Local radio stations often have 'chat shows' that are keen to give a few minutes' exposure to local authors. Phone up your local stations and find out which shows offer these opportunities and ask for the names of the presenter or producer. Listen to the shows to get a feel for the format and attempt to understand the type of audience they are trying to attract.

Initially send a review copy, press release and personalised covering letter. Make sure it goes to a named person – there is no point in sending it otherwise.

Radio is a world where everything is *news* so try to offer a *worthwhile* story or 'hook'. Do not expect anyone to have to read your book to find out if there are any good stories lurking! Make sure the press release and/or covering letter give so clear clues as to why the publication will appear to their listeners.

Interviews can be 'live' or recorded. Either may be done by phone but most stations prefer you to come to the studio. Being interviewed in the studio is much to be preferred as your voice will come across more clearly than via a telephone. Even more importantly you have eye contact with the interviewer which greatly helps you to 'sync' the start of questions and answers.

Live interviews can be fairly nerve-wracking but have the advantage that your words cannot be taken out of context (inadvertently or otherwise) in the editing process.

Do not drink alcohol before the interview (although you will almost certainly need a stiff one afterwards!). I even avoid coffee as this sends my heart rate helter-pelter as The Moment becomes imminent.

Speak more slowly and more clearly than you think you need to (nervousness and the limitations of radio reception will make 'normal' speech into a gabble).

Few interviews will last for more than 5 minutes – that is about 750 words (assuming the presenter does not interrupt often). Promoting a publication is the opposite of practising to be a politician – so keep to the point and make the point clearly. You really do have to focus on the essential points and resist any temptation to 'waffle'. Make every sentence say something important and 'sexy' – well at least make the listeners more curious about wanting to read the book.

Never worry about 'drying up' or losing track of where you were going – the interviewer will be used to working with inexperienced interviewees and will swiftly but subtly come to your aid. If you get something wrong or have to back track, just take a deep breath and correct yourself in a confident voice. The listeners will forgive 'honest errors' but will be much less forgiving of people who become hesitant or apologetic for their foibles.

Do not regard the interview as a commercial. You will not be invited back if you 'blot your copy book' by doing a selling routine. The presenter will almost certainly introduce you and your book and (hopefully) provide a reminder about the price and how to obtain a copy at the end (if they don't it may be because you waffled on and time ran out before the news or some other key event in the rest of the programme).

The most exciting part of live radio for me is dealing with phone-in questions. I will freely admit that having to ad lib on air about topics that may be two steps removed from the previous topics of the interview can be something of a challenge. Thankfully not all radio presenters expect their guests to rise to this challenge but, if you have little or no previous experience of doing live radio I suggest that when you are arranging the interview with the programme's producer you tactfully enquire whether you will be expected to take phone-in questions. If you think this will be a challenge too far then make this clear to the producer who should then agree that you will not be subjected to this particularly effective way of sending adrenaline levels sky high.

Despite the challenges and the 'nerves', radio interviews can be thoroughly enjoyable. If you do well, the station may even offer you regular opportunities to discuss your speciality subject.

After the launch

Following up with the local papers

Odds are that no one from the local papers or radio stations made it to the launch. Now the ball's back in your court. Prepare yourself with lots of good reasons why you think the book will interest the readers or listeners – and try to make them good reasons, not just 'puff'.

The day after the launch *phone* the editor, news desk or the producer of the local radio 'talk' programme. Yes, I said *phone*. Do not write or email as these will be ignored and you will miss out on a crucial chance for publicity. State that the launch took place and give one or two 'snippets' that are the basis for a story suitable for the paper. Be as concise and to the point as you can – although you will have put aside all morning for contacting the media always remember that whoever is at the other end of the phone probably has at least six other things that should have been done an hour ago.

Think of interviews with the press as a bit like job interviews – you need to make a good first impression then highlight the most relevant aspects, not give your complete life story.

Before you start speaking to the press make a list of specific attention-getting 'snippets' that can be developed in more detail if the journalist 'bites'. These may be especially interesting anecdotes from the publication, or about how the research of the book, or – best of all – something interesting or quirky about the author. Journalists are most likely to be interested in stories that affect other people or have a genuine 'human interest' angle.

If a journalist picks up on any of your story suggestions then do not simply respond by telling the tale at length. Allow him or her to ask lots of questions and answer these as concisely as possible. Resist all temptation to get on a 'hobby horse' and ramble on. Instead try to get a feel for what sort of story the journalist is trying to develop – and do as much as possible to help them develop that story. All journalism relies on simple stories that relate to basic aspects of human nature; without them the journalist would quickly be out of a job. The more you understand what the journalist is trying to achieve, the more likely you are to end up with a published story rather than one that gets dropped by the editor.

State that you could email some photographs taken at the event (they probably will not want to use them, but at least it shows you are keen and well-organised). With luck they will interview you over the phone, or perhaps send a journalist or photographer round.

Never make 'throwaway' or 'off the record' remarks to journalists – even at the end of the 'formal' interview – as these could be used to your disadvantage. *Always* assume that anything you say to a reporter could appear in print (even if you say it should not). So a very tongue in cheek reference to the people who helped put your book together as a bunch of boring old farts will appear a lot less amusing when it ends up in the paper...

If you have had a successful interview then there is a good chance of an article being published. Be patient, this may not be in the next issue. Unless there is something very topical about your book you may have to wait for a 'slow news' day. One of the tricks of the trade of editing local papers is to have a few stories 'up your sleeve' that can be used to fill the paper at the last minute. If, after a few issues, your story has not been used in this way then it will appear before it goes 'stale' (a useful article is unlikely to be just wasted). Phoning up the journalist or editor to ask why it has not appeared is counterproductive. No matter how keen you are to see some valuable publicity in the local paper, bear in mind you stand to gain far more from this free publicity than the paper does. Be patient and do not make yourself unwelcome – you are going to want 'follow up' publicity in the coming months!

The excitement of seeing your publication mentioned in the local paper is usually dampened by the way it has been 'dumbed down' or even by some 'unnecessary' mistakes. Local papers are notorious for misrepresenting facts and spelling names incorrectly. So long as there are no major mistakes, just be grateful for the very useful publicity. Only if there is a real problem – such as details of the price or availability are wrong – should you ask for a correction. Don't castigate the journalist – we all make mistakes and journalists work under intense pressure. Indeed, the reporter may have got his facts right and the error came resulted from someone else 'interfering'. Regard such mistakes as not something to get upset about but rather as an opportunity to get a second round of publicity. If a real mistake has been made then the journalist will accept that he 'owes you one' and, even if a correction is not forthcoming, you may stand a better chance of some other follow up publicity.

Do not chase the editors of monthly or quarterly periodicals, especially those run as part-time activities. Most specialist magazines will review books received, so long as they are reasonably relevant to their subject, but not necessarily in the next issue. Annual 'transactions' type journals are often about two years in arrears with reviews (a quick skim through the reviews section of a recent issue will reveal how recently – or otherwise – the books were published). This is not a lot of help for promotion but bear in mind the primary purpose of these publications is not to provide publicity for other publishers.

Book signings

Even if a bookshop does not act as the venue for the launch, they may offer to promote a book signing. The rewards are probably slight and, unless the author is already a local 'celebrity', the rewards will probably not justify the effort.

Book signings usually take place from mid-morning to mid-afternoon. Saturdays are normal, although there may be reasons to chose a mid-week date.

Check that the bookshop will organise all the necessary publicity and provide a table and chair for the author's use.

However assume that book signings will not draw in any noticeable crowds. The author and publisher should make every effort to encourage friends and passing acquaintances to 'pop in' (even if they already have a copy of the book) just to make the place look busy.

Book signings can end up rather depressing when the actual act of signing a book is an infrequent occurrence.

As with book launches at shops, offer the shop a bigger discount on copies sold during the signing, to defray any expenses. Despite my pessimistic expectations, do make sure that there are enough copies 'out the back' (or in the boot of a nearby car) to cope with unexpected demand.

Follow up promotion

This is the tricky part! The initial publication should result in reviews and maybe prominent display in bookshops. But after about three months such attention-attracting activity has probably subsided. Sales have hopefully been good. Yet, with any luck, you will sell at least as many books again in the next year or so. And ideally you want to sell many more than this.

There are several possibilities. If any of the publicity has been especially successful or had intriguing outcomes or involved 'famous people' then send out another round of press releases to the media. If the news is very topical then follow up more or less immediately with phone calls to the news desk of the papers or radio stations.

Normally however once a book has been out for a few months considerable imagination is needed to come up with a 'story line' for a press release that is likely to engage the attention of a news editor. Aim for making 'human interest' aspects more important than the book itself. 'Local book sells 1,200 copies' simply will not work whereas 'Local author delighted with sales of new book' is better (though perhaps not perfect) – even though the reason the author being pleased is because he or she has sold 1,200 copies.

Promoting the book in conjunction with other events is also helpful. So a local history book could be co-promoted with fund raising for village projects. Offering a few copies as prizes in a raffle is worthwhile, especially if the publicity for the raffle clearly mentions the book. Try to be as imaginative as possible to take full advantage of opportunities that crop up.

There is one option for follow up promotion that does not require too much imagination, and rarely requires too much effort. This is writing short articles (rarely over 3,000 words and often half that length) about aspects of the book to appear in specialist magazines. While you are unlikely to get any fee for writing the article, think of this as better than even a full-page advert in the periodical. The next section is devoted to preparing and submitting articles.

Promotional articles

Articles in specialist magazines are one of the best ways of promoting books. Even if these magazines are likely to review your publication, an article (preferably in the issue before or after the review rather than the same one) will be more likely to generate sales.

However very few magazines are interested in a simple 'sales pitch'. Either attempt to summarise the key aspects of your book or simply concentrate on one aspect that will be especially relevant to the magazine.

Always (and I said 'Always', not 'Sometimes' or 'If you feel like it') read a recent issue of the magazine. Check how long the longest article is and get a 'feel' for the writing style. Something written for, say, *Local History Magazine* will be much shorter and need to be much more readable than, say, a submission to the local county transactions. Also check how references are cited and *exactly* how bibliographical details are listed, down to the finest aspects of punctuation.

Short articles will always be more welcome than long ones. Again, go back to the issue of the magazine and check what sort of length is typical for articles.

You must adapt your writing style to fit in with the publication. If, like me, you normally write in an accessible, 'friendly' style then you need to be deliberately avoid colloquialisms and be more 'dull and boring' than usual when writing for transactions and the like. In contrast, if you are accustomed to writing for academic periodicals, or your day job has accustomed you to writing 'corporate-speak' reports, then make sure you avoid impersonal sentences (see page 35) and all the dreadful clichés and pomposities (see page 38) when writing for non-academic magazines and newsletters.

Articles need to start in a way that both introduces the subject matter and intrigues the reader. A friend of mine, Jeremy Harte, has got this off to a fine art. Some of his articles are on-line and together are excellent examples of how to create strong openings:

www.indigogroup.co.uk/edge/gtree.htm
www.indigogroup.co.uk/edge/hollow.htm
www.indigogroup.co.uk/edge/pussycat.htm
www.indigogroup.co.uk/edge/fairies3.htm
www.indigogroup.co.uk/edge/fairies4.htm

Conclude the article with details of how to obtain the book, including whether post and packing is included and to whom cheques should be payable.

If you are not sure whether your article will be of interest to the editor then email or post a synopsis. Bear in mind that most editors of specialist periodicals are busy people; most only do the editing in their 'spare' time. So replies may be slow or non-existent; wait three or four weeks before following up.

If you have a suitable article already written then email the text (but *not* the pictures, no matter how relevant they are to the text – the editor can easily come back to you requesting the images but will not thank you for filling his email box and losing emails from other people as a result). Never submit the same article to more than one editor until a definite rejection has been received (or a follow up has remained unanswered for a couple of weeks). Just occasionally a 'multiple submission' might be appropriate but make sure this is clear from the covering letter. In practice, a short press release sent to all relevant editors is almost certainly more appropriate than multiple submissions of an article.

Submitting an article

Check the magazine and its Web site to see if the editor expresses any preference for how articles should be submitted. Some academic periodicals will ask for two or three printed copies, double-spaced. A few will say that an email attachment is acceptable. If no preferences are given then print the article out *with double-spacing and wide margins around all four edges of the text*, using only on one side of the paper and with Arial as the font (*not* Times Roman which is less easy to read, and certainly not anything you think makes it look 'fancy').

If there are no illustrations then enclose a floppy disc with the article in both Word DOC and RTF formats. If there are illustrations then both the filename and caption should be the relevant part of the text. Burn all the images on a CD-ROM; the Word DOC and RTF versions of the text should also be on the CD-ROM. *Never* (that means 'Never', not 'I'm going to make the editor's life awkward by ignoring this advice'...) insert images into the text of the document.

Images should ideally be at least 600 dpi *reproduced size* and never less than 300 dpi; you will have to make an intelligent guess as to how big the periodical usually prints pictures to work out how many inches are appropriate – for example a photograph reproduced 4" across requires 2400 pixels for 600 dpi (see Chapter 3 for more details of preparing illustrations for reproduction).

After submission

If your article is accepted then some editors will respond with detailed suggestions; others will accept the article as drafted. Minor changes will often be made to fit the publication's 'house style'; more significant changes should be (but are not always!) referred to the author first.

Be patient. If you have not heard from an editor after a month then check it has been received but do not chase for acceptance. And after you have been formally accepted you may have to be even more patient. Many magazines have a back log of articles and also work to quite long lead times. Your contribution will almost certainly not appear in the next issue and a couple more may pass by before you see it in print. Delays are especially likely with longer articles which are more likely to get held over, whereas shorter text might be exactly the right length to fill an awkward gap. Do not chase your article until at least three issues have come and gone. By politely enquiring if the editor intends to use it or whether you can submit it elsewhere (even if you do not have any such intentions!) will usually get a clear enough indication of whether publication is probable.

A final suggestion

Although not actually promotion, there are two organisations that should also be informed about your publication. These are the Public Lending Right Office (which administers payments made in proportion to the number of times your book is borrowed from a library) and the Authors' Licensing and Collecting Society (who distribute payments made by academic institutions, libraries and the like for photocopies made from your publications).

In practice the Public Lending Right (PLR) discriminates badly against local and regional publications because it is based only on a sample of a few county library services. So, unless your county is one of those in the current year's survey, then even a high number of loans of a local title will go unnoticed. They also have an inflexible registration system which means they need to be informed about new titles before 30 June otherwise you miss out on a whole year's loans.

In reality the sums paid by PLR and ALCS are fairly modest – you will be doing well if you get more than £5 per year for each title registered. However every little helps!

Public Lending Right
Richard House
Sorbonne Close
Stockton on Tees
TS17 6DA

telephone: 01642 604699
fax: 01642 615641
email: authorservices@plr.uk.com
Web: www.plr.uk.com

Authors' Licensing and Collecting Society
Marlborough Court
14-18 Holborn
London
EC1N 2LE

telephone: 020 7395 0600
fax: 020 7395 0660
email: alcs@alcs.co.uk

Final thoughts

Successful promotion requires both imagination and hard work. A wide range of skills are needed. Fortunately the tasks can be shared out between several people, assuming that everyone knows exactly what the others are doing. Such teamwork will also be beneficial for the most important part of publishing, which I have for good reason termed 'the hard part' and discuss in the next chapter.

Further reading

Marketing for Small Publishers, Bill Godber, Robert Webb and Keith Smith, Journeyman, 1993

Chapter Nine

SELLING

The hard part

So far we have discussed all the easy parts about publishing. The hardest part is the last part. Publishing a book is *about selling*. If you can't or won't sell, you will have simply spent your money on a pile of books that will simply carry on taking up space.

Publishing is ultimately *not* about writing, editing, typesetting, liaising with printers and promoting. In the final analysis all these different functions could be subcontracted to suitable specialists (indeed, in an ideal world where money is no object you would be best to employ such experts). What cannot be 'subcontracted' is the selling part, simply because there is no one out there to whom you can subcontract this part of publishing. Few commercial book distributors are interested in local history books, and never in booklets or CD-ROMs. In local history publishing, the publisher *must* be the sales person.

Be warned that the selling stage is usually where group publication comes apart – often argumentatively. This may mean that previously good friends are no longer speaking to each other and a large pile of books is just sitting in someone's house without generating any income to pay the printer's bill. Make sure that everyone involved realises in advance that the real work starts *after* the book has been launched – think of the earlier stages as just the 'fun' part. Nevertheless, if approached in a professional way, the selling part can have its own rewards too, although it is fair to say it may only seem like fun a few weeks or months afterwards!

To reiterate, if you (either as an individual or as a group) are not willing or able to put in the effort needed to sell your publication then you should not be thinking of publishing.

Trade terms

If you have no prior experience of selling then you need to become familiar with the terms of business used in the book trade – and how to avoid being lumbered with terms unattractive to you.

Firm sale

Many shops will agree to you supplying on 'firm sale, 30 day invoice'.

This means that the shop agrees to buy, say, 5 copies and they will pay against an invoice which is due for payment 30 days after the delivery date. Well, that's the theory. Most shops will take 60 to 90 days to pay.

Even the words 'firm sale' are regarded as meaningless by some bookshop managers. To counteract this put 'Returns only accepted if sale or return agreed at the time of ordering and books are in as-supplied condition' on your invoices (see page 249).

Sale or return

Many shops will try to get you to supply on 'sale or return'. This means that you leave, say, 10 copies and go back a month or so later to find out how many have been sold, then raise an invoice. The shop will, inevitably, take at least 30 and probably 60 days to pay this invoice which means that there is a very long time between dropping the books off and getting paid.

Furthermore, any copies damaged will be given back to you. And, unless you regularly pass the shop, then going back to stock check can become time consuming and expensive.

Only agree to sale or return when the potential sales at that shop are likely to exceed 50 copies and if you can easily go back to check stock. Otherwise wriggle and squirm about sale and return. Insist that you will not offer a discount bigger than 25 percent for sale or return (and stick to this!). Offer a *slightly* bigger discount (see next section) for firm sale. If you really cannot get any alternative then, without risking appearing rude, leave the shop owner with the distinct impression that you are doing them a really big favour by even thinking about agreeing to sale or return (you are).

Trade discount

Offer 33 percent discount for two or more copies. (Few shops will ask for only one copy but, if they do, offer no more than 25 percent discount.) Nine times out of ten shops will be happy with this offer. A few shops will ask for more discount, but be prepared to negotiate.

Respond with 'If you order more than 10 copies at a time, I'll offer 35 percent.' (When doing this type of negotiating, adjust the number of copies to whatever you think the shop is most likely to take. No shop will take more stock than it wants just for the sake of a small increase in discount. Worse still, in a few months time you may end up having to take some grubby copies back *and* raise a credit note.)

Confirm that this is for firm sale. If the shop owner wriggles and says they want sale or return then *immediately* say you only supply sale or return at 25 percent discount. Expect various negotiating tactics to ensue but only supply on a sale or return basis at more than 25 percent discount if the potential sales are sufficiently great, for example for a 'one off' special function. The best way to resist bigger discounts than 25 percent for sale or return is to offer a slightly bigger discount as a way of converting the order to firm sale. So, maybe respond with 'If you take 5 [or whatever] copies on firm sale, I'll invoice at 35 percent'.

Do not consider that the negotiating is over until you have discussed both discounts *and* payment terms. The serious negotiator will wind you up to, say, 40 percent discount and, just as all seems settled, ask 'Of course, I only ever pay after 90 days'. Just take a deep breath and start as if from the beginning. Be equally emphatic. 'Oh no, I've never agreed to 40 percent for *90 days* terms' – and make sure you really sound pained as you briefly contemplate having anything like 90 days. The feeling of pain should be genuine as people who say 'They only ever pay after 90 days' are usually the ones that will keep you hanging on for much longer than that.

Never go over 40 percent discount without *much* protesting and only for orders worth at least £100 after discount. Make it clear that future orders will be at lower discount rates, unless they are for as many copies.

Some bookshops will ask for 60 days (or even 90 days) instead of 30 days to pay. Accept this reluctantly (avoid 90 days unless there are exceptional reasons) and do not accept delayed payment and more than 40 percent discount.

If you end up negotiating on any aspect of an order always make concessions in small steps and make it clear that you expect something (such as a bigger order) in return. Always give the impression that the final deal is really as far as you were willing to go (even if the reality is that you *might* have gone further if you had to).

Selling to bookshops

Plan a route to visit all the bookshops, tourist information offices, museums and heritage centres in the area. Dress smartly. Take sample copies of the book and a notepad for taking details of orders. Take with you some spare covers as smaller bookshops may be willing to put them up in the window. A duplicate book for delivery notes (see page 248) is *essential*.

Remember that books are heavy and, with luck, shops will be asking for ten or more copies. Pedestrianised town centres prevent easy access to shops by car. Anyone with an 'iffy' back should invest in a sturdy luggage trolley or ask for help from someone fitter.

You will almost certainly want to have a good stock in the back of your car. If you have published a book (rather than a booklet) just enter the shop with a sample copy.

If you get an order then drop off the necessary number of copies later. With booklets it is probably worth taking a reasonable supply with you (although ensure that you carry them in a way that will prevent covers getting scuffed or creased).

Under no circumstances try to sell to shops on a Saturday and avoid busy days (such as market days in small towns). Some bookshop owners and managers will ask that you make appointments, but most will see you there and then if it is convenient to them.

Major bookshop chains

The major chains of booksellers (such as Blackwells, Borders, Menzies, Ottakers, W.H. Smith and Waterstones) each have their own ways of doing business. Some require all suppliers to be approved by their head office and for suppliers to agree to their terms of business.

At the time of writing the branch managers of these chains have a certain amount of autonomy with local interest titles (whereas the large proportion of their stock is supplied to them by a central purchasing team). The response to local history will depend on the manager – within the same chain one manager may be enthusiastic and take six or ten copies at a time whereas another branch manager will take merely a perfunctory interest and take only one or two copies.

When you supply a branch that belongs to a chain always check where invoices and statements should be sent. Sometimes this is the branch but is more often a central accounts department. *Always* send monthly statements, showing which invoices are due for payment and still unpaid. Be prepared for slow payment and invoices to be frequently lost – although my experience is that a friendly phone call to the accounts department will speedily resolve matters.

Although the branch staff at Waterstones and W.H. Smith are usually friendly, invoices are paid by their head offices which are notoriously difficult to do business with and expect ridiculous discounts for small orders. Rather than supply these two chains direct simply advise the relevant staff that your books are available via their usual distributor (at the time of writing that is Gardners) and leave them with a promotional leaflet or flat cover. So long as your book has an ISBN and you have informed Nielsen (see page 217) then TeleOrders from Gardners (at your usual discount rates) should result (see page 250). It may seem odd posting books all the way down to Gardners in Eastbourne when they will end up on the shelves of Waterstones or W H Smiths a few miles away from you, but this is the only way you are likely to get paid. You will not be the first small publisher offering books to these two chains in this way.

Walk up to the counter and . . .

Smile! Ask to see the person responsible for buying books (but do not assume that the 'youngster' behind the counter is *always* just the assistant!). In chains, such as Waterstones, specifically ask for the person responsible for the local history section.

Keep smiling. With people I have never met before my opening words are usually 'Hello. *[Even bigger smile]* I have just published a new local history book and was wondering if you may be interested.' Have a copy of the book in your hand and offer it (the right way around for the other person to see the cover). *Then shut up* (but keep smiling).

The response is invariable. A brief glance at the cover (yes, everyone in the book trade *does* judge a book by its cover) then the 'three-flick' test – opening at three different pages at random. This is exactly what customers are most likely to do when browsing and shop staff intentionally form their first impressions of a book the same way.

Buying signals

The shop's buyer may respond with a question. 'What discount do you offer?' is the dream response, showing clearly that the person is seriously thinking about buying. There are other 'buying signals'. The most awkward one is 'Yes, I'll have some – on sale or return' (see page 242 for advice on how to get out of that unwelcome situation).

Note that the answer to the question 'What discount do you offer?' is another question. *Do not state any figure. Simply ask how many copies they had in mind.* If they say one or two copies then you may want to suggest a different discount than if the response is 10 or 20. (See page 243 for details of negotiating discounts.) Except for single-copy orders (and less than about 5 copies of booklets with a cover price under, say, £5) offer '33 percent 30 days for firm sale'. Try to get a bigger order if these terms are not acceptable.

Tactfully make it clear you are talking about firm sale, not 'sale or return'.

Many shops will accept '33 percent 30 days'. The problem is that, if you have not dealt with someone before, you do not know whether they are happy to accept this 'normal' discount or are in the mood to negotiate till the cows come home.

When to start your 'sales patter'

If you get a 'buying signal' then concentrate on getting a useful sized order on good terms. If not (and *only* if not!) is it time for you to start your sales 'patter'. State two or three reasons why you think the book is exciting, interesting, ground-breaking or otherwise likely to appeal to the shop's customers.

Pause to let the other person respond. If the answer is 'Yes, but . . . ' then come up with one or two *different* reasons. Try to avoid arguing with the other person's opinion (unless you know for sure that they are factually incorrect and the point is an important one).

When to shut up

If you get an order, and have agreed on terms, there is only one more thing to say: 'Thank you'. You will also need to confirm quantity, discount terms and invoicing arrangements. But under no circumstances keep on with your 'sales pitch'. You have said all that is needed to get the order. There may be a thousand and one other sales arguments that you meant to use but *keep them to yourself.* Only keep on chatting if the shop owner asks you further questions – some owners of smaller bookshops have a genuine interest in the history of their locality. Even then, avoid anything that sounds like sales spiel.

Never contradict or argue – there are plenty of other ways to persuade people you may be right! The strongest form of disagreement should start 'Yes, but... '.

Do not take refusals personally. Bookshops operate in a competitive market and, unless new to the trade, owners or managers have an accurate idea of what their customers will buy. (Smaller bookshop proprietors probably know exactly which regular customers are likely to buy a particular title and order accordingly, with perhaps one or two 'extra' copies.)

Tact, good manners and patience

Until you get to know shop proprietors always assume your presence is, at best, barely welcome. Smile at every opportunity. Tact and good manners are essential at every stage.

Patience is indispensable. Shop staff will continue to serve customers while dealing with you, sometimes several in succession. Under no circumstances keep talking (even if you are just building your sales patter up to the 'punch line') – the staff need to concentrate on stock procedures, counting change, and the like. Above all, do not start to look agitated about being kept waiting. Fiddling with keys or coins in your pocket, tapping the counter or your briefcase, and all similar annoying habits will not have a beneficial effect! Smile and appear truly grateful that the person has condescended to even talk to you at all.

When the customers have gone, start you sales patter from a step or two back and keep going until the next customer needs serving...

Leaving sample copies

With small shops the person who buys stock (invariably the owner) may not be there every day. Be willing to leave a sample copy and find out when is a good time to catch the owner by phone. Be sure to get hold of this person within a week or so, even if this means several phone calls.

Learn from your mistakes – and successes

After every encounter with shop staff re-run the conversation in your mind *immediately,* while walking to the next shop or back to the car. Do not go into the next shop, or start driving, until you have done a full 'rerun' and analysis.

Was there a particular 'sales pitch' that seemed to get the order? Did you fail to get the order because something you said (or, more likely, did) could have been construed as bad mannered? Did you give away too much discount?

Keep a mental track of what worked and try to understand why things went wrong (more difficult!).

Nothing succeeds like success

At the next shop build on your successes. However, it is *not* the done thing to say 'Your rival up the road has just taken 20 copies.' If, as may happen, you are pumped for information about a competitor, then respond vaguely but positively – 'Yes, she gave me a useful size of order' or 'Oh, no problems there, I'm really pleased to get orders like that!'. The reality may be that it was quite a small order, but economy with truth means that you will never need to say an untrue word while still giving a positive impression.

Always appear successful and happy – *especially* if you have had a run of 'no thanks' responses, it is pouring with rain, your feet hurt like hell, and the car is probably about to get a parking ticket. The person you are about to meet knows nothing of this. *Smile,* be enthusiastic and give the impression that you are having a great time and have never sold so many books in a day before. Nothing succeeds like success. Make sure you *always* appear and act successful.

At the risk of stating the obvious, the more effort you put in to selling, the more you will sell.

Follow up visits

When you get back from a repping trip, use your word processor or database software create a list of all the shops you have visited, the name of the key person, their phone number, the date of the order and what they bought. Never assume you will remember any of these details at a later date – you almost certainly will not. This list is your 'bible' and one of the most important files you will ever create. Make sure it is kept up to date (e.g. with dates of follow up phone calls and subsequent sales) and, equally importantly, that is regularly back up and/or printed out.

Unless you book is selling very fast – usually as a result of publicity in local papers – then resist the temptation to phone up or visit bookshops every week. You will soon wear out your welcome with the staff. However, if you happen to live near a bookshop then by all means pop in to keep an eye on stock, without speaking to the staff if there is no need.

Normally monthly telephone calls will suffice to check on stock levels. However just before Easter and early September it is well worth phoning all shops in your area to make an appointment to make sure they have appropriate stocks ahead of the tourist season and the Christmas spending spree. Monthly phone calls through the summer and up to mid-December are often all that is needed to maintain stock levels. Unless there are exceptional reasons, do not bother to phone during January and February – customers tend to hibernate at this time of year.

With both follow up phone calls and visits be sure to be enthusiastic about your book. Remember that nothing succeeds like success (see previous section). Do not invent 'success' but make the most of what success you are having. Even if most shops are reordering less than six copies, should one shop take ten then you can safely casually drop into the conversation that 'some shops are taking about a dozen copies' (but never name names!) If the shop manager you are talking to was thinking of taking three copies it might just tempt them to take four or six instead. Never lie, but use the truth selectively and always to your advantage...

When you set off to revisit shops, make sure you have your list with the names of all the people you met before, what they bought, and when. Express your appreciation to the relevant shop staff if you notice that your book is 'face out' on the shelf or, even more remarkably, there is a copy in the window display. Such 'favours' are not bestowed on all books and show that the shop has done everything possible to promote your work.

In contrast, if you find that your publication has been hidden behind a rival publication placed face out then do not assume this is the bookshop staff's doing – it probably means their rep has visited recently and intentionally hidden your book. Return the 'favour' in like manner. If the rival seems to be playing really dirty then consider moving all their stock into the wrong section of the shelves – for example few people browsing for village history titles are likely to find a booklet tucked away out of sight behind the cookery books. However remember that what you do unto others they will probably do unto you, so only play these sort of tricks in response to clear provocation. I do not condone such dirty tactics but mention them simply because there are people out there with few scruples.

Other follow up promotion

If you have any especially good reviews of your publication – and especially if there are two or more – and the geographical scope of the interest in your books is fairly far-flung then consider putting together an 'flyer' with details of the book and scanned copies of the reviews (a exact scan is better than typing it out because it proves that you've not merely included the good bits), perhaps with a short attention-getting quote as the headline. This can be posted to relevant shops. The trick is then to follow up with a phone call about 5 to 7 working days later (but never on a Saturday). *Never* assume that a shop will order simply as a result of seeing the flyer.

Paperwork

Delivery notes

When you leave stock at a shop then it is essential to make out a delivery note in duplicate (using carbon paper) and leave a copy with the shop.

Ask if the shop wants to include an order number or order reference on the delivery note and/or invoice. If they do not need a reference then make sure you have the name of the person who gave you the order (this can be helpful for future visits too).

Delivery notes should state:

- Your name and address
- Your reference number (essential)
- The shop's name and address
- The shop's order number (if required by the shop)
- The quantity of books delivered and the title(s)

If I have agreed to sale or return I will state this and also indicate the discount agreed, to prevent any confusion at a future date.

Someone in the shop should sign *your copy* of the delivery note.

Invoices

When you get back home then make out the necessary invoices and post them. Invoices should look smart and business-like. They need to state:

- Your address and phone number.
- Your reference number for the invoice.
- The date.
- The customer's exact trading name and address.
- *Either* the customer's order number *or* put 'verbal' and the name of the person who placed the order, the name of the person who took the order (probably yourself) and the date the discussion took place.
- Details of the books supplied, especially the cover price and ISBN.
- The total price *before* discount.
- The discount rate.
- The amount due after discount.
- When the invoice is due for payment (30 days unless agreed otherwise).
- Who to make cheques payable to.
- At the bottom of all invoices state: 'Returns only accepted if sale or return agreed at the time of ordering and books are in as-supplied condition' (to prevent 'firm sales' becoming anything but firm).

Chasing payment

Some shops will pay invoices promptly (often at the end of each month) and others only pay invoices when they have received a statement. Make a note of these and ensure that they receive statements as soon as invoices are due for payment.

By and large small bookshops are run efficiently and honestly. Most problems with non-payment result from genuine mistakes and can almost always be resolved by phoning or popping in when you are passing by. Above all, be polite and keep calm when chasing payments.

The usual 'try on' is 'Oh, I don't think we'll sold all the copies yet'. Unless you really did agree sale or return then the answer is a firm, but polite, 'But we agreed you would pay after 30 days and it is now over 90 days'.

Credit stops

If, after several reminders, payment is still not forthcoming then under no circumstances keep supplying that shop, or any sister outlets. Should you receive an order by post or TeleOrdering (see next section) then phone and, politely, tell them that they are on 'credit stop'. It may or may not result in the non-payment being sorted, but will stop you being taken for a ride once more.

TeleOrdering

If you sent Advance Information to Nielsen (see page 217) then you may start to receive trade orders sent by TeleOrdering. If you have advised Nielsen of a fax number, expect them to arrive that way, otherwise they will come by post. The order will clearly show the name, address and phone number of the shop which has ordered the book, their order number, the quantity required, the title, and the author.

Almost inevitably orders received via TeleOrdering are for single copies. It is up to you what discount you offer. Generous publishers (such as Heart of Albion!) offer 25 percent post free. The normal discount for single-copy orders is 10 percent post free or 25 percent plus the cost of postage.

For multiple copies (or multiple title orders if you have more than one book) then 33 or 35 per cent post free is normal (unless you have previously agreed different terms with the shop).

TeleOrdering is used by bookshops and by various distributors and library agents. Among these are Bertrams, Cypher, Gardners, and Lindsay and Howes. Gardners (who currently supply Waterstones, W.H. Smith and Amazon) are by far the biggest of the UK distributors. Simply invoice all of these organisations in the same way, with the same terms, as you would a bookshop.

Telephone orders

Some bookshops will telephone to place orders. Apart from details of how many copies they want, make sure you have their correct name and address, the name of person you are speaking to, and an order number.

Write down all the details and read them back. Ask for a phone number (you will need this if the shop is slow to pay the invoice).

Selling to local shops

As you may expect, village history books usually sell extremely well in the village's newsagent shop or Post Office, even if these do not usually sell books. This is one instance where sale or return can work well. Agree a discount (offer 33 percent) and then leave 50 or 100 copies. Keep in contact every couple of weeks and restock as necessary. Once a month do a stock check and raise an invoice.

Guide books and village history booklets often sell well in tourist outlets such as craft shops, antique shops, tea rooms, and even pubs. In one Leicestershire village without other shops, the petrol station sells local history publications. Always ask the owners or managers of such promising but unusual outlets, as many are willing to take a few copies to see how well they go. Avoid sale or return if the stock is likely to get grubby (in places serving food, for instance).

Always offer local shops and other outlets spare front covers to use as posters. Not everyone will take up the offer, but those that do will often place them where they get plenty of attention.

Door to door publicity and selling

If you have published the history of a village that is now without a newsagent or Post Office, selling directly door-to-door may be necessary. However, this is something of a last resort as it is time consuming and many people dislike anyone knocking on their doors to sell something, and may say 'No' even though they may, in reality, be quite interested in your book.

If you get good publicity in the local paper then word of mouth will probably be enough to ensure good sales through bookshops in the nearest towns. If the village has a parish magazine (especially if your book contains information about the church) then you may either be able to get a 'mention' in the magazine or do a deal whereby a leaflet about your book is included with the next copy. The leaflet should say where the publication is available from (ideally a village shop but it could be a willing resident).

If your book includes information about the local school then ask if the headmaster will arrange for the children to take home a leaflet that you supply. A small number of complimentary copies of the book for the school library is usually sufficient bribery!

If these options fail or are unsuitable then consider delivering a leaflet to every house. If there is a reasonably local shop (or the aforementioned willing resident) stocking the book then this should boost sales. If there is no local stockist then you may want to consider going back about a week later (in the evenings or weekend) and go around door-to-door selling. People will have had a chance to read the leaflet and your chances of sales are greatly improved over simple 'cold selling'.

Start with the more affluent-looking houses and those where retired people are likely to live (such as bungalows) as these are the people most likely to read local history books.

If your village history book costs much more than £5, and certainly if it costs more than £10, door-to-door selling *soon after publication* may be quite important. What you want to avoid is a few people buying the book and then lending it to their friends. Try to get people to buy before they find out that their friends have got a copy!

Library sales

There are two people you need to get to know (at least by telephone) at your county library headquarters. Usually there will be one person who buys books for the loan stock and another person who buys books for selling in the small 'shop' areas that many libraries have.

Copies supplied for lending can be invoiced at full cover price (historically libraries expected 50 percent discount but that is one tradition I conveniently ignore). Copies for sale will, of course, be subject to exactly the same sort of terms as you would agree with a bookshop (see page 242).

Mail order selling

Except for village history booklets, quite probably you will make more money from selling single copies by direct mail order than by selling through shops.

When the various reviews of your book appear in monthly and quarterly magazines then the first thing you will know is that the postman is covering your door mat with envelopes – each of these with a cheque inside. It's a great feeling!

Make sure you send the books well packaged (see page 228) and, if you have any other publications on related subjects, then include a simple but attractive catalogue. A copy of an AI leaflet (see page 220) for forthcoming publications is also appropriate.

Keep a record of everyone's name and address on a database. As and when you publish more titles you can send a leaflet or catalogue.

Data Protection Act 1998

If you maintain a database of customer information you *may* need to register the database with the Data Protection Registrar; at present this costs £35 per year. Currently the activities of small specialist publishers who do not make their customer records available to anyone else (and do not infringe other, less probable, criteria) are exempt from registration. However at the time of writing the Data Protection Act is being revised so you will need to check whether registration is needed.

Clear guidance about whether registration is necessary is on the Data Protection Registrar's Web site at www.dpr.gov.uk; at the time of writing guidance on the need for notification is at www.dpr.gov.uk/notify/4.html

If you need to discuss this guidance contact:

> Data Protection Registrar
> Wycliffe House
> Water Lane
> Wilmslow
> Cheshire
> SK9 5AF
>
> telephone 01625 545740

Finally, watch out for scams by unscrupulous types who send official-looking paperwork with requests for more substantial payments.

Keep records

If your first book is successful then you may want to publish more or, as was the case with Heart of Albion Press, you will be approached by people who want you to publish their work. Keep records of information that will make things easier next time, including:

- Individuals and organisations who have been helpful.
- Details of any mail shots or adverts that proved to be successful.
- Details of any mail shots or adverts that proved to be unsuccessful.
- The amount spent on promoting the book (advertising, postage and packaging for review copies, etc.).
- Details of contacts at local papers, radio stations, libraries, shops, etc.

Follow up publicity and sales

After the initial excitement has worn off it is necessary to use some imagination to generate renewed interest. Has your book won an award, or been recognised in some other way? Has the book brought unexpected interest in the subject? If so, prepare a press release and circulate it to everyone you think will be interested.

Unless your book was launched in September or October then it is essential to revisit the shops in late September or early October to ensure that they are stocked up for the Christmas season. Local history books end up in many people's stockings, probably as a result of impulse buying.

Do not assume that bookshops will automatically reorder from you at this time of year – far too many trade representatives are trying to get their business already and your book risks being completely overlooked.

As already noted in this chapter (see page 248), if you have especially good reviews of your publication put together an 'flyer' with details of the book and photocopies of the reviews. Post this to relevant shops then to follow up with a phone call about 5 to 7 working days later.

Chapter Ten

Go forth and publish

If you are simply planning your first publication and have read this book from beginning to end you may well feel that there is simply too much to do to become a publisher. This would be a very foolish response simply because so many people have become publishers for the first time – most of them without the benefit of the help in this book.

There are indeed many different skills needed to write, edit, illustrate, design, typeset, promote and sell a book. But each of us in our own lives already have a far greater range of skills. Each of the skills relating to publishing can usually be built up independently.

I wrote *How to Write and Publish Local History* about six years ago to pass on some of the knowledge and details which I would like to have had when I started publishing ten years previously. In the last six years printing technology has changed, which in turn has made illustrated books much more feasible. Likewise Web sites and CD-ROMs have ceased to be exotic and are a normal adjunct to publishing and sharing local and family history research. So I have attempted to pass on what I would most like to have known when I started working with illustrations and HTML. As a result this book is more than double the length of its predecessor.

My hope is that this book helps you avoid some of the pitfalls encountered by novices to writing and publishing. This should ensure that your first publication will be a more successful than it might otherwise have been. And, as nothing succeeds like success, this will encourage you to take on further publishing projects. So, I wish you every success with all your writing and publishing!

Index

Also from Heart of Albion Press

Explore Folklore

Bob Trubshaw

'A howling success, which plugs a big and obvious gap'
Professor Ronald Hutton

There have been fascinating developments in the study of folklore in the last twenty-or-so years, but few books about British folklore and folk customs reflect these exciting new approaches. As a result there is a huge gap between scholarly approaches to folklore studies and 'popular beliefs' about the character and history of British folklore. *Explore Folklore* is the first book to bridge that gap, and to show how much 'folklore' there is in modern day Britain.

Explore Folklore shows there is much more to folklore than morris dancing and fifty-something folksingers! The rituals of 'what we do on our holidays', funerals, stag nights and 'lingerie parties' are all full of 'unselfconscious' folk customs. Indeed, folklore is something that is integral to all our lives – it is so intrinsic we do not think of it as being 'folklore'.

The implicit ideas underlying folk lore and customs are also explored. There might appear to be little in common between people who touch wood for luck (a 'tradition' invented in the last 200 years) and legends about people who believe they have been abducted and subjected to intimate body examinations by aliens. Yet, in their varying ways, these and other 'folk beliefs' reflect the wide spectrum of belief and disbelief in what is easily dismissed as 'superstition'.

Explore Folklore provides a lively introduction to the study of most genres of British folklore, presenting the more contentious and profound ideas in a readily accessible manner.

ISBN 1 872883 60 5. 2002. Perfect bound, demi 8vo (215x138 mm), 200 pages, **£9.95**

Also from Heart of Albion Press

Masterworks

Arts and Crafts of Traditional Building in Northern Europe

Nigel Pennick

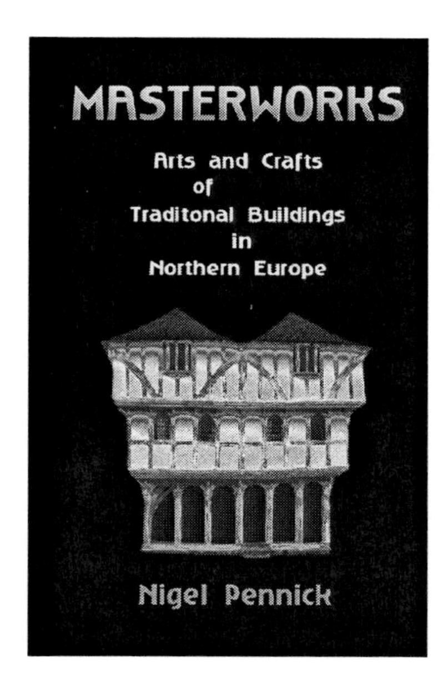

Masterworks is about the traditions of arts and crafts in northern Europe, taking as a starting point the use of timber in building. Timber frame buildings have been constructed over a long period of time over a large territory, mostly northern and north-west Europe. Various regional and local styles have come into being.

Timber buildings display a rich diversity of techniques, forms and patterns developed by generations of master craftsmen working with local materials under similar limitations. The 'arts and crafts' used in the construction of these buildings acknowledge and celebrate the knowledge, traditions, abilities and spiritual understanding of how to work effectively with natural materials. They are living traditions that remain relevant today.

Masterworks is a celebration of this arts and crafts ethos that is present in the traditional buildings of northern Europe.

> "*Masterworks* ... is written by a man who is not only in tune with his subject matter but is, in fact, a master wordsmith in his own right and deserves credit for this. I personally found this one of his most intriguing and important works to date and cannot recommend it too highly to the discerning reader."
>
> Ian Read *Runa*

ISBN 1 872883 63 X 2002. Perfect bound, Demi 8vo, 163 + viii pages, 23 b&w photos, 15 line drawings **£9.95**

Also from Heart of Albion Press

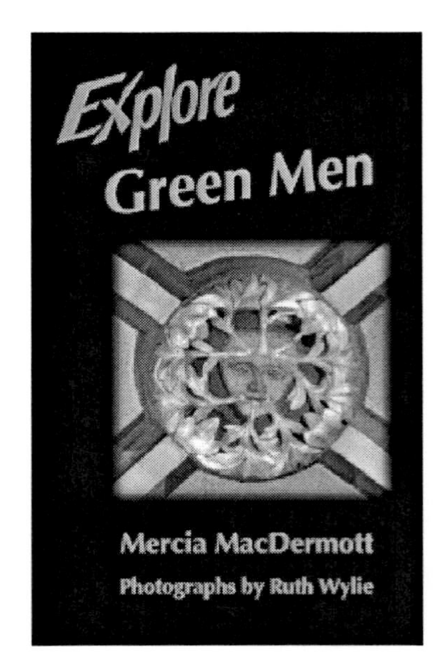

Explore Green Men

Mercia MacDermott
with photographs by
Ruth Wylie

Explore Green Men is the first detailed study of the history of this motif for 25 years. Dr MacDermott's research follows the Green Man back from the previous earliest known examples into its hitherto unrecognised origins in India about 2,300 years ago.

The book starts by discussing the 'paganisation' of Green Men in recent decades, then follows backwards through the Victorian Gothic Revival, Baroque, Rococco and Italianate revivals, to their heyday in the Gothic and the supposed origins in the Romanesque. As part of this discussion there is background information on the cultural changes that affected how Green Men were regarded. The author also discusses the comparisons that have been made with Cernunnus, Robin Hood, Jack-in-the-Green, woodwoses, Baphomet, Al Khidr and Bulgarian *peperuda*. She also investigates which pagan god Green Men supposedly represent.

Explore Green Men is illustrated with 110 photographs and drawings, mostly of Green Men who have never before showed their faces in books.

This book will appeal to all with an interest in Green Men and to art historians looking for a reliable study of this fascinating decorative motif.

ISBN 1 872883 66 4. 2003. Perfect bound, demi 8vo (215 x 138 mm), 216 pages, 108 b&w photos, 2 line drawings **£9.95**

Also from Heart of Albion Press

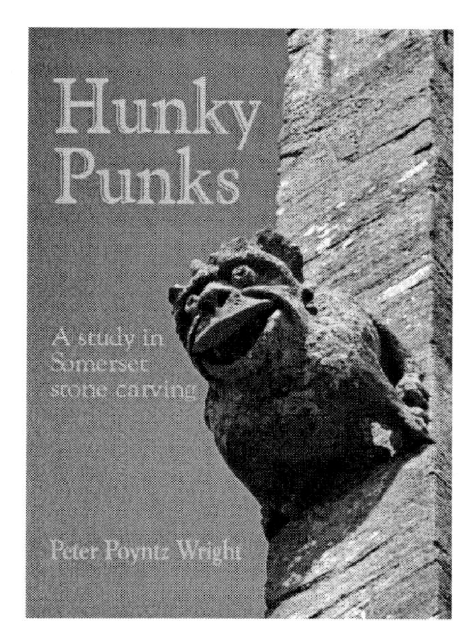

Hunky Punks
A study in Somerset stone carving

Peter Poyntz-Wright

High up on the famous church towers of Somerset, almost lost to the eye except for their silhouettes, are an amazing series of grotesque stone figures. Carved in the fifteenth and sixteenth centuries, to ornament corners and break up straight sections of masonry, these figures are known in some rural areas at hunky punks.

This book combines a fascinating historical and architectural study with a stunning collection of photographs. Peter Poyntz-Wright's research provides the first thorough account of the hunky punks and gives us a direct insight into the medieval mind. He examines the techniques and influences of the medieval masons, and considers methods of attachment and the effects of weathering.

The author has recorded a host of hitherto unknown and inaccessible medieval carvings the first time – and possibly for the last. They include such creatures as dragons, griffins, hounds, stags, heraldic creatures, a basilisk, the devil, a woman in childhood, and many others. However many of the hunk punks are suffering seriously from the effects of wearing, and some, without costly restoration, may not survive for many more years.

Peter Poyntz-Wright is author of *The Parish Church Towers of Somerset* and *The Rural Bench Ends of Somerset,* and is currently writing a biography of the early sixteenth century Somerset woodcarver, Simon Warman. He lives in Somerset and lectures widely on medieval architectural, archaeological and historical topics.

ISBN 1 872883 75 X. 2004, A5, perfect bound, approx. 160 pages, 76 full page b&w photos, 3 line drawings. **£9.95**

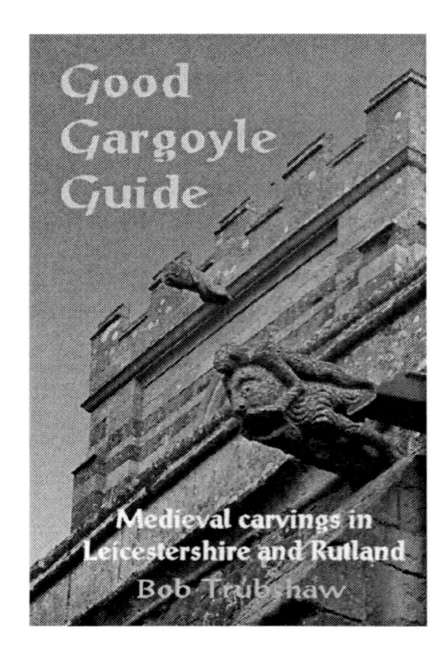

Good Gargoyle Guide

Medieval Carvings of Leicestershire and Rutland

Bob Trubshaw

Grimacing gargoyles adorn many of the churches in Leicestershire and Rutland. Alongside them are a wide range of imaginary beasties, foliate faces and Green Men, face-pulling heads, contortionists, and other imaginative figurative carvings. While those on the outside of the churches may be badly weathered, their counterparts inside are usually near-perfect examples of the medieval mason's skills.

Leicestershire and Rutland is fortunate in having more such carvings than in adjoining counties, although this wealth of medieval art has been unjustly overlooked by church historians. These depictions provide a unique insight into the often rather disturbing thinking of the craftsmen who carved them many hundreds of years ago, people who are otherwise almost entirely invisible from historical records.

The aim of the *Good Gargoyle Guide* is to encourage people who would not normally take an interest in church architecture to get out and about hunting further examples of these extraordinary sculptures.

'This excellent guide... is a typical Heart of Albion publication: thoroughly researched, nicely presented and also affordable!'
John Hinks *Leicestershire Historian*

ISBN 1872883 70 2. **2004.** Demi 8vo (215 x 138 mm), 100 + xii pages, 151 b&w photographs, perfect bound. **£6.95**

Also from Heart of Albion Press

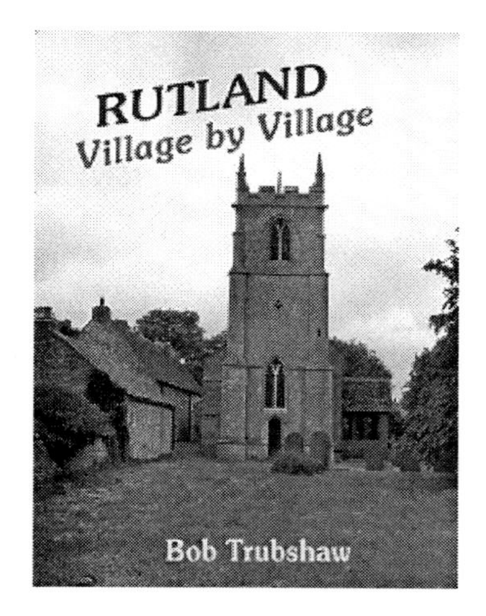

Rutland Village by Village

Bob Trubshaw

A guide to the history of all the villages in Rutland, with the emphasis on places that can be seen or visited. Based on the author's sixteen years of research into the little-known aspects of the county.

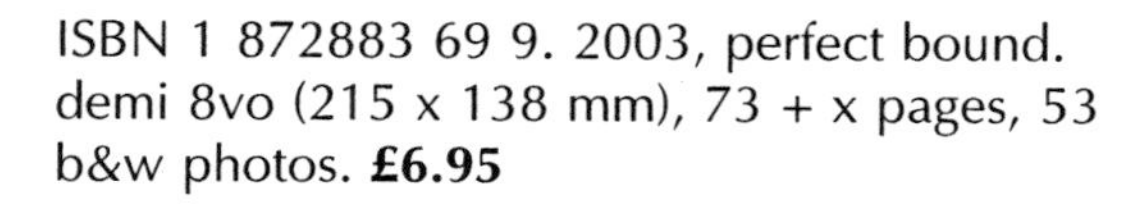
ISBN 1 872883 69 9. 2003, perfect bound. demi 8vo (215 x 138 mm), 73 + x pages, 53 b&w photos. **£6.95**

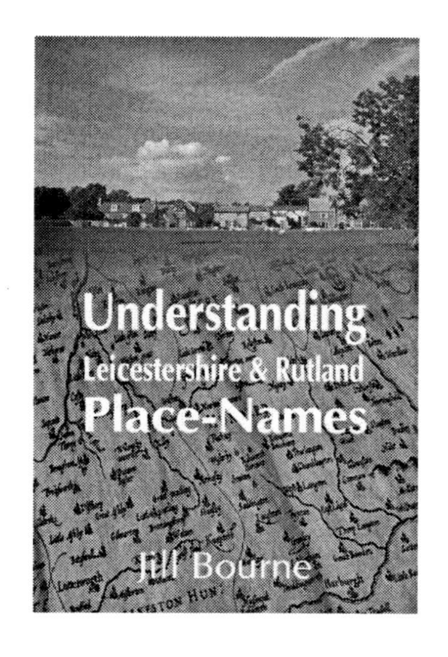

Understanding Leicestershire and Rutland Place-Names

Jill Bourne

We take for granted the names we use for places. Yet these names are a valuable part of our cultural heritage, providing a detailed insight into the early history of the region. Place-names reveal the otherwise lost voices of our forebears who settled here.

Understanding Leicestershire and Rutland Place-Names analyses the whole range of place-names which occur in Leicestershire and Rutland, most of which were coined between 1,000 and 1,500 years ago. These place-names describe, often in fine detail, the landscape, geology, rivers, buildings, flora, fauna, boundaries, meeting places, roads and track-ways. This book also looks at the distribution of the names, the languages from which they are derived, the successive waves of conquerors and migrants who fought and settled here, and the society they created.

ISBN 1872883 71 0. 2003, perfect bound. Demi 8vo (215 x 138 mm), 145 + viii pages, 5 maps. **£6.95**

Interactive Little-known Leicestershire and Rutland

Text and photographs by Bob Trubshaw

For seventeen years the author has been researching the 'little- known' aspects of Leicestershire and Rutland. Topics include holy wells, standing stones and mark stones, medieval crosses, and a wide variety of Romanesque and medieval figurative carvings - and a healthy quota of 'miscellaneous' sites.

Some of this information appeared in early Heart of Albion publications (mostly long out of print), but this CD-ROM contains extensive further research. The information covers 241 parishes and includes no less than 550 'large format' colour photographs (all previously unpublished).

There are introductory essays, a glossary and plenty of hypertext indexes.

Runs on PCs and Macs.

ISBN 1 872883 53 2. Published 2002. **£14.95** incl. VAT.

Special offer!

Mail order customers save 17.5% (because Heart of Albion is not VAT registered) = **£12.70**

Sepulchral Effigies in Leicestershire and Rutland

Text by Max Wade Matthews
Photographs by Bob Trubshaw

This CD-ROM makes available for the first time
details of the wealth of sepulchral effigies in Leicestershire and Rutland - from thirteenth century priests, thorough alabaster knights in armour and their ladies, to the splendours of seventeenth century Classical aggrandisement. There are even a number of twentieth century effigies too.
350 photos depict 141 effigies in 72 churches, all with detailed descriptions and useful hypertext indexes. Runs on PCs and Macs.

ISBN 1 872883 54 0 Published 2002. **£14.95** incl. VAT.

Special offer!

Mail order customers save 17.5% (because Heart of Albion is not VAT registered)
= **£12.70**

Glad for God

A history of the Bousfields of Newark and Bedford to 1903

John Hamilton

Glad for God is the history of the Bousfield families of Newark and Bedford from the late eighteenth century to the beginning of the twentieth. It first traces the origins of the Newark families they married into and then tells the story of two brothers, Edward and Thomas Bousfield, and their descendants. Charting their triumphs and disasters, their loves and losses, their jobs and good works reveals how some of these descendants found a new religious ideal which transformed their lives, while others stayed with the faith of their fathers.

As the years passed, their differing beliefs and lifestyles led to a widening gap between the two families. In Newark one family remained Anglican and became publicans. The other converted to Methodism, moved to Bedford and became energetic Temperance campaigners. By the early twentieth century all contact between the two had been lost.

Glad for God includes an account of the career of Edward Tenney Bousfield. During 45 years working for J. & F. Howard of Bedford, he was at the forefront of the development of agricultural equipment internationally, making major though unacknowledged contributions in many areas including both steam ploughing and sheaf-binding reapers.

This is the story of nineteenth century England in microcosm, showing how the lives of both ordinary and extraordinary people were fundamentally reshaped by the new society that emerged and by the new opportunities and new beliefs that helped to form it.

ISBN 1 872883 72 9. **2003**, 234 x 156 mm, 260 + xiv pages, 26 b&w photos, 1 map, perfect bound. **£16.95**

Also from Heart of Albion Press

Low Seams and High Vistas

Baddesley Ensor of yesteryear

Albert Fretwell

A wonderful first-hand account of this north Warwickshire village and its coal mines from an author who lived and worked there for 80 years. Illustrated with the author's attractive drawings which recreate lost buildings and village scenes.

ISBN 1 872883 26 5. 1994, A5, 130 pages, 50 illustrations, tinted paper, perfect bound. **£6.95**

Further details of all Alternative ALbion and Heart of Albion titles online at **www.hoap.co.uk**

All titles available direct from Heart of Albion Press.

Please add 80p p&p (UK only; email **albion@indigogroup.co.uk** for overseas postage).

To order books or request our current catalogue please contact

Heart of Albion Press

2 Cross Hill Close, Wymeswold

Loughborough, LE12 6UJ

Phone: 01509 880725

Fax: 01509 881715

email: albion@indigogroup.co.uk

Web site: www.hoap.co.uk